The
UNFORGIVING MINUTE

The UNFORGIVING MINUTE

TIM JARVIS

BANTAM
SYDNEY • AUCKLAND • TORONTO • NEW YORK • LONDON

THE UNFORGIVING MINUTE
A BANTAM BOOK

First published in Australia and New Zealand in 2004
by Bantam

National Library of Australia
Cataloguing-in-Publication Entry

Jarvis, Tim.
The unforgiving minute.

Bibliography.
Includes index.
ISBN 1 86325 434 X.

1. Jarvis, Tim. 2. Antarctica – Description and travel. I. Title.

919.8904

Transworld Publishers,
A division of Random House Australia Pty Ltd
20 Alfred Street, Milsons Point, NSW 2061
http://www.randomhouse.com.au

Random House New Zealand Limited
18 Poland Road, Glenfield, Auckland

Transworld Publishers,
A division of The Random House Group Ltd
61–63 Uxbridge Road, London W5 5SA

Random House Inc
1745 Broadway, New York, New York 10036

Typset by Midland Typesetters, Maryborough, Victoria
Printed and bound by Griffin Press, Netley, South Australia

10 9 8 7 6 5 4 3 2 1

Contents

South Pole Route

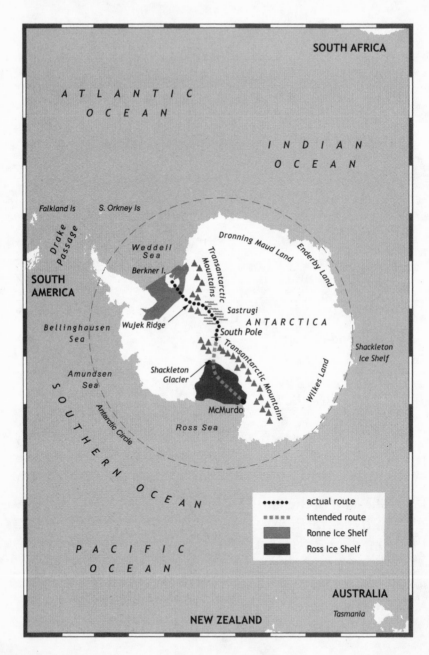

North Pole Route

PACIFIC
OCEAN

Bering
Sea

Sea of
Okhotsk

Gulf of
Alaska

Bering Strait

ALASKA (USA)

East
Siberian
Sea

Siberia

Beaufort
Sea

CANADA

ARCTIC OCEAN

Laptev
Sea

Victoria
Island

Predominant ice drift

Khatanga

North Pole

RUSSIA

Cape
Articeskiy

Sredniy

Ellesmere Island

Average permanent extent of sea ice

Baffin Island

Kara
Sea

Baffin
Bay

Novaja
Zeml'a

Davis Strait

Greenland

Spitsbergen

Barents
Sea

Greenland
Sea

Denmark Strait

Norwegian Sea

ICELAND

FINLAND

SWEDEN

ATLANTIC
OCEAN

NORWAY

ESTONIA

LATVIA

LITHUANIA

BELARUS

••••••• actual route

DENMARK

••••••• intended route

IRELAND

UNITED
KINGDOM

POLAND

——— by air

GERMANY

If

If you can keep your head when all about you
Are losing theirs and blaming it on you,
If you can trust yourself when all men doubt you
But make allowance for their doubting too,
If you can wait and not be tired by waiting,
Or being lied about, don't deal in lies,
Or being hated, don't give way to hating,
And yet don't look too good, nor talk too wise:

If you can dream – and not make dreams your master,
If you can think – and not make thoughts your aim;
If you can meet with Triumph and Disaster
And treat those two impostors just the same;
If you can bear to hear the truth you've spoken
Twisted by knaves to make a trap for fools,
Or watch the things you gave your life to, broken,
And stoop and build 'em up with worn-out tools:

If you can make one heap of all your winnings
And risk it all on one turn of pitch-and-toss,
And lose, and start again at your beginnings
And never breathe a word about your loss;
If you can force your heart and nerve and sinew
To serve your turn long after they are gone,
And so hold on when there is nothing in you
Except the Will which says to them: 'Hold on!'

If you can talk with crowds and keep your virtue,
Or walk with kings – nor lose the common touch,
If neither foes nor loving friends can hurt you;
If all men count with you, but none too much,
If you can fill the unforgiving minute
With sixty seconds' worth of distance run,
Yours is the Earth and everything that's in it,
And – which is more – you'll be a Man, my son!

Rudyard Kipling

To Caroline and my parents for their love and support, and to my parents for instilling in me a spirit of adventure that they never seem to give themselves credit for.

Introduction

I've always been interested in trying new things and I'm not sure I know exactly why. What I do know is that a natural progression of this way of thinking has led me to attempt the most extreme journeys imaginable. This book is about the three polar journeys I have undertaken to date, including attempts to reach the North and South poles on foot and unsupported. It is about what happened along the way, what these journeys have taught me and why I continue to attempt them.

I've given a lot of talks about my polar expeditions. Two questions seem to crop up more frequently than any others, asked by everyone ranging from kids to senior business people. First, just how do you go to the toilet at the South Pole? Second, why attempt these kinds of things?

The first question is easy. When you're hanging out in the breeze at −35°C the answer is, of course, *quickly*. Why do these kinds of trips? That's not so straightforward.

I was a guest speaker at a psychology conference a couple of years ago and a bearded professor stood up to thank me. He summed up my talk, and took the opportunity to say a few words about my psychological profile. I can't recall exactly what he said, but he called me something like, 'a neotechnic man with suicidal tendencies'. I remember being disappointed that I was so easily pigeonholed and thinking at the time that perhaps the desire to do these kinds of journeys is pretty common – hard-wired into our psyche. Maybe it's a response to the modern world in which we live, which forces us to look for interesting ways to commune with nature and to try to find our place in it.

I undertake expeditions for a combination of reasons, many of which I'm sure I'm not even consciously aware of. They include the resolve to be clear about what I want to do with my life and what I want to be remembered for. My childhood and upbringing also play a part, along with a desire to participate in something that is bigger than me, the camaraderie I experience when on a journey with another, and the fact that expeditions provide an unparalleled opportunity to test oneself and to discover new capabilities.

None of these realisations came to me overnight. A series of events made me wake up to the idea of having some real self-belief and increasingly wanting to see what my potential was. I began to realise the world was full of opportunities that before I had never had the confidence to tackle. Unfortunately it seems to be rare for people to tell you what you're capable of and so the way you tend to discover this sense of your own ability is when something happens to you out of left field. I was lucky to stumble upon some kind of self-realisation via a combination of good and bad luck and have never looked back. Now there doesn't seem to be enough time to try all the things I want to. I live by the line from the Kipling poem 'If': '[…] fill the unforgiving minute/With sixty seconds' worth of distance run'. In other words, life is short, so be sure to cram in as much as you can while you can.

I recall reading an article about the great endurance runner Pat Farmer, who discovered his fantastic ability fairly late on.

The interviewer was quoted as saying, 'You must be mad to do the things you do,' referring to Farmer's epic run all the way around Australia. His response was, 'Mad to do it? I think I'd be mad not to. I've just discovered this ability and I'm going to take it as far as I can.' I couldn't agree more.

So why the Poles? For some reason they seem to have been witness to some of the most eccentric and heroic acts of exploration ever undertaken, from the attempt by the Swedish explorer Andree to reach the North Pole in a balloon to the Australian adventurer Hubert Wilkins's attempt to take a World War I submarine beneath the northern ice.

For eccentricity you can't beat these journeys.

Then there were the polar greats like Shackleton, Mawson, Amundsen and Scott, who undertook journeys for a whole range of reasons during the 'heroic era' of polar exploration in the early years of the twentieth century. Scott and Amundsen travelled for king and country, Mawson for science and discovery, and Shackleton – whose reasons I identify with most – for the challenge, a love of camaraderie and a healthy dose of ego. Regardless of their individual reasons for being there, they were responsible for some of the most heroic acts ever recorded. Who can forget Mawson's will to live against terrible odds, after surviving the death of his two colleagues, described in his book *The Home of the Blizzard*? Amundsen, having been the first man to reach the South Pole and negotiate the fabled North-West Passage, died trying to rescue an old adversary, leaving on a plane to search for him and never being seen again. Then there was Scott who along with all his men died just 17 km from the safety of their final food depot, having been narrowly beaten to the South Pole by Amundsen. Finally, of course, there was Shackleton, who against almost insurmountable odds undertook a journey of almost 1300 km across open ocean in a small rowing boat to rescue all 28 of his men from certain death after being stranded for almost a year and a half.

He describes reaching the relative civilisation of a remote whaling station on South Georgia so evocatively, saying that he and his companions did not bring:

> *tangible things, but in memories we were rich. We had pierced the veneer of outside things. We had suffered, starved, and triumphed, grovelled down yet grasped at glory, grown bigger in the bigness of the whole. We had seen God in his splendours, heard the text that Nature renders. We had reached the naked soul of man.*

Certainly then regardless of motive, there is something mystical about trying to reach these points at the end of the world. It is perhaps because they are situated in the least hospitable places on earth, making any attempt to reach them so desperate that it attracts people to try. The Antarctic has been described as the continent least suited to human habitation, and the conditions there as the least favourable for the development of complex forms of life. As a result it is the only continent never to have had a native population. The North Pole, on the other hand, is no more than a point at the top of the world situated amongst a swirling mass of treacherous sea ice. The Pole – if you should get there – is simply the piece of ice that happens to be situated at 90° north on that day.

Both Poles, then, represent places where you must rely on your own resources; it is either you or your teamwork with others that gets you through. People have tried for many reasons – fame, ego, money, nationalism, the list is long – but most of all it is the challenge of trying to see if you are capable of making it.

The polar regions are the stage on which some choose to act out the most challenging journeys of their lives. I know it's the main reason I do it. I embarked on the journeys not for the fascination of seeing Spitsbergen or the Poles per se, although they were of interest, but because I wanted to find out about myself there. I wanted to see whether I could make it without any help of any kind. That's what keeps me going. Not the fleeting recognition of people who don't know me, or a fascination with the piece of pack-ice that happens to be at the North Pole the day I arrive.

This goes back to the origins of why I do things. I don't do something where I think success is a foregone conclusion; rather, I do something where the opposite is the case. Failure to achieve a goal then is not failure, rather it tells me that at least I'm pushing my own personal envelope. It's about trying to find out where my limits lie and about looking back and having as few regrets as possible.

The more I've done, the more I want to do. The old adage about getting it out of your system has become increasingly fallacious in my mind. I'll always enjoy challenges and I guess it will simply be a case of trying different types of things as I go on. As I gracefully age, perhaps I'll be as interested to see how far I can travel in a hot-air balloon or something that requires less physical exertion. I'll just cut the cloth to suit. In the meantime I'll tell you about my polar journeys.

1

London Cloudy

As good a place as any to start is back in 1973, when as a seven-year-old I lived together with Mum and Dad in a small house in Coulsdon, near Croydon, on the wooded outskirts of the southern fringes of London. Two things happened in 1973 that changed my life completely. First of all my brother Dan came along, which was really exciting. Second, Mum and Dad sat me down and explained that we were going to live in what they referred to as the Far East – in fact Malaysia.

Dad had heard of a great opportunity, a management position running a company in Kuala Lumpur. Malaysia at the time was going through a state of change. It had cast off the last of its colonial shackles, having been known as Malaya until the 1960s, was trying to find its identity and had recently experienced bad race riots between the Chinese and Malay populations. To add to all this it was under serious threat from communist 'insurgents' in the north of the country and the region overall was pretty 'active', with the infamous Pol Pot about to take power in Cambodia and the Vietnam War still with another two years to run.

On the other hand, we could stay in Croydon. Croydon ain't no holiday destination, that's for sure. It is miserable, grey,

windy and soulless – a living testament to man's lack of design
nous back in the 1960s where everything for some reason had
to be made of concrete. Dad was working as the accountant for
a paper manufacturer and his journey into work was through
London's sprawling southern suburbs. In the winter he would
often leave and return home under cover of darkness.

The prospect of drinking Singapore slings on the verandah of
an old colonial house with the fan revolving slowly overhead, or
30 more years of slogging out an existence in the concrete
jungle in Croydon helped them make up their minds. We were
on our way within three months. I remember the day we left
getting up in the darkness to drive to the airport and thinking
it was all a big adventure. I still wasn't sure where we were going
or why, but getting up in the dark was what you did at Christmas and that was exciting. I think what my parents did was
adventurous in its own way; leaving London with a young family
to live in Malaysia when they'd barely heard of it six months
before. I feel their decision has had a profound influence on
my life.

We settled into our house in the suburbs of Kuala Lumpur or
'KL' and I began the academic year at Alice Smith School with
classmates of every nationality. It was all a far cry from my early
schooling at St Anne's School, Coulsdon, where we were all
white Anglo-Saxon kids who recited our lessons parrot-fashion,
religiously consumed our milk each day at break time and played
conkers with one another under the old oak tree in the play-
ground.

Our neighbours in KL were members of Malaysia's royal
family – or at least members of one of Malaysia's State royal
families. There are thirteen states in Malaysia and the deal is that
everyone gets a shot at being sultan of the whole lot every so
often. Bordering our house on the other side was jungle, and
opposite was a slightly ramshackle old Chinese school, with
loads of space for me and my friends to run around in with

access to the playing fields via a hole cut in the fence. All in all a great place for a kid.

Just like at school, my neighbourhood friends were a mixed bunch of Chinese, English, Malay and American kids. About half a dozen of us formed the core members who organised various activities for everyone else, like bike rides and building jungle camps after school. We decided to make our club official and called ourselves unambiguously the Adventurers Club, although we weren't exactly sure what we were going to do to live up to our tag. Some months later we set up camp on a disused tin mining gantry, a huge wooden structure about 30 metres high with a long ramp of wooden sluices leading down to the ground. You could see for miles around, and as far as we were concerned it was a perfect defensive position. We set about devising all sorts of passwords and means of defending our base against all comers. Of course there were no comers, and all of our enemies were imagined.

During this period I was in the Cub Scouts too, but it never quite lived up to the sort of stuff we used to get up to in the Adventurers Club and may have been the beginnings of my ongoing aversion to organised adventure activities. I sometimes wonder how much of those early days in KL really helped mould my thinking and set the scene for my being more interested in trying to do things my own way and learning from my own mistakes.

Ironically one of the most dangerous activities I involved myself in (looking at the statistics) was butterfly collecting. I probably sustained as many injuries catching them over a five-year period than in my journey to the South Pole. At every available opportunity I used to head off with my net. In the process I was stung by hornets, had some narrow escapes with snakes, and on one occasion managed to break my arm after a 15-metre fall from the upper branches of a tree whilst pursuing a Rajah Brooke – king of all the butterflies. It was a bad break, and I never did catch a Rajah Brooke.

Soon Dad got the news he was being promoted and we moved to Singapore. There I went to the United World College or UWC. It was an incredible school with 90 different nationalities amongst its 1300 or so kids. Although academic achievement was on the agenda, the main emphasis was on growing up as a balanced individual. That meant lots of sport, drama and 'extra-mural' activities as they were known. I loved it and was soon involved in drama classes, as many sports as I could lay my hands on, putting my hand up every time there was an offer of a trip to the school's jungle camp 'Belunta' on the east coast of Peninsular Malaysia.

There was one particular occasion at Beluntu that I will never forget. It was an adventure/drama week of sport, jungle walking and acting in 1980 when I was thirteen years old. As part of a role-play game for drama we were given an envelope containing an identity that we were meant to assume for the day. I forget the exact details, but recall we were members of a scouting party whose goal it was to get back to base and, using cunning, get to the top of the water tower without being seen by the teachers. We were taken by Land Rover some 10 km from Beluntu in different directions on old logging tracks and told to get on with it. The only rules were that we were a mixed group, and should at no time leave the tracks. To add an extra dimension to the exercise one of our group was a 'spy' whose role it was to thwart us from achieving our goal.

I think the idea of the game was to see how differently we felt about ourselves when we reached base, having assumed a different character for a few hours. Unfortunately for us, however, the spy in our group took his spy role too literally and after a couple of hours we were off the tracks and beating our way through dense undergrowth on a 'short cut' suggested by him, designed to confuse. We were lost.

After five or six hours, members of the group began to panic. Soon our role-playing went out the window and we realised we were completely lost. A night out in the jungle beckoned. Then I remembered I had a compass. Peninsular Malaysia is a long north–south orientated country, to the east of which lies the South China Sea. Therefore if we headed east we had to reach the coast. We set off on a new easterly bearing in the late afternoon, having been travelling north before we checked the compass. After about an hour and a half on the new bearing the jungle began to thin and we emerged on a coconut-fringed beach. Given that we'd been heading north before, I decided we should head south along the beach as I had a gut feeling we were probably north of base. Almost two hours later, during which time I frequently doubted my judgment but remained outwardly confident, we arrived back at Beluntu in failing light.

I learnt something about myself that day. It had felt good being in charge of the group and having everyone fall in behind me. I'd never really experienced it before and didn't know where my resolve had come from. It felt good too, to have had the confidence to go with an instinct and have it work. It was a big deal for a thirteen-year-old and it did my credibility with the girls at school no harm at all.

Singapore was full of experiences for a young teenager back in the 1980s. There was 'drain sliding' when soccer or cricket was rained off, where we all jumped into overflowing storm drains and got washed along by the torrential flows. Then there was going running through fields and jungle with the Hash House Harriers with my dad and his friends and there were of course the old characters like our landlady Pam Hickley – a dignified old English lady who'd lived in Singapore since she was a little girl. All this was juxtaposed with a Singapore that was modernising more rapidly than just about anywhere in the world under the benevolent fascism of then Prime Minister Lee Kuan Yew. His Singapore was going to be the phoenix rising from the flames of the old British colony. As a sign of the changing times, even UWC switched from the old British 'A'

Level exams for eighteen-year-olds to the International Bacca-laureate system or IB. It was to spell the end of my time living in Singapore. My folks were told that it would be a good idea if I went back to boarding school in the UK for my 'A' level exams. Within a few months I was on my way.

What followed were two years of corporal punishment, cold baths in the middle of the night, sexual frustration, isolation and regimented church attendance – life at a 500-year-old British public school. I'd like to say that I at least came out of it with some good academic achievements, but in actual fact they were pretty average. Instead I actually mostly enjoyed boarding school with its heavy emphasis on sport and by the end could at least claim to be an old 'Wit' as all who survived King Edwards, Witley, were known. In actual fact the school was closer to the village of Wormley, but this would have meant we were all 'old Worms'.

Nevertheless, those two years were something of a culture shock for a kid who'd grown up in Malaysia and Singapore. The vestiges of beatings and fagging still clung on. I'll not forget the sight of young kids being told to do menial tasks by the ruling class of prefects under threat of violence if they didn't comply. It was like something out of *Lord of the Flies* and although I didn't like it, I would have been powerless to change anything even if I'd tried.

At the end of my stint I decided to seek some advice from the school careers adviser who had a new whiz-bang software package designed to plot career paths for confused youths such as me. My parents were also now in the UK, having just left Sin-gapore for good, and so we all sat patiently in a musty old room off the old school library waiting for the verdict. The results were spat out of a computer, the careers adviser analysed them carefully, and with the glasses on the end of her nose looked up and said, 'Has Tim ever considered a career in costume design?' It was another defining moment. Shortly afterwards I embarked on a course in Geography at Brighton Polytechnic.

I had a few months before the academic year began so had some time to catch up on what it was like to really live in the UK. Now I had time to do what most teenagers do, and so I chased girls, got drunk, watched bands, learnt to drive, and of course promptly managed to crash Mum's car.

Childhood friends had developed into different people to those that I had played with as a kid. I felt quite isolated living back in the old house in Coulsdon and I remember the period to be very disorientating until I started my course. Around this time I heard a funny story about some African villagers who actually thought London was called 'London Cloudy' based on the fact that the two words were always used together on the BBC World Service weather forecasts. London . . . Cloudy, Paris . . . Sunny, etc. It just about summed up the way I felt.

I chose Geography at Brighton Polytechnic down on England's south coast – or rather it chose me, as with my results beggars couldn't be choosers. I felt at home in Brighton as a student; it was a melting pot of nationalities. I was in the company of students from all walks of life and backgrounds. By a strange twist of fate quite a few of my friends from the old Singapore days ended up there too. Brighton had a large gay population, and this made for some pretty interesting nightlife. It was an uninhibited existence, big on self-expression and was a refreshing change from the somewhat formal world that is English life.

Brighton wasn't about pushing any academic envelopes, but my pool playing certainly got pretty good. After three years of pretty ad hoc studying, I emerged with a bit of paper that said I'd been awarded an Honours degree in Geography. I collected my degree certificate and now had to think about what I was going to do to earn my keep. I tried my hand at everything from fruit picking to packing underpants (a low point) and finally managed to get a job as a Securicor driver (probably due to being 6 feet 4 inches tall), picking up and delivering money and valuables in an armoured car. This paid well and, incident-free, I retired with my danger money two months later.

With the money I'd earnt and supplemented with various jobs along the way including a stint as a *homme a tout faire* (man who does everything) in a ski resort in France, I caught up on the bits of Europe I'd never seen. A year later I was back in the UK, again considering my options. Travelling had at least distilled a few of my thoughts about what I wanted to do and I came back determined that it should be something in the environmental field. Competition was stiff and after countless job applications with councils, charities and research organisations I ended up back in Brighton, working as a volunteer countryside ranger.

It's fair to say the Geography degree wasn't quite the dooropener I'd hoped for. I finally had to abandon hopes of a paid environment position and sell my soul instead. I got a sales and marketing job in London working for a marketing magazine and moved into the city. It was okay for a couple of years, especially as I managed to get a role promoting the magazine in Europe that saw me travel to Italy and Scandinavia, but otherwise it left me cold. Although I performed the role diligently, I didn't really give a damn who got the biggest market share. A casual conversation with one of my colleagues in the pub after work one day finally cemented my decision to leave. 'I'm a bit fed up with it, but it's difficult to leave the money. I always thought I'd only be here a year but that was five years ago. Maybe next year,' she had said to me. Bugger that, I thought to myself, and set to work finding a suitable course to supplement the Geography degree.

Stressful, rewarding and fun, 1992 was a hell of a year and I managed to score a Master's at the end of it. It was great because I had the courage of my conviction to give the Master's a try, not knowing whether I'd be up to it, particularly given my academic track record. It was worth it for that feeling of waking up in the morning and knowing I was driving my own destiny. More to the point, I was actually managing the Master's okay with a bit of hard work. I had that wonderful feeling of pushing my personal horizons and it felt good.

Back in the uni scene I fell in with a group of folks who were into the outdoors and we organised climbing and mountain biking trips throughout the UK and to France. The year went quickly and as it was drawing to a close I had a piece of really good luck, just as the familiar spectre of having to look for work was again rearing its head.

It took the form of Mike Shawcross, a gruff, bearded Englishman with a broad Yorkshire accent who came to visit the college. Mike had been travelling the world and had found himself in Guatemala. He'd fallen in love with the place and the people and had never left. Although he loved Guatemala, he hated what was going on there, principally human rights violations by the army against the local people backed by people like the CIA. And so, as no-one else would do it he started an aid organisation, the Shawcross Aid Programme for Highland Indians (SAPHI), to help these persecuted people to help themselves.

I was recruited to the program based on my qualifications and the fact that I had travelled widely and lived in a number of different overseas countries. It was the first time I think I won a job based on my diverse background and again it was a good feeling. Two months later after a few weeks of one-on-one language training and armed with an old military map, I was sent off into the mountains of northern Guatemala to find a village called San Pedro La Esperanza, where I was to help build gravity-fed water systems for the local Mayan Indians. My arrival in the village caused much amusement among the diminutive inhabitants over whom I towered. They seldom saw a foreigner and when I uttered the famous words, 'Donde Esta el Jefe, por favor?' (the equivalent of 'take me to your leader'), they burst out laughing. He was off hunting and wouldn't be back for several days.

After an uncertain start I became accepted, integrating into all aspects of village life. San Pedro was set high up in the isolated mountains of northern Guatemala in a fantastic natural limestone amphitheatre with views over the valleys below. It was a day's walk to the nearest unsealed road and the village had no electricity. My job was to install the running water . . .

I had my own hut made of rough-hewn logs, which in a concession to the twentieth century had a tin roof, unlike many of the others which were banana-leaf constructions. The villagers were wonderful people, persecuted by the authorities essentially for being pure-blood Mayan Indian stock – a Central American form of ethnic cleansing. The atrocities committed against this peaceable people were horrific. Estimates place somewhere in the region of 200 000 as having been killed since the mid-1970s at the hands of the army; burnt, dismembered and shot indiscriminately. A guerilla movement had grown up to fight for the rights of the people but amazingly most people just took it philosophically as if it was their lot in life.

On one occasion I climbed the mountain behind the village so that I had pretty much an aerial view of it. From my viewpoint I could now see clearly the plots where houses had once stood, where undergrowth had grown to obscure them at ground level. When I asked about this, I was told that the army had been through several years before and killed 60 or so of the villagers. The rest had fled to the jungle and only returned months later to rebuild.

Adjusting to the slow pace of village life meant that I had plenty of time to think. I found myself looking back on all that had gone before and realising that the richest life experiences seemed to be those where I was trying new things and learning what I was capable of. I was determined to do more of that when I returned to England, although I wasn't yet sure what it would entail.

When my year in Guatemala came to an end I felt as though I had crammed ten years' worth into it, such was the richness of the experiences. Even my Spanish was pretty good, as long as I stuck to certain topics like, you guessed it – gravity-fed water systems. I'd fallen in love with the place – the people, the excitement and the unbelievable beauty of the country, with its active volcanoes, mountains, jungles and spectacular coastline.

It was now the summer of 1994 and I'd decided to turn up unannounced to surprise my folks. In a few days' time I would be back at their place in England's Cotswolds amongst church spires, ploughman's lunches and village green cricket.

I was somewhere over the Atlantic when I noticed it. I stretched and rubbed my stomach and there was something under my skin. It was strange and lumpy and sore to touch. I put my hand up my shirt and followed the line of it with my fingers. Whatever it was ran in a line from my stomach up to my chest, and was long and thin like an electrical cable. My heart started to race. I released my seatbelt and headed to the toilet for a better look in the mirror.

Sure enough there was something there. What was worse was that it emanated from a weeping sore that had appeared on my stomach after a night spent rough in the jungle in Guatemala some ten days before. I went over the facts. There was a bite mark that had become a weeping sore; there was a long, thin, dare I say it, *serpentine* thing under my skin; and it seemed to come direct from the wound. Shit, something had got in and was growing inside me.

Five interminable hours of worrying later and we touched down at Heathrow. I think everyone around me was relieved. Fellow passengers would have been forgiven for thinking I was systematically assembling a device to hijack the plane, such was the frequency of my visits to the toilet.

Heathrow was at its customary grey, miserable and impersonal best, and that just about summed up how I felt. I collected my bags and went through the green channel trying to look as innocent as possible with a scruffy beard, a 60-cm machete in my bag (I'd used one every day in Guatemala and forgotten to take it out), and some strange creature growing under my skin.

I scanned the meeting area but my friend Matt was nowhere to be seen. I heard my name called out, and turned to see a familiar face. I double-took, and then realised that the face of course belonged to my ex, Anne.

'Hi, Anne, how are you?' I managed, and we embraced uneasily due to our changed status. Lack of sleep, seeing Anne again unexpectedly for the first time since our breakup and my experiences over the last few hours had left me feeling buggered.

'How are you, Tim?' she asked, looking at my dishevelled state.

'Actually not that great,' I replied.

'Matt couldn't make it so I said I'd pick you up.'

'That was good of you.'

We walked, saying little until we reached the car where I lifted my shirt for the tenth time that day. I got the reaction I expected and we went straight to the hospital.

The drive back to London was slow. It was crappy weather, I'd had no sleep for 36 hours, we were stuck in gridlock on the M4 motorway, Anne wanted to dissect the reasons behind our breakup and I was about to hatch some alien. It wasn't the triumphal return I'd imagined.

We pulled up outside the old Victorian red brick building that is the Hospital for Tropical Diseases in Kings Cross and I was directed to a waiting room. The place was full of people with strange ailments. A couple of bewildered-looking African guys shuffled past, wheeling trolleys holding drips of coloured liquid attached to their arms. All around were people with strange lesions. Opposite sat a couple of backpackers glumly reading year-old copies of *Women's Weekly*, whilst the guy next to me was in with painful knee swelling since crawling through old Vietcong tunnels four months before.

After an hour's wait my name was called and I went in to see the doctor. The shirt was lifted again and he winced slightly as he saw the lesion on my stomach. 'Obviously a parasite and obviously linked to this lesion.'

'Do you know what it is?' I asked.

'Not at this stage, no,' he replied, 'but then again that happens quite a lot round here. Let's do a biopsy.' He stabbed me with a needle, anaesthetised the skin around the lesion, took some pus and skin from the wound and put it in a dish. 'Okay, come back in two weeks and we should have some answers for you.'

'Is that it?' I stammered.

'Yes, it's obviously a parasite, but we need to work out a bit more before we decide on treatment.'

I sat in the car as Anne negotiated London's traffic to Matt's place where I had a bed for a few days. We had plenty of time to talk and the conversation soon turned again to our breakup.

We'd been together for three years when Anne had finally got up the courage to write to me in Guatemala announcing she could wait no longer, and that she wanted to end things between us. I didn't blame her as I'd been characteristically selfish. At that stage I'd been in Guatemala for six months and the time apart had made her realise she couldn't wait any longer for me to decide what I wanted to do with my life. She had a career in marketing in London, was 28, going places and had no interest in going off and working in the overseas aid scene. I'd gone proclaiming I needed to do something more meaningful with my life. I stand by what I said but I think as much as that was the prospect of life in Latin America, not knowing what was going to happen from one day to the next. That was real living, although I can imagine it must have sounded a bit trite to Anne. I'd known for a while that we had drifted apart since meeting as students in Brighton but something – cowardice, compassion or a combination of the two – had stopped me from saying anything. Instead I went for the easy option of leaving the country and putting off doing anything about it – effectively hedging my bets.

Now that she had ended our relationship I felt a tremendous respect for her, for her strength and presence of mind.

I heard Matt's familiar voice and soon we were in front of the fire drinking tea and the cold of London and the events of the last few hours receded into the background as I caught up on the year's news. That night and much of the next two weeks went by in a bit of a blur. I went to see my folks, spent time catching up with friends in London, and the creature settled in. By the time of my next visit the lesion was now a hole some 7 cm across, 2 cm deep and growing every day and the doctor was obviously taken aback at the deterioration when we met for the third time. He informed me that the biopsy had been unsuccessful, and that he would need to do another one. Before leaving I asked if he had anything I could use to try to keep the wound dry and reduce the smell of decaying flesh that was now emanating from the sore. I left with reams of bandages and antiseptic ointment with no real instructions on how to usefully apply them. He had looked at me incredulously when I'd asked for them and I wondered how he'd handle being in my shoes.

And so as this thing grew inside me I patched the growing hole with bandages and medical tape as best I could. In the middle of the night when even the most trivial problems loom large, I would wake and be unable to get back to sleep, fearing the worst until finally exhausted with the worry I would drift into slumber. Each night I hoped I would sleep through to morning where the affairs of the day would divert my attention. I developed something of a routine, partly stemming from a desire to forget about it and lead as normal a life as possible, but for the most part from a genuine resolve to overcome the problem and a stubborn determination not to be beaten. One that I would call upon when faced with self-imposed hurdles in the form of polar journeys in the future.

Ten days passed and I went through the routine again. The biopsy had again failed and the doctor, now joined by three colleagues in lab coats, prodded my stomach and took photos of the hole for a medical journal. 'Any royalties from that?' I joked nervously.

The medicos pronounced their diagnosis: I had fallen victim to an aggressive (and therefore primitive, as it affected the health of its host) parasite. There were two options for its removal. The first option, a drug with potential side effects on the heart, would confine me to bed for six weeks. It also involved the installation of a permanent line into my chest with a stop valve to administer the drug. The second option was a drug called amphuteracin that can cause permanent kidney and vein damage due to its aggressive nature. Neither option appealed.

'What about cutting it out?' I asked. But it wasn't that simple. The 'creature' was more a collection of parasitic nodes. The thought of these nodes spreading under my skin was sickening – not to mention potentially life-threatening if left untreated according to the doctors. The next day I plumped for the amphuteracin treatment, thinking it would allow me to continue life as usual. From what I was told, amphuteracin is like a parasitic/fungal disinfectant kill-all. I had been warned that it was pretty toxic with side effects that left you feeling exhausted and sick much of the time. The urine-coloured bag of amphuteracin was duly hooked up and I was given a trolley so I too could shuffle around the hospital corridors and reach the depository of old *Women's Weekly*s.

A week later and the initial optimism following my first infusion had evaporated. Now I was on the full dose, having to work hard to keep food down, and my veins ached with the toxins they were pumping in. It didn't take much to tip me over the edge and make me extremely nauseous, which the pungent urea smell of the hospital disinfectant often did. Adding to this misery were bloodcurdling screams from the mental institute next door, making the whole scene pretty damn unpleasant. Really I had no choice, though, so I just had to get on with it.

Six weeks after treatment commenced one of the doctors gave me the bad news. 'We need to stop the treatment immediately. Your kidneys won't handle another infusion, Tim. You'll need to rest up for a month, let your body fully recover and then we'll have to commence treatment with the other drug.'

I was devastated. After six weeks of treatment, the hole had almost closed up, and although I felt terrible, I felt sure I could hold out long enough for the drug to kill the beast before my body could no longer tolerate it. I went home feeling utterly dejected and shed a tear with the frustration of it all, feeling annoyed that someone who prided himself on physical strength and resilience could be so easily beaten. That night I resolved to take control of the situation and turn the medical equation on its head. All along the doctors had said the decision was mine to make, and so the next day I suggested they allow me to have additional doses of the drug. After half an hour's discussion they reluctantly agreed that if my kidney function had stabilised to a particular level they would administer the drug every three days instead of the previous regimen. By the same time the following week I had received three additional infusions and was again feeling lousy.

I was called in the following day for a consultation and had a meeting with the renal specialist who told me predictably that my kidney function had deteriorated and that I would need to cease the treatment. This time there were no buts. Ten minutes later and with a heavy heart, I fronted up for my appointment with the doctor who monitored the creature. I sat down and took off my shirt. He looked at the hole on my stomach, which had now scarred over, prodded around for a while, wrote some notes and then asked me to put my shirt back on.

'I think you've beaten it, Tim.'

'What?'

'I think that scabbing-over of the entry point may indicate that it is dead.'

I could have kissed him.

2

Every cloud . . .

I excused myself, pushed the microphone out of my face, undid the straps that held my feet down and made a break for it. I must have looked green, as the crowd parted like the Red Sea before me without any prompting. I reached the changing-room, saw a sink on the far wall and threw myself at it, reaching it just in time before vomiting copiously. I felt guilt as I recognised chunks of my mother's beef bourguignon appear partly digested in the bowl inches from my face. A minute later, I splashed water on my face, rinsed out my mouth and went back to continue the interview. 'Sorry, where were we?'

It was 1996 and I'd just won the first heat of the UK indoor rowing titles and taken some pretty big scalps in the process. The indoor titles are conducted on rowing machines in a sports arena in front of the cameras and a large crowd. They were certainly prestigious with the world record-holder Greg Searle and many of the British squad present. I'd been rowing for six weeks.

The road to here had been an unusual one. Just six months earlier on a cold winter's night I had lain sweating and in pain under the orange floodlights of an all-weather football pitch, my right leg buckled sickeningly. I had been playing a friendly game of soccer, had attempted a slide tackle and caught my out-stretched right foot on the all-weather surface of the pitch. All my weight had been thrown into the tackle and my momentum had snapped my right leg out sideways. I had retched from the pain and people around me too were sickened by the sight of my injury.

Ten days later I had been to see the doctor with my knee still ballooned to twice its size, with purple and grey bruising all around the cap.

After looking at my injury and at an x-ray of my leg he delivered his verdict. 'You have no anterior cruciate ligament in your right knee, severe trauma to your knee joint, a displaced patella, and severe cartilage damage. Basically you need a knee reconstruction operation or that's the end of sport for good.' I was shocked, but I still didn't really take on board what he'd said and, like an expectant child, waited for him to pull a cure-all option out of his kitbag. 'There is no other option,' he said, reading my mind.

'An operation is a must and they can be quite successful. I would suggest going to see Greg Keane in Adelaide.'

'Adelaide?' I was hoping he would say Birmingham or somewhere in the UK at least. Why Adelaide? He explained that it was a common Australian Rules footballers' injury and that Australian surgeons were best at dealing with it. 'If you get the operation carried out in this country you'd have to wait eighteen months and then they'd be using less refined techniques.'

I hobbled out of the hospital muttering under my breath, the ball now well and truly in my court. 'What the bloody hell are less refined techniques,' I thought. I had images of a Forrest Gump style metal brace as my future and was at a loss as to what to do. Go to Australia for an operation? I don't think so. I was on a pretty modest wage working for an environmental consulting firm and had debts from my time in Guatemala, so simply couldn't afford it.

The scars from my alien encounter had only just recovered and now this. I sat in the pub a few days later, wearing my full leg bandage, crutches at my side and feeling like I'd been dealt a really dud hand in the last couple of years. I was pretty much incapacitated, hobbling everywhere on crutches and feeling despondent. The knee injury served to remind me how much I took my physical health for granted.

It also forced me to slow down and take time to think – and that was a good thing. The combination of events started shaping my thinking, instilling a sense of urgency that I needed to get on with really living and testing myself. For a start I had a pretty much 'take it or leave it' attitude to the work I was doing. The environmental consulting firm I worked for was a far cry from my idealistic vision of saving the world. On the other hand I'd had some wonderful experiences in recent years, including the satisfaction of doing my Master's and the incredible adventure that was Guatemala. Both had been beyond the bounds of my normal life, both had pushed me to new limits, and both had worked out well. The common denominator was that they involved my doing something more worthwhile with my life. I couldn't help feeling that what I was doing now wasn't really living at all.

Many years later, I've spoken to lots of people about the journeys I've been on. I've met some truly exceptional people, including many who after suffering major accidents or a near-miss, have changed life direction, and gone on to achieve more with their lives than before their 'misfortune' befell them. Although what had happened to me was far from what many of them went through, it seemed to be a wake-up call to get on with things – a reminder of what I already knew, that life is short.

Despite coming out the other end of both injuries, having seen some kind of light, physically I was still pretty buggered. I was limping around with all-time low fitness levels and carrying a few extra kilos courtesy of an unchanged regimen of beer consumption. Now the first priority was to get myself mobile and fit again and that meant building up my leg.

Several months later and I was walking everywhere in a bid to get fit again. My friend Nick suggested I join him down at his gym for a training session that evening. 'It'll be good for you – you can do specific exercises and go easy on your leg.' I'd never been to a proper gym before and images of beefcakes wearing muscle tees and fatsos in fluorescent leg warmers popped into my head.

It was only six o'clock but the shadows were already long. It was autumn in Chester, the leaves were turning golden brown, winter was not far off and I needed some other way to get fit. One thing was for sure, my running circuit atop Chester's old Roman wall – as spectacular as it was with views over the surrounding countryside – would soon have a treacherous cover of ice and wet leaves on it. With my knee the way it was it would be out of the question. I conceded that the gym wasn't a bad idea.

Half an hour later, we pulled up outside a big 1960s-style leisure centre set amongst a blighted industrial landscape on the outskirts of town. Inside was an indoor pool, squash courts and the pervasive smell of chlorine that seems to go with all leisure centres. We got changed and headed for the gym. Inside was a cross-section of folks and nowhere near as bad as I'd thought it would be. We warmed up and did some upper body weights.

After about half an hour my interest was waning. On the far side of the gym opposite a mirrored wall were some strange-looking instruments of torture, and I went for a closer look, unaware that Nick had followed me over. 'Have you ever been on one of these?' he asked, sitting down on the seat of one of the machines. 'They're rowing ergometers – ergos to us rowers. I still row a couple of times a week. You should have a go, I reckon with your height and strength you're an ideal build.'

I sat down on the sliding seat of the machine next to his, strapped in my feet and grabbed the handle, pushing down with my legs and pulling the handle in towards my chest. An electronic display burst into life with the first pull and recorded a score. 'Is this any good?' I gasped to Nick after a 30-second burst. He glanced over. 'It would be if you could keep it up for six minutes at that pace,' he joked.

It was hard work but I quite liked it and decided I'd try to see whether I could match the scores on the wall of the gym. The top ten were held by firemen from the local station. Now I had a goal to aim for, plus Nick reckoned it would build up my knee. Within three weeks I was top of the ladder and others were trying to topple my score.

I joined the local rowing club, the Royal Chester, and ended up in a four-man boat team. Our technique was pretty 'agricultural' and we weren't going to win any races on the water, that was for sure. On the ergo, though, it was a different story, and I soon became one of the best at the club. One evening I was joined by a guy on the machine next to me who seemed very strong. He was doing the same distance as me so we agreed to row along together to make things a bit more interesting. Before long the intensity had picked up and we found ourselves in an impromptu race. I was working as hard as I could to beat him, as a small crowd gathered to watch the spectacle. We matched one another pretty much stroke for stroke and after twenty minutes finished even, gasping for breath.

In the changing-rooms he asked me how much rowing I'd done and I told him I was a novice. He seemed surprised and couldn't suggest strongly enough that I take up ergoing a bit more seriously, both for training and because the national titles were coming up in six weeks' time. He reckoned I'd go well and promised to give me a few pointers on technique in the lead-up to the comp. I thanked him, and we agreed to meet a few nights later for a training session down at the club. As I was leaving, one of the guys I rowed with told me who he was. He was Mike Harris, the reserve for the British Men's Olympic 8, recently returned from the Barcelona Olympics!

^ ^ ^

I finished the interview and went outside for some fresh air. I had flogged myself in the heat, having no idea of the amount of effort I should put in to ensure I got through. Now I was into the final for the over-29 category and had just an hour to regain energy. The thought was appalling as I sipped gingerly on an energy drink and walked round trying to compose myself.

I pushed open the changing-room door to behold a vast sea of bodies in various stages of undress and was instantly hit by the pungent aromas of liniment and body odour. I was now conscious of the other competitors eyeing me suspiciously. There were reputations at stake and there would be no holds barred in the final.

Even with my limited rowing knowledge I recognised some of the faces from photos that adorned the wall of the rowing club. The guy opposite was Johnny Searle, one of the England squad and brother of Greg Searle, Ergo world record-holder. Next to him was Steve Redgrave's old doubles partner Simon Berrisford – winner of a couple of Olympic gold medals in the late 1980s. All around were the navy and light blue of Oxford and Cambridge rowers – England's best. I began to wonder what the hell I was doing there.

A voice crackled over the loudspeaker system and snapped me back to reality. 'Competitors in the final please proceed to the arena for warm-up.' It couldn't be time but it was. Aching from the exertion of the heat and its aftermath, I walked down the long tunnel and into the bright lights of the main arena to a deafening, baying, chanting crowd. The scene was gladiatorial as we were met with a roar from hundreds of spectators. A number of the competitors gave practised waves to the crowd and climbed onto their machines to warm up. I felt like a fraud as I took the applause of the audience, being introduced as a winner of one of the heats.

I jumped on my machine, pulled the handle towards me and the body responded. Amazingly I felt like I might still have something left in the tank. I can do this, I told myself. 'Five minutes,' came the voice again.

The machines were set up three deep by about a dozen across, and a commentator called the action enthusiastically via a computer display that gave him readouts from all of the machines. We too could track our own and others' progress via a little electronic boat on a virtual course on a screen in front of us. The adrenaline began to pump as one minute to go was called. The gun went, I clenched the handle like my life depended on it, leaned back with all my strength and pushed my legs down. The machine responded sluggishly, but by the third pull I had managed to get the momentum going on the flywheel and I was away. In six or so minutes this whole experience would be history.

Once you have some momentum going, rowing is a bit like the game with the stick and the hoop, where you keep the boat (or in this case the flywheel of the ergo) moving by tapping it along. Don't take this analogy too literally; it is a desperately gruelling sport. Pundits rate rowing a 2000-metre rowing race as the most aerobically challenging sport in the world, and I wholeheartedly agree. When you finish you are utterly spent.

The first twenty seconds of the race are okay. Then the pain starts. First it is the raw, searing pain in your lungs as you try to suck in enough air to supply your muscles, then the horrible sensation of oxygen debt that takes over your body, and finally the sensation of muscle heaviness as they become full of lactic acid and begin working less and less efficiently – that sensation many of us will have experienced where muscles lock up after the repetitive strain of doing something for too long. In a 2000-metre rowing race you reach the point where all of these things start to affect you after about a minute. Then it's a case of hanging on through a combination of mind games for the remaining five or so interminable minutes.

I looked at my digital display, convinced I must be approaching halfway through. Disappointingly the display only read 350 metres, 360 metres . . . 370 . . . Christ, why did I put myself through this? I began breaking down the task ahead of me as I always did when the whole was too much to contemplate. I decided I'd just aim for 750 metres. It was as much as I'd just done, but I'd be there in less time as the wheel was now up and moving. I reached 750. Now all I need to do is reach 1000, halfway, and then I'm on my way home.

My boat was creeping up on some who had gone out too hard and were now beginning to flag. I was conscious of the big guy next to me labouring under the effort as his technique began to get ragged and sure enough his electronic boat slowed on the screen in front of me. I passed 1000 and convinced myself I only needed to get to 1500. At 1500 the end would be in sight and I could endure any amount of pain for a minute and a half. It was all smoke and mirrors, of course, as the workload wouldn't change.

Sure enough, my little electronic boat began to pull level with the leaders. By 1350 metres, I was level with Berrisford, and still had something left. A fear of being caught rather than the glory of winning drove me to push harder as my boat pulled away from his and that of an SAS guy who had led for much of the race. I gasped deeply with the effort, trying to get enough oxygen into my lungs to fuel my workload, my face contorted in a painful grimace as I tried to keep going, my body protesting desperately; 1810, 1820, 1830 . . . The SAS guy made a late surge, but now no-one was going to beat me, and I sped up my work rate to edge clear again. The last seconds seemed to take as long as the previous minutes until finally the display read 2000 metres and I fell off exhausted, narrowly missing six minutes.

Two things flashed across my mind as I fought to catch my breath. First, that I didn't ever want to sit on one of these bloody things again. Second, why hadn't anyone ever told me what I was capable of? I stood on the victory dais and was awarded the winner's medal. The crowd was clapping, and the praise felt wonderful and undeserved at the same time.

My time had been good enough to beat several members of the Men's Olympic squad, including Johnny Searle and Steve Redgrave's old partner Simon Berrisford, and was only fifteen seconds off world record-holder Greg Searle's winning time in the open final. What topped it all was that I was told that I'd recorded the third-fastest time ever for a 30-year-old in the UK. The only two faster were recorded by the British armed forces champion and by none other than Steve Redgrave himself, the most decorated rower ever.

As I drove home, thoughts flew around in my mind. Why had nobody told me about my potential? If I can do this, what else am I capable of? I was determined I would find some more challenges to pit myself against. My perspective was shifted and suddenly life appeared to be full of boundless opportunities to test myself and find out where my real limits lay. It was a Sunday night and I became stuck in traffic on the outskirts of Birmingham with all the other nine to fivers heading home before the beginning of the working week. I looked at people and wondered how much undiscovered potential they had, and thought to myself, they might never find out, but I will.

^ ^ ^

A few weeks later I was at a lecture at the Royal Geographical Society in London (or RGS as it's known). The RGS is something of an exploration institution. It was from here that Burton set off to find the source of the Nile, Shackleton planned his attempt to cross Antarctica, and to here that Edmund Hillary returned as a conquering hero following his ascent of Everest in

1953. The building is impressive; a stately old red brick Victorian mansion opposite London's Hyde Park, with the Royal Albert Hall next door, and an interior reminiscent of a Raj-era hunting lodge, complete with lions' heads and tribal paraphernalia from darkest Africa.

My election as fellow of the society (one used to have to be elected, you know!) was via a spurious request made to a couple of my geography lecturers at uni that I needed to borrow some books from the RGS library. By early 1987 I was in, reducing the average age of membership by about 30 years when I joined.

The RGS tends to place the feats of explorers on pedestals, which in many cases is well deserved. The effect of this, however, is to make you feel pretty insignificant sitting in the audience. The lecture that night was by someone famous and I was one of five or six hundred who filled the old oak-panelled lecture theatre. The audience was an odd mix of armchair adventurers, genuine outdoor types, academics, overweight professionals and people with double-barrelled surnames that typically make up the membership of the RGS. I was feeling anonymous as I sat watching the lecture. Tonight it was about a polar trip and, although it was interesting, by the end I felt restless. I could do what the guy lecturing had done, I was sure of it. By the end of the talk I was fired up and determined that I should attempt something serious in the exploration line to see how I coped.

After the lecture a few people hung around, one of whom was an old friend, Alison, who worked for the RGS. She had done the same degree as me and was living testament to the fact that a geography degree could actually get you a job. We had a couple of drinks and got talking.

'I need to do something that really tests me,' I told her.

'Give me a clue,' she replied.

'I don't know, something really challenging like a polar trip. I've always been interested in the polar regions and in Scott and

Shackleton. The stories of their journeys are filled with adversity and challenge and acts of extreme heroism and that appeals to me.'

'A polar trip? That's a big first step,' said Alison. 'Not just anyone can up and do a polar trip.'

She had a point. Life in the UK is very structured in many ways, with protocols that need to be observed. In order to get your polar credentials you should really spend your childhood climbing through the ranks of the Duke of Edinburgh Award scheme, or the cadets, then spend time with the British Schools Exploration Society, including attending a series of outdoor leadership and climbing courses along the way. You should then undertake a couple of low-key, unambitious exploratory expeditions to somewhere like northern Scotland or Norway to get a feel for cold, mountainous environments. This might be followed by a stint with the British Antarctic Survey on one of its Antarctic bases for a year (if you can beat the intense competition to secure a glamour job like cook or diesel mechanic). Then one needs to spend time hobnobbing with people at the Polar Club and RGS for a period of several years to get yourself known. Finally, of course, you must secure RGS approval (but never any money) for any expedition that is attempted. If you are unsuccessful, you can pretty much guarantee never to be heard of again. If you are successful, this may still be the case.

My CV wasn't a perfect match – in fact it in no way approached these credentials. I weighed up all the facts and decided it would be a real coup if I could pull off a big trip. I definitely had to try something.

3

Miss one of them,
you deserve to die

The fabric was stretched to breaking point against the force of the wind that poured down on us like a mighty torrent of whitewater funnelled through a narrow gorge. As the maelstrom shrieked around us searching for a way into our little tent, inside we sat with our backs wedged against the tent's windward side, trying to ensure it didn't tear under the wind's terrible force. I had seen images of Sir Douglas Mawson and his men down in Antarctica literally crawling along the ground using ice-axes just to move short distances horizontally against the force of the wind and had thought it an exaggeration. Now, too late, I realised that it was not.

The same primeval forces that now threatened to sweep us from the face of the earth had seen Scott and his men tent-bound for days, finally costing them their lives as their food ran out. They had been unable to move through a combination of the terrible cold and zero visibility caused by the wind. We too had no choice but to stay put, as to venture outside would have been suicide. Clinging to the frozen surface of the Lomonosov Ice Cap, our tent was tied down to everything we had, including our sleds and our ice-axes buried to the hilt and threaded through four of its eight guy lines. Its thin layer of fabric represented our only means of survival in this harsh Arctic world; if it failed we would not survive the night.

I looked at Ed and couldn't think of anyone I would rather have been with under the circumstances. He was a great friend with a character brimful of all the traits needed for a journey of this type. Boundless energy and optimism, a quick thinker, a good sense of humour, a bloody-minded ability to put up with unrelentingly shitty conditions and above all, someone you could trust with your life. And at an athletic 6 feet tall, good at hauling heavy loads to boot.

We'd first met when we'd played in the same rugby team at university. We'd only had fifteen turn up to fill the fifteen positions and so everyone was in. Rugby is something of a specialist game with certain positions suiting certain body shapes and there are positions that no-one wants to fill, top of the list being 'prop'. Props are the two guys who form the first row of the scrum either side of the smaller 'hooker'. They're normally pugnacious guys with cauliflower ears, no necks and about as wide as they are tall. They need to be like that as the whole weight of the remaining five guys on their team is pushing them from behind against the full weight of the opposition's eight men pushing the other way. The chances of neck and back injury are therefore pretty high.

There were no short, squat guys to fit the bill amongst our fifteen. There were, however, Ed and a Portuguese guy called Luis who couldn't speak more than a handful of words of English. Luis got prop by default. Ed, on the other hand, said he'd give it a go even though he'd never played there before. Four months later, without complaint Ed and Luis had still been our props despite a harrowing season, several concussions and a couple of near shoulder dislocations. I had a tremendous amount of respect and admiration for Ed.

My enthusiasm to try new things had resulted in our deciding to attempt to cross the Arctic island of Spitsbergen. Neither of

us had any first-hand experience of polar regions. We had limited
experience of fundraising, planning, cold weather survival, navigation or the other skills necessary to survive in a place like this.
Instead we had determination, enthusiasm, and a lot of information about polar travel gleaned second- and third-hand.

Now we were fighting for our lives on Spitsbergen's ice cap
high up in the northern Arctic Ocean, courtesy of climbing
friends of mine, Dave and Andrej, who said it would be an
'interesting' place to cut our polar teeth. Spitsbergen is about
the size of Ireland and the biggest of a series of islands of jagged
peaks and glaciers in the Arctic Ocean known collectively as
Svalbard or 'cold coast'. Sixty million years ago it sat near the
equator in the Atlantic Ocean until slowly but surely at a rate of
about 100 km every million years it crept up to its current
position at almost 81 degrees north where Dutchman Willem
Barents stumbled upon it in 1596, while searching for a
northern route to Asia.

It is almost the most northerly land in the world, with only
the uninhabited islands of Canada's extreme north and a couple
of islands off the north coast of Siberia being closer to the
North Pole. North of Spitsbergen is nothing but the ice of
the frozen Arctic Ocean extending to the Pole itself some
1000 km away; to the south the closest land is Bear Island – a
remote, windswept rocky outcrop in the Arctic Ocean some
300 km south.

Barents found little to recommend Spitsbergen with its
rough ocean, ice and jagged inaccessible mountains, and it's fair
to say his views were shared by the few others who set eyes on
the place. Probably the only reason anyone went there at all was
because of the two commodities discovered there – coal and
whale blubber. Whales were in abundance in the frigid waters of
the Arctic Ocean, such that by the eighteenth century they were
already being summarily plundered by whaling fleets. Within the
space of only a few years whalers had not only mapped much of

Spitsbergen's treacherous coastline but had even been involved in a war over whaling rights.

None of that mattered now as we sat in the tent trying to keep positive about things. We'd trekked across several hundred kilometres of ice sheet, had our first experience of walking on the surface of the frozen Arctic Ocean and negotiated several heavily crevassed glaciers just to get to where we were. That was an achievement – one that we could be proud of. Now we were only 50 kilometres from the far side of the island and would have just enough food to get ourselves to the coast and back again if the weather was kind to us. If not it would be risky to try to go much further.

I remembered my reasons for coming here. Buoyed with enthusiasm I'd felt sure I could manage the journey and that a combination of luck, willpower, bravado and four months of pretty rushed planning would get me through. The polar regions can, however, ruin even the best-laid plans – as the Swedish explorer Salomon Andree who embarked from Spitsbergen discovered to his cost. I just hoped we weren't going to suffer the same fate.

He and his companions had used Spitsbergen's desolate north coast as the point from which to set off on his bid to reach the North Pole in his air balloon back in 1897. After several close shaves where Andree was almost tipped into the frigid Arctic Ocean, the massive 50-metre balloon finally took off and within a couple of hours had disappeared over the horizon, heading north towards the Pole. That was the last that anybody saw of Andree, his two companions, and their 30 or so carrier pigeons. It remained one of the Arctic's great mysteries until 33 years later their fate was revealed when whalers stumbled upon their skeletons and Andree's diary on a desolate rocky outcrop known as White Island, some 400 kilometres to the east of Spitsbergen.

In the sunlight the gas in their balloon had heated and

expanded, the balloon had risen, entered cloud and become laden with moisture. The weight of water caused the balloon to drop to the surface of the ocean and within three days the men had been forced to abandon the balloon and try to make it back to safety on foot. This they did by trekking across the frozen surface of the Arctic Ocean with as many provisions as they could carry pulled behind them in a makeshift boat.

Exhausted after 35 days of wasted energy trekking against a conveyor belt of ice drifting in the opposite direction, they finally conceded to head with the flow of the ice. After a further two weeks of drift and painful progress pulling the heavy boat over towering pressure ridges of ice, they spotted a low island. Despite appearing close by it still took them ten days to reach it, their boat breaking up just as they reached its rocky coast. There they fell ashore, built a crude shelter and, without even the strength to unload the boat or hunt for food they died in the bitter cold. Andree's skeleton was found propped up against a rock – the last to die, with his diary in his lap. Within five years balloon travel had become obsolete.

Andree had planned meticulously. We hadn't. Our wilderness training for the journey had consisted of a single weekend in Scotland practising cross-country telemark skiing, and pulling the sled along. All in all it had been a fantastic weekend but scarcely enough to say we were now equipped to take on something like Spitsbergen.

That was two months before, but it seemed a world away now. A strong gust hit the tent, its intensity so great that it forced snow like talcum powder through the very seams, covering us in a fine dust. My bones ached from the cold and exertion. We had been stuck here for almost 36 hours sitting in the same position and I had lost much of the sensation in my toes. I had no more clothes to put on, so just had to put up with it.

We were at least lucky that as we'd seen clouds gathering on the horizon and felt the freshening of the bitter wind on our faces we had sensed the storm was approaching. That had given us time to dig ourselves in, placing blocks of snow in a horse-shoe-shaped wall on the windward side of the tent, and pitch it in the hollow made by our excavations before the wind hit. Had we not done this, the wind we were now experiencing would have blown us off the ice cap.

We'd had no chance to even make a meal. I munched miserably on a high energy biscuit and had some more chocolate. Toilet duties were performed into our piss bottle, which at least meant we could stay inside. We sat sullenly watching it as within twenty minutes it began to crystallise right before our eyes into a solid yellow block.

At least there would be no bears out in something like this. They'd been a concern ever since we'd arrived; Spitsbergen was home to some 5000 of them. I had phoned the Norwegian Polar Institute in Spitsbergen's capital Longyearbyen some months before to ask advice on the issue. Speaking in hushed tones from my open-plan office I asked if they had a gun I could hire and whether it would be big enough to kill a bear. The voice at the other end had said, 'Of course it will be plenty,' adding 'as long as your aim is good,' and I was conscious of my workmates chuckling quietly in the background at my whispered request.

Sensible bears hang around down on the coast anyway, where the seals were, not up in the frigid mountainous interior. That was reserved for fools like us who tried to survive against nature at its most extreme. At the coast the bears emerging from hibernation could satisfy their insatiable appetite, preying on seals when they surfaced at breathing holes. Polar bears are so immense at anything between 350 and 700 kg that they lift 100-kg seals out of the water with one swish of their mighty paw, like a grizzly catches salmon. I weighed about the same as a seal and it made me nervous.

We had several lines of defence in the event that we met a

bear. The first was trip wires and explosive charges, which we set each night to stop polar bears falling on us as we slept. I would stand the skis upright in a triangle around the tent, pushing them into the snow until they stood firm, then attach the wires to each one to form an enclosure. I was unsure how high to set the wires, and plumped for about 50 cm off the ground, assuming that a bear would stumble through them at that height. Any lower and I had images of such a massive creature stepping right over them.

The fine metal of the trip wires reminded us just how difficult it was to keep circulation going in your extremities in the Arctic. The wire, malleable when shown to us at room temperature, was now brittle with the cold and difficult to unravel. Even when we wore two pairs of gloves contact with the cold of the metal caused the little remaining circulation in our fingers to ebb away, leaving them numb. Pulling the small pins from the explosive charges to render them live each night was a painful and difficult exercise when performed by fingers that were virtually anaesthetised.

With the sleds safely outside the perimeter so that bears might visit them rather than us, we would remove the three pins to activate the wires and then dive inside the tent out of the incessant wind, like commuters trying to get the last spot on an overcrowded subway train. There we'd lie motionless for several minutes, in amongst the expedition equipment and sleeping bags, numb hands thrust under our armpits in an effort to restore circulation before getting the stove going. It was vitally important to make camp quickly and get warm before the cold slowed your body to the point where you couldn't accomplish anything.

Our ultimate bear deterrent was our rifle and my experience of firing guns had been an afternoon's training with my next-door neighbour back in the UK. He was a captain in the army and relished his role as weapons adviser, finding out all sorts of stats about what it would take to down a bear. The one he loved was that a bear's cranium is apparently a couple of inches thick and a head shot could simply deflect off. I didn't want to rain on his parade by telling him I had no intention of firing a shot in anger if I could possibly avoid it, especially to kill a wonderful creature like a bear. What's more, during the planning of the trip I had also been sent a letter on 'Polar bear protocol' from the Sysselmann or Governor of Spitsbergen. 'In the event of shooting and killing a polar bear you must remain with the carcass and notify the authorities. A full written explanation must then be prepared detailing the circumstances under which you had cause to shoot the bear.' Basically if we'd killed one it would have been the end of the expedition.

I unzipped the door of the tent just a fraction to see that the gun was still there. Its green canvas cover was just visible under the snow that had accumulated under the tent fly. Even though the gun was nothing like what I had practised with and didn't exactly instil confidence, I would still have felt safer with it in here in the tent. But to bring it in risked the warm moisture from our breath during the night freezing inside the barrel, rendering it useless. It was a Lee Enfield 303 that looked like it had been unearthed from a First World War battlefield. Looking on the positive side I stood a half-decent chance of clubbing a bear to death with it, as it weighed about 4 kg. It was a bolt-action rifle with one bullet in the breech and one in reserve. When handed the gun I asked, 'What happens if I miss?', meaning how would I reload. The grizzled old hunter I rented it from had replied, 'My friend, if you miss one of them, you deserve to die,' referring to the fact that missing a bear would be like missing the side of a barn from two paces.

The following day all was quiet. Wearily I unzipped my sleeping bag, put on my jacket and boots and emerged from the tent to a changed scene. Although the temperature was still low, the sun was shining and the wind had dropped. Our tent had snow piled up behind it to a height of almost 2 metres. Downwind, there was a shadow about 30 metres long – a deep trench where no new snow had been permitted to fall. We dug out the sleds and skis and assessed our situation. Our two days stuck in the tent meant that our food was now close to half-gone. We decided to continue east for another two days and then turn around to head back to Longyearbyen as quickly as possible.

∧ ∧ ∧

Ahead was a spectacular waterfall of turquoise ice, hanging from the valley side to the snow hundreds of metres below. It looked like a frozen burst dam, a raging torrent of water frozen impossibly in full flow as if captured in a photograph. It had been just ahead of us since the day before, but despite our efforts we had not reached it by day's end. Now, approaching midday after a 7 am start, it was still some kilometres away. I'd learnt just how slow progress was because of the cold. The air being so dry and clear meant that objects appearing only a few kilometres away were in reality three to four times that distance. The main effect of this was that one seemed to travel incredibly slowly. Hours and whole days seemed to make little impression on the vast frozen landscape. Speed now, however, was of the essence. We had twelve days' worth of food left and a good ten days of travel to reach Longyearbyen and the end of our journey back from the east coast.

I slumped down onto my sled, dog-tired, back to the wind to eat some biscuits and soup. It had been a hard day – much like every day before it. I went through the ritual of wrenching the balaclava from my face, pulling out clumps of beard which had become frozen to it by my condensed breath. The thermos too was frozen shut and I struggled to break the seal and get it open, holding it clumsily in my mittened hands. I got it loose, tipped it back to my mouth and awaited the sensation of warm soup. Instead a lozenge of congealed lard slipped down my throat. Cold and slippery it would have made me retch under normal circumstances, but here I needed the fat to fuel my body and it didn't bother me. The thermoses were made from stainless steel but after three weeks of crashing through the ridges of snow and ice had become dented and lost some of their insulating capacity. Now we used them more to keep our drinking water or soup from freezing than to keep their contents hot.

Three days later the familiar Frondheim cliffs that marked the beginning of the Sassendalen Valley back to Longyearbyen finally began to loom into view as we headed down off the ice cap towards the west coast. Below us snaked the Tuna Breen Glacier leading steeply down to the frozen sea a few kilometres away and the inevitable crevasse field that would mark its snout. We kept going for another hour then decided to pitch the tent safely away from the end of the glacier and negotiate it in the morning when we had more energy.

Ed got the tent out and pegged down one corner as we always did. The wind was blowing hard and tonight we were anxious to get into the tent. Our haste almost ended in disaster. Before we could get another peg into the ice, the first one came out and the tent started to blow away. With lightning reactions Ed dived on it immediately, lying there getting his breath back partly from the exertion and partly from the adrenaline of thinking what might have been had he not reacted so quickly. From that point on we tied the tent to his sled with a piece of rope.

We had a panoramic view that night as we cooked with the door of the tent slightly open, the mountains around us forming a spectacular backdrop to an unspectacular meal of beef broth and noodles, which within 20 minutes was bubbling away and ready to eat. Even though we'd had virtually the same meal each night, Ed cut two large chunks of lard from a 5 kg frozen block and dropped them in with mock panache. The fat from the lard had provided us with much-needed extra calories to sustain us in the cold throughout the three weeks of our journey and we watched intently as the chunks dissolved in an oily slick on the surface. We turned the stove off to preserve fuel and ate our meal watching the orange glow of the Arctic sun sweep slowly across the massive 300-metre cliff face of Frondheim still far below us.

Later that night I was woken by the sound of a loud crack and took a few seconds to realise where I was. Sure enough, the ground beneath my head was creaking and groaning ominously. Spitsbergen is home to surging glaciers that remain static for days on end then lurch forward unpredictably. The glacier we were now on, Tuna Breen, had decided to continue its inexorable move down the valley towards the frozen ocean – with us on it. It was an eerie sensation listening to the sound of its grinding and moving, scouring out the massive valley.

To put things in perspective, we were still a couple of kilometres from the end of the glacier, known as the 'snout', so at least we weren't in danger of being cast off the cliff face into the ocean. Rather it was the prospect of the ice deforming, cracking open and swallowing us up in a crevasse that concerned us. We had no choice but to lie there and hope that all would be well. After a couple of hours I drifted off to sleep, too tired to care.

We emerged to a largely unchanged scene. The glacier was a few hundred metres across, its surface chaotic waves of snow and ice littered with angular icy rubble. Our path ahead down the side was fortunately smoother and we hoped that by midday we would be down to the relative safety of the frozen ocean.

We roped ourselves together, put on our crampons, took out our ice-axes and began gingerly to descend. For all the noise during the Arctic night, no new crevasses appeared to have opened up ahead of us. Down below somewhere, though, was the glacier snout. Although we could not see it, we could certainly hear the sound of great rafts of snow and ice breaking off with a crack like a gunshot and then the delay before they crashed into the ocean, forced over the edge by the imperceptible movement of the glacier.

The thought of a similar fate if we should slip kept us focused. A fall from here would have sent us skittering down the icy surface of the glacier and over the edge of the cliff that marked its snout – if a crevasse didn't claim us along the way. If we fell, the only choice would be to roll onto the butt of our ice-axe and dig its point into the ice and hope we could arrest our fall, being sure to keep our crampons up in the air. To snag them as we fell would have sent us tumbling head over heels and make an ice-axe arrest impossible.

Occasionally I looked to my right into the mouths of gaping crevasses with hues of brilliant turquoise and white that ran at right angles to our route down the glacier's side. Deep and menacing, they were every climber's nightmare and a fall into one with a heavy sled attached would have meant little chance of rescue. The sled, too, exerted its will. Still containing some 70 kg of food and equipment, it would try to head off down the glacier, pulling you off balance if you lost your concentration. If it began to move, you needed to lean into the face of the slope as quickly as possible, hoping your crampons would remain fast, calves burning.

Encrusted in frozen sweat we arrived at the top of a steep chute of snow to the side of the glacier snout. It seemed to offer a way down to the ocean 100 metres or so below us. From where I stood I could see the telltale wrinkles that ran across the full width of the snowy slope below us. That meant there were likely to be crevasses, but there seemed to be little option. I looked at Ed some 20 metres away. 'Safer to ski it!' he shouted across. I agreed. If we unroped, put on the skis and just went for it at speed we might stand a good chance of jumping straight over the top of the mouth of any crevasse that might be there. As long as it wasn't too big.

I cut a platform on the steep snow slope with my axe, parked the sled on it, slipped the skis from under the straps on the top of my sled and managed with a bit of difficulty to get them on. Ed did the same and was ready first, turning his skis down the slope, screaming and whooping as he careered down towards the ocean a few hundred metres away. A minute later and he was down, waving his ski pole to signal it was okay. I turned my skis down the slope, seriously wondering whether it was a good idea but before I had time to think felt the shove from my sled in the small of my back and began to accelerate rapidly downwards. I must have gone over a number of crevasses as at times the ground surface seemed to drop away from beneath me, revealing thin chasms below, but my speed carried me safely over them all. Thirty seconds later and I was down on the sea ice, laughing with a mixture of elation and relief.

Now the ocean surface that had seemed so alien when we had first set foot on it felt thick and reliable, unmoving even with the weight of man and sled on it and with no danger of crevasses. It felt like an old friend. All that concerned us now were bears and weather. The ice was easier to pull the sled on and we made good time clattering over its solid, frictionless surface. Our little caravan of two men walked beneath the cliffs of Frondheim, home to thousands of birds that screeched noisily as they nested on a high ledge that ran the full length of the cliff line.

The steep cliff afforded few places for the snow to get a purchase and the horizontal rock bands remained clearly visible, jet black against the white of the snow. It was 5 pm as the sun sank large and red on the horizon and the temperature in the tent was −22°C on the thermometer as we entered the Sassendalen Valley for the last time. It was day 30, we had about 20 kilometres to go and three days' food left.

By late afternoon we arrived at a cairn on the outskirts of town. This was not a memorial to a polar explorer – rather it marked the spot on the outskirts of Longyearbyen where two girls had been attacked by a bear the year before. Both had fled in terror, and the slower of the two had tragically been caught and torn to pieces by the animal. It must have been a terrible way to die and was a grim reminder that man is visitor here and not the other way round.

An hour or so later we came to Spitsbergen's one and only road. Town now was only 3 or 4 kilometres away. One month earlier we had been dropped here and it had felt like the end of the world; now it seemed like civilisation. The sensation of looking into the vast white nothingness of the Arctic had been similar only to the sensation I got when I had driven to the end of the road in south-eastern Morocco years before, when ahead had lain the vast erg dunes of the Sahara Desert. There a sign in French had said 'Timbouctu 52 jours'. Here there wasn't even that.

4

Subterranean cows

Our polar solitude evaporated as we walked back into the middle of town to stares from the townspeople going about their everyday lives. A car beeped its horn as it sped past, unintentionally spraying us with brown slush as we toiled along the side of the road with the sleds. The gesture seemed to be taking the piss after what we'd been through. No matter how I tried, I couldn't now capture the feelings and sensations of the past month of survival amongst the splendour of the Arctic. Yesterday I had been checking the gun and taking compass bearings in a vast frozen wilderness, now I was saying good morning to the postman and avoiding traffic. As we knocked on the door of Lars's lockup it felt like we were just paying a casual Sunday afternoon visit to a relative. In fact Lars was the closest thing we had to a polar mentor. He worked for Spitsbergen's wildlife service and had given us some valuable advice on polar survival.

'Shit, how are you guys?' Lars took a moment to register it was us before inviting us in. We kicked the snow from our boots, shut the door on the snow flurries that tried to follow us inside, and sat down. I hadn't sat in a chair for a while and although it was great to take the weight off, after a month of either standing or lying down, it took me a few minutes to get used to the position. Lars casually handed me a cup of tea as we chatted and it occurred to me just how much we take for granted in our modern world. Yesterday it would have taken an hour to make one after setting up the tent, getting the stove going, digging out some snow, melting it and waiting patiently for the water to boil. A month out in the Arctic had certainly given me a new perspective.

I slurped my tea. It was bliss to stop and rest out of the wind and cold, without the need to move to generate warmth, without the incessant sound of the wind in my ears. 'So what happened? How did it go?' Lars asked impatiently.

We took it in turns to fill him in. We had made pretty slow progress in the initial stages which was frustrating as we were trying to get as much distance from the coast as possible due to the heightened risk of polar bear attack. Despite our efforts it had taken us until day 3 before we had managed to clock up a double-figure distance. Much of this was due to having to pull 100 kg through the deep snow, but certainly added to by the fact that our sleds were different widths, which made breaking a trail through the deep snow more difficult. Ed's sled was narrower and so formed a narrower, deeper furrow. Mine was wider and, as its weight was distributed more evenly, formed a shallower furrow. Neither sled was properly forging a trail for the other, and belatedly we realised our sleds had added an unnecessary burden to our already difficult task.

We hadn't spotted any bears, but we had seen tracks near the tent and couldn't understand why we hadn't been attacked. 'Maybe it had just eaten,' suggested Lars. 'Or maybe you were just lucky.' Yes, maybe.

We told him about the movement of the Tuna Breen Glacier, the storm on Lomonosov that threatened to blow us off the ice cap, the incredible sensation of isolation where we had felt as though we were walking off to an uncertain fate and the extreme cold that sapped our energy each day. The cold had been particularly bad, and it had seemed a crying shame to have to cook outside the tent where the valuable heat was lost.

'You cooked outside the tent?' said Lars incredulously. 'Why?' We explained that we'd been told on good authority that it was best to cook outside the tent. Cooking inside causes the steam to build up and rise to the roof of the tent, where it freezes. As soon as you get the stove going again or your body heat escapes from your sleeping bag in the morning and temporarily warms the tent, this ice melts and drips all over you and then refreezes, making you cold and wet.

'Yes, but the warmth from the stove also dries things out and makes you warmer, doesn't it? Whenever I camp I always cook inside, it's madness not to.' I had to admit he did seem to have a point, and I couldn't even specifically recall who'd given me the advice that you shouldn't cook inside. Now though I just didn't have the energy to argue the toss and Lars sensed it.

'Why don't you take a shower?' he suggested.

It was fantastic. The warm water running over my body felt almost indescribably good. As I stood there considering what Lars had just said I realised that the whole expedition had been a steep learning curve and we'd been extremely lucky. As novices in the field we'd taken as gospel whatever advice came our way. Bugger it though. The whole point after all was to try to push the envelope, and that by definition means being a bit out of your depth at times. And we'd made it.

Ed was still chatting to Lars when I came down after my shower. They were talking about our original plans to climb the highest mountain, Newtontoppen, en route to the eastern side of the island. 'Yeah, we decided against it,' I chipped in from the other side of the room.

As I got changed I thought to myself that quite honestly it had been pretty stupid to even think of doing it. It might have been possible but it would have meant leaving the sleds with all the food and equipment behind whilst we did. Spending a day and possibly a night climbing the peak and leaving the sleds open to polar bear visitation, or worse, losing them if the weather deteriorated, was pure folly and would have been frowned upon by anyone who knew the first thing about polar travel. If we'd lost the sleds we would have been dead. It had been lucky that lack of time had given us no choice but to abandon the idea.

^ ^ ^

Strictly speaking getting to Lars's place hadn't been the first taste of civilisation during the trip. We'd stopped at the emergency hut at Frondheim whilst still about two days out from Longyearbyen on our way back. We'd kept a few hundred metres away from it on the way out, not wanting to compromise the unsupported nature of our trip. Actually we had only come in for a closer look now out of curiosity. There was a whisper of smoke coming out of the chimney and we wanted to see who was inside. The combination of seeing who would be staying in such a remote place, plus the prospect of talking to someone who had news and views from the outside world was too great a temptation to pass up.

It was a sturdy hut with solid oak beams, a metal roof and an outhouse that surely rated as one of the most spectacularly situated crappers in the world, perched on the edge of the frozen Arctic Ocean beneath Frondheim's towering cliffs. Opposite we could see glaciers in U-shaped valleys cascading down to the ocean on which we walked.

The Arctic had played a final trick as we approached the hut from the base of the Tuna Breen Glacier across the frozen sea surface. It had appeared only the customary kilometre or two ahead and yet it had taken us a full day's walk to reach it. On arrival we undid our ski bindings, kicked the worst of the snow from our boots and pushed the door open, as if in a Brothers Grimm fairytale, wondering who would be inside. A wave of warmth hit us as we opened the door. Inside it was musty and dark. Cans of provisions with varying dates of expiry sat on the wooden shelves – emergency rations for travellers on their last legs. It reminded me of images I had seen of Scott's hut in Antarctica.

We called out a greeting and there was silence. Some clothes were draped over a chair inside but there was no sign of anyone. It is the law of the Arctic that you should really only use emergency huts such as this if you are in trouble. Our journey was, however, essentially over, and we had enough food so needed none from the hut. We were even spared the moral dilemma of wondering whether or not to light the fire, as one had been lit. It would have been a crime not to have enjoyed the heat.

The fire was in a small inner room containing two bunk beds. We sat on one of the beds soaking up its heat, agreeing we would not add any wood to it, in order to observe Arctic protocol. The warmth made us drowsy, but after a few minutes I managed with effort to drag myself away to bring some food and the sleeping bags in from the sled. I opened the heavy door and looked at the sleds on the snow in front of me. They looked insignificant and it amazed me that contained within them was all we had needed to survive in this most harsh of places for almost a month.

The hut seemed to have a presence, cluttered as it was with old equipment and provisions from another era. Our surroundings and the anticipation of waiting by the fire for the hut's inhabitant to return were quite surreal. I felt as though I was waiting for the return of a colleague lost in the snow. I recalled the tale of Douglas Mawson in his book *The Home of the Blizzard* where he fought his way back to the safety of a hut much like this one against incredible odds, his two colleagues having tragically died, one from a fatal crevasse fall, and the other from vitamin poisoning, as a result of consuming the livers of his sled dogs.

Suddenly the door burst open and a figure appeared, silhou-etted against the snow outside. We shouted a greeting, wondering what reaction we would get having invaded this person's space. The tall figure approached, pulling off layers of clothing. Standing in the doorway of the inner room he removed an old woollen balaclava to reveal the lined face of a man in his late fifties.

'Good, you have the fire stoked. I'm John Hay.' He took off his multiple glove layers and we shook hands flesh to flesh – strange after a month of wearing gloves.

He hung up his gun – a Magnum 45 – and sat on the bed next to us. John was a Scottish country solicitor with his own practice and this allowed him the time to do what he really enjoyed – visit the polar regions. Granted, he never strayed far from towns but then again that wasn't necessary in order to get a good taste for the Arctic. I admired him for coming out this far on his own. He was staying in the hut for a couple of days and each day would ski out into the wilds nearby to get his fix of solitude. We apologised for encroaching on his space, but he insisted it was no problem and asked us if we wanted to join him for dinner. An academic question really, and I offered to help him bring in some food from his small sled.

He unzipped the cover to reveal a treasure trove of delicacies. Pâté, cheese, chocolate, canned fish and several half-bottles of whisky. Feeling guilty, I delved into our sled, bringing in some of our packets of soup, chocolate and somewhat stodgy high energy biscuits. We placed the provisions for our feast next to the fire to thaw and began to chat.

We talked for hours, with the odd infusion of whisky to fuel the conversation. John was fascinated to hear of our journey, as it provided a window into the world of unsupported polar jour-neying of which he had little experience. He on the other hand knew his polar literature inside out, rattling off story after story about explorers from the heroic era. These tales of derring-do all seemed more real given our location and having completed a journey ourselves. With the heady sensation of warmth, whisky and good company I thought this was definitely not the last of my polar journeys.

Almost on cue he asked what we intended to do next. Neither Ed nor I knew, but were open to suggestion. He mentioned a number of journeys he thought were worth attempting, and I detected a distinct hint in his voice that he would love to come along for the ride. There were some epics – travelling through Alaska's mighty Brooks Range, dog-sledding from Spitsbergen to Greenland across the frozen ocean, and the ultimate – the unsupported crossing of Antarctica that Shackleton had attempted back on the eve of the First World War.

'So what do you take away from something like this?' he asked. There had been many things, but the main ones were the realisation of how little we knew when we embarked on the journey, and the confidence to try more, based on the fact that things had actually worked out okay. With this in mind I decided that one of the most important factors is to have a very discrete goal to aim for. At the end of the day you go to do what you set out to do and once you've done your dash, you get out fast. You'll never beat the Arctic or Antarctic, these places just tolerate you – nothing more. With all the best-laid plans, equipment and CV of previous accomplishments you can at any time be subject to a freak storm, crevasse, extreme cold or bear attack and snuffed out by the place without remorse. Recounting the story of what we had set out to do, both Ed and I left out any mention of an ascent of Newtontoppen, realising more than ever what an unrealistic side goal it had been.

∧ ∧ ∧

I saw a scraggly, weather-beaten bearded face with cracked lips staring back from the mirror, legacy of 31 days living in the wilds of Spitsbergen. With a sepia hue, a bit of imagination, and perhaps an accessory like a pipe, I wouldn't have looked out of place standing next to Mawson or Shackleton on the deck of an ice-encrusted boat barging through the pack-ice.

As a matter of fact in a moment of weakness I'd actually bought a pipe and about a kilo of tobacco at Heathrow. Exactly what possessed me to do so I'm not sure. Perhaps I secretly hoped that by assuming aspects of the outward appearance and countenance of the early explorers I would inherit some of their strength and resolve. Whatever the case, we decided not to take it on the expedition partly in a bid to keep weight down, and partly in the interest of continued respiratory function.

The beard, unlike the pipe, was the real McCoy, but I didn't like the way it made me look, and contrary to conventional polar wisdom it actually contributed to more frost damage of the face than it prevented. It did this by giving the ice from your frozen breath something to cling to, holding it close to your face where over time it killed the tissue, causing the telltale blackness of frostbite.

On the floor at Lars's lockup down by the harbour was five-star accommodation compared to the tent, despite being unheated. It made me realise just how much of the difficulty of trying to survive on a trip like this is about the misery of the daily routine of living in a tent in the Arctic, trying to eat, sleep, keep warm and go to the toilet. It is the unrelenting unpleasantness of routine in such conditions that wears you down as much as the effort of pulling the sled and watching out for crevasses.

I woke at 4.30 the following morning, body still on expedition time and peered out of the iced-up window. From it I could see the frozen sea, the sun shimmering on the ice as it sat low and red behind the mountains on the far side of the valley. In the harbour were a dozen or so little fishing boats locked in the ice, waiting patiently for the spring thaw that would release them in a month or two's time.

Ed's voice emanated from behind some boxes on the far side of the room where he'd set up camp, revelling in the personal space after a month in the two-man tent. 'Let's eat, I'm bloody starving.' I agreed. Since arriving back the previous day, apart from sleeping and having a shower all we'd done was eat – constantly hungry as the body repaired itself after the exertion of the trip. We got up, donned our cold weather gear and headed downtown in search of food. 'Downtown' was a café, a supermarket, a skidoo sales centre and a shop selling various bits of reindeer, enterprisingly turned into handbags, shoes, ashtrays and coat hooks.

We wandered into the supermarket and it was almost too surreal after a month in the wilderness. The piped music, the girl behind the till asking in near-perfect Scandi-English if we were having a good day, the warmth, and the ease of just taking food off the shelf and eating it, rather than having to dig up snow, boil it and rehydrate it. The adage of not going food shopping when you're hungry could be applied about a hundred-fold to our situation. We left with bags of biscuits, cheese, chocolate and fruit, and that was only to keep us going until we got to the café.

The supermarket I'd discovered was also a fount of knowledge on polar bears, with a noticeboard dedicated to the subject next to the checkout counter. I stopped to browse the advice and was glad we hadn't read it before the expedition.

Apparently polar bears are perfectly adapted to life in the Arctic as carnivorous hunters at the top of the food chain. They are serious adversaries, weighing up to 700 kg, able to run at speeds of over 40 km/h in short bursts, unafraid of humans as they seldom meet them and yet able to smell them from miles away. Normally they comb the coastal areas of the islands where seals are most abundant and these are their principal food source. Recently, however, they had supplemented this diet with a couple of Homo sapiens in the form of the young girl whose memorial cairn we had passed and a French glaciologist who'd discharged a full clip of bullets from his pistol into the bear before it tore him to pieces.

All was not lost. In addition to the scary bear stats there was a section giving useful tips on how to deal with bears. Apparently, without the use of a gun there are three principal techniques available to the novice to foil a full-on attack from one of nature's most perfectly honed killing machines. First there is the old trick of removing an item of clothing and throwing it over your shoulder as you are running frantically away from the bear. Apparently the bear will stop to smell the item and this will give you valuable time to escape. The second technique involves running down whatever slope you can find. Bears apparently aren't that good at going downhill as their front legs are shorter than their hind ones and this throws them off balance, slowing them down, and allowing you to make a getaway. The pièce de résistance is the cunning ploy of making yourself appear larger than the bear such that it thinks twice about taking you on. If you get this method absolutely right, the bear will in fact run away and not disturb you again.

I never did get an adequate explanation of the shortcomings of these techniques. Firstly, the one thing you don't want to do in −30°C is start discarding clothing. It may well slow a bear down but depending on how long the chase goes on and how many clothes you have to discard, the cold may very well kill you first. Although you may survive the bear's attack, you sure as hell won't last long in your underpants at that temperature. The second technique involving finding a slope steep enough to slow a bear down is also problematic, as much of the surface of an ice cap is a long slow gradient with not a steep slope in sight. You would inevitably be dead long before you found the short sharp slope you wished for. And the final 'make yourself appear bigger than a bear' technique is also a bit scant on the detail. Specifically the bit where you transform yourself into something that looks bigger than a creature that might well weigh over half a tonne and stand over 3.5 metres tall. Standing on the sled to give you extra height to scare a bear was more likely to just crush the chocolate.

Back at the lockup we wondered what to do with the remaining 48 hours before our flight home. To be honest, since finishing the expedition I felt I hadn't had the time to stand back and really appreciate what we'd achieved. Spitsbergen's capital Longyearbyen, as small and remote as it was, now seemed like a heaving metropolis with people everywhere encroaching on our brain space, preventing us from coming to terms with the whole experience. We needed to get out to the wilds again before we left.

We informed the Sysselmann that we were back safely from our expedition and went to see Lars at the Svalbard Wildlife Service to return the explosive charges. He was an authority on all things Spitsbergen and we took the opportunity to ask him what we could do with our remaining time. Without a moment's hesitation he suggested we might go to one of the seldom visited Russian settlements to the north – Pyramiden and Barentsburg. From there we could either spend the night in the tent or try our luck at the weather station on the west coast. These isolated communities, largely forgotten by their former communist masters and able to be reached only by boat in the summer and via snowmobile in the winter, were the legacy of the rival claims to Spitsbergen made by Russia and Norway in the early part of the twentieth century.

The area contained coal, courtesy of the dense forest that had covered Spitsbergen when it was close to the equator 60 million or so years ago. As a result the Russians had established a coal mine at Barentsburg; not because it was a profitable venture, but because it improved the case for their claim to the islands. In a historical irony their gambit was unsuccessful and the islands were ceded to Norway in 1920, based not on the merits of

Norway's case, but due to Norway posing less of a strategic threat. And yet Pyramiden and Barentsburg remain to this day, with Barentsburg eking out a meagre, unprofitable existence as the most northerly coal mine in the world 1300 km north of the Arctic Circle.

Barentsburg is home to some 900 people from Russia and the Ukraine. According to Lars it not only had its own power station, hospital, hotel, and sports hall, but also a large underground facility where pigs and cows are reared. It sounded surreal and just what we were looking for. Lars reckoned to get to Barentsburg and back by skidoo – a small motorised oversnow vehicle that is similar to a jet ski – would only take a day. If time became tight for whatever reason we had the opportunity to travel through the twilight of the Arctic night. It was a bit tight but we decided to do it.

We went down to the snowmobile showroom and made some enquiries. Scraping together our remaining money we had enough for two skidoos for 36 hours. It was advisable to use two machines as a skidoo's range is so great that if we took only one and it broke down we could end up miles from anywhere and in serious trouble.

We aimed to pick up the skidoos at 7 the next morning and decided to go for a celebratory beer and slap-up feed that night before setting off. The former miners' union building, or Huset, now doubles as a drunken disco and restaurant and is Spitsbergen's only night out. We opened the door to a scene of drunken excess and gluttony, the locals staggering around with plates piled high with reindeer and tables creaking under the weight of beer. Just like at the supermarket our eyes were bigger than our stomachs and we paid our krone and got stuck in at the 'all you can eat' buffet.

If you didn't like venison you'd have been in trouble, as upon closer inspection each tray of the buffet contained reindeer as the principal ingredient. We hoed in and after three or four beers and two hours of grazing rolled out bloated with lager and reindeer meat. I felt ill walking back to the lockup, but the cold, crisp air cleared my head. Ed on the other hand punctuated the twenty-minute walk back with bouts of projectile vomiting until there was nothing more coming up. We attributed it to our stomachs having difficulty with meat after a month of de-hydrated food.

The following morning Ed seemed recovered and we picked up the skidoos from the showroom. We packed the tent, sleeping bags, maps, food for four days and thermoses into the compartments on the skidoo, I slung the rifle over my shoulder and we were off. I pulled in at the petrol station to fill up, sliding up to the bowser on a carpet of petrol-stained slush. It felt strange pulling up to the pump on a skidoo and not in a car but then again a lot of things about Longyearbyen were strange. There were few cars – little point when there are only 30 km of roads in the whole place. Most cars sit dormant in a car park in the middle of town plugged into a power supply that stops the engines from freezing up. Most transport takes the form of boats in the summer, and skidoos in the winter. The rest of the year little contact takes place as the valleys inland become impassable quagmires with the snow melt, while the sea remains choked with ice.

Since 1920 Norway has had sole sovereignty over the islands. But the country stands by itself, the taxes are different to those of Norway and the money from Spitsbergen stays in Spits-bergen. There is no tax on alcohol and tobacco, so the prices are much lower than in Norway. It is ruled by the Sysselmann, who is locally elected.

In the two minutes it took us to get through Longyearbyen's 'suburbs' and out into the wilds of the Arctic it struck me just how many of Longyearbyen's 1000-strong population have ceiling-to-floor windows and houses full of tropical plants, such is the abundance of coal-fired power. While the temperature outside hovers below −20°C, Longyearbyen's inhabitants swelter in +30°.

Once away from the houses we opened up the throttle on the skidoos, accelerating up to 70 km/h effortlessly, the sun glinting off the visors and polished paintwork as we carved fresh trails through the deep virgin snow. After a month of pulling the sled it was going from the ridiculous to the sublime. Manhauling – the term used to describe putting all our food, fuel and equipment in a sled and pulling it using our bodies alone – is about the slowest means of travel I have ever subjected myself to, accentuated by the vastness of the landscape through which I travelled. The skidoos on the other hand were turbo-charged. The equivalent of a powerful road bike at 500cc each, they were like driving jet-propelled dodgem cars, and had a huge amount of grunt. The handlebars were as much something to hold on to as the steering mechanism as we screamed out of town on a heady combination of fuel and adrenaline. It was just the antidote I needed after a few days of sitting on my backside eating.

Within 45 minutes we were 30 km out of town – more than we'd covered on our best day of nine hours of manhauling. Ironically, despite the heated handlebars and foot wells, sitting motionless on the skidoo was cold work and we needed to stop periodically just to warm up.

The Arctic assumed a different character altogether, now that we were able to divert some of our energy towards appreciating it rather than just pushing through it. A few days ago it would have absorbed all of our mental and physical energy. Now I was free to think about the trip as I sped along – we'd been lucky. Had we fallen into a serious crevasse we probably wouldn't have had the right technique to get one another out. Our different-sized sleds had caused constant problems when breaking trail through the often deep, heavy snow and yet we had managed to keep to our schedule and get back safely to Longyearbyen.

We'd also been lucky in making the right judgment about how far we could travel each day, having loosely arrived at a figure of around 20–25 km a day, based more on educated guesswork than the application of science.

Under normal circumstances we agreed we could both walk comfortably at 6 km an hour, and so we assumed we'd do no worse than half that speed. In lay terms, 3 km/h is about the speed you'd do on your average weekend shopping trip, dawdling along, stopping to look at things as you go. We figured we could comfortably do that speed and planned to walk for seven or eight hours a day, hence 20–25 km. To build in a little bit of margin for error because it was our first foray into polar regions and we'd be pulling heavy sleds we took the lower end of the range as a 'conservative maximum'.

Into this we'd built a certain amount of contingency time, for anything from blizzards where the wind is so strong that the temperature becomes life-threatening, to where visibility is virtually zero. In such zero visibility or white-out conditions, stumbling into bears, crevasses or wandering over the edge of cliffs would have been very real possibilities. Then there were more day-to-day issues such as the possibility of equipment or injury problems ranging from stoves not working properly to skis breaking to frostbite, blisters, broken limbs and snow blindness. By the end of our planning, I remember thinking that perhaps a camping trip to Wimbledon Common would have been more prudent. All, however, had ended well.

Now we sped across a vast icy plain with mountains to our right and ice-choked ocean a few hundred metres to our left, ink-black and full of a jumbled mass of turquoise and white blocks of pack-ice. Ahead of me and to my right two strange shapes loomed into view. I signalled to Ed that I was going to go and have a closer look, cutting a swathe through the deep virgin powder and leaving a trail behind me like the wake of a boat as I veered away. Closer examination revealed that they were the rusted hulls of two large boats sitting next to one another in the ice, utterly incongruous in the setting. The boats had presumably been frozen in by successive winters such that they now sat stranded some 2 kilometres away from the 'open' sea. All around us was wilderness but with a bit of imagination I could now appreciate that we were in fact in a bay filled with solid pack-ice, disguised as land beneath a blanket of deep snow. Ahead, a kilometre or so away was a headland, and just protruding from above its ridgeline something that again looked distinctly man-made – a chimney stack. We gunned the engines and went round the headland to investigate. As we rounded the rocky outcrop that marked its seaward side there in front of us stood a large stone building that would not have looked out of place in a Dickens drama – easily posing as a nineteenth-century poorhouse. Except of course for the rusty hammer and sickle insignia on the side of the building.

We pulled up to the front, and after several attempts managed to open the solid oak door. Inside all was quiet and deserted. The shadowy corridors were cold and smelt dank, leading to a succession of rooms that were even less hospitable. There was scarcely an intact window in the place. Stumps of bolts that probably once held machinery in place protruded from the floor, indicating that the building had perhaps been a factory. Now the sounds of whirring machinery and human voices were long gone, replaced by the wind whistling through the building. For some reason it was reassuring to have the gun with us as we crept through its icy corridors, unsure what we might find.

We ascended the stairs to the next floor and the scene was even more intriguing. Here we found rooms with bunk beds, old wooden furniture and even an old Russian technical manual dating back to the 1950s, complete with oily fingermarks where a machinist would have leafed through its pages. There was a changing-room too, where wire lockers stood, some of them even complete with overalls stiff with the cold, hanging on old coathangers. The scene was reminiscent of the *Mary Celeste*, as if the siren had gone for the morning tea break and for some reason no-one had returned even to take their clothes with them.

From the second-storey windows I could see a dock a couple of kilometres away, presumably once a loading bay for coal, but the hammer and sickle on the side of the building had me imagining much more sinister things. It had been a place locked in the cold of the metaphorical war and the literal ice. Perhaps people had looked out of these windows conspiring against the western world. Whatever the case, the doom and gloom made us feel glad to be outside again and able to escape quickly with a flick of the thumb on the accelerator.

The vigilance of looking out for bears now became a thing of the past as I cranked the skidoo up to over 100 km/h. If we saw one now we could simply outrun it. How different that was to the sensation of having to rely on ingenuity and manpower to outrun or outsmart a bear. Looking back I was surprised how easily I had coped with the claustrophobia of travelling on foot.

Another couple of hours of high-speed travel and – I was sure I wasn't imagining it – the snow was definitely assuming a greyish tinge. And then for the third time that day a man-made structure encroached upon our Arctic solitude as another chimney appeared on the horizon. This time, however, it was very much in use, acrid smoke billowing out of it and then being blown sideways across the sky by the chill Arctic wind.

As we approached, the snow transformed from grey to dark grey, and finally to black as the surface became covered in an increasingly thick blanket of fine coal dust from what was obviously a power station. We motored on across the dark snow, the sound of the rasping engines echoing off the buildings so that by the time we ground to a halt a crowd of several dozen had instantly assembled around us.

It was like viewing footage from an old black and white Pathe newsreel as we looked at the crowd. All were dressed in heavy coats and drab colours, and pallid complexions peered at us from beneath hats of Arctic fox and timber wolf. We parked our skidoos next to a sombre-looking bust of Lenin and removed our goggles and face masks, smiling broadly to elicit a similar response from the throng. This was Barentsburg, home to people from the Ukraine who mined coal here at one of the most isolated Russian settlements in the world.

Slowly the group inched towards us, exchanging comments to one another, presumably about us and our skidoos, both of which looked embarrassingly ostentatious in the austere surroundings.

A tall man with a drawn face and a full ginger moustache stepped forward to act as spokesperson for the group. 'Welcome to Barentsburg,' Dmitri offered. Encouraged that he could speak English I asked if there was anywhere we could get in out of the cold and have a bite to eat. He looked at me, bemused, and I realised that his opening line may have been the full extent of his English. I pointed towards the cluster of buildings behind him, suggesting we go and have a look. He smiled, 'Please,' and gestured over to them.

We opened the door of a large building and once inside realised immediately from the old polished wooden floorboards and well-used items of sports equipment lying all around that it was a sports hall. I remembered back to the 1980s and communism when the Soviets had somehow always managed to pull amazing sporting performances out of the bag and wondered if any champions had been reared here in this secluded, secretive place.

We smiled appreciatively and continued the tour complete with our entourage, being taken to the accommodation blocks, the school and then on to the power station. The accommodation had an Eastern Block austerity about it, with small rooms, small ice-clogged windows, grey walls, and heavy metal radiators that clunked and rattled as coal-fired hot water was forced through them. For all intents and purposes it felt like a prison, a point reinforced by the fact that on all sides was Arctic wilderness with roads that led nowhere, making escape impossible.

The boilers of the power station billowed out dark smoke whilst an army of men fuelled the burners manually with coal, digging it from the large pile heaped behind them. The coal dust, fire and smoke from the burners, cigarettes in the mouth of virtually every man, and frozen breath combined to create a surreal scene of smoke, dust and flames amongst the ice.

Just when we thought that things could get no more weird, we were taken down the steps of an adjacent building to a vast subterranean cavern. I knew something was afoot before we even opened the door to the basement of the building, as a strong earthy, composty smell hit me. As I opened the door, I was confronted by a heaving mass of animals, steam rising off them as they grazed unconcerned by our presence. I looked at Ed incredulously. There in front of us under strip lights was a large underground herd of cows, mooing and occasionally farting noisily. Our guide looked at them with pride, seeing that we were impressed. In fact we were amazed. The temperature outside was –20°C and here were cows feeding on fodder grown under solar lamps, all made possible by electricity which came from burning coal – a distant legacy from when this remote Arctic island had been situated at the equator.

We finished our 'tour' and went for an obligatory vodka with Dmitri. He was an engineer, but more than that I couldn't work out. Sitting in what was presumably Barentsburg's sole watering hole, we were again the centre of attention, and out of nowhere came Cold War Russian medals and knick-knacks made from bits of reindeer. We bought a couple of medals, conscious that we might be depriving a family of the legacy of a heroic ancestor, but the current generation were insistent and we gave them the asking price out of respect and as thanks for their hospitality. Now we needed to be on our way, as the day was drawing on and we still had to find the weather station on the west coast, some 20 kilometres distant.

We asked for directions and Dmitri pointed out to the south, gesturing that we should then make a loop back round to the north-west. Barentsburg was, however, only just on our map, and to venture south would have taken us off the map and into unknown territory. We were still in the Arctic, skidoos or no skidoos. In fact if anything, skidoos mean you can get yourself lost more quickly as you speed across the ice.

'What about across there?' I asked, pointing directly west where I knew the weather station to be according to the compass. This route appeared to take us over a wide bay a couple of kilometres across. 'Is it solid enough to cross or is the ice too thin?'

Dmitri's response, 'Da', left me lacking. I resorted to sign language to get my point across, pointing first at the skidoos and then down at the ground as if to say, will we break through the ice? There was discussion amongst the small crowd and although there was no definitive answer, the consensus seemed to be that it was quite thick ice.

We decided we would try it. Like crevasses, if we sped across weak sea ice quickly enough, spreading the weight of us and our skidoos, we presumed we'd be safe. We said our goodbyes, gunned the engines into life and turned to the west. Within a couple of minutes Barentsburg had receded into the distance and we had reached the edge of the sea ice. Its surface seemed smooth, and small upturned sections around its edge looked to be 20 or so centimetres thick. It seemed strong enough and so we decided to pick a point on the far side of the bay and head for it. Although it was token, at least we were lighter. Despite eating a diet of over 5000 calories a day during the trip Ed had lost 5 kg and I had lost over 7 kg.

For the first kilometre or so we were fine, travelling in single file at about 50km/h. Suddenly icy cold spray whipped against my face mask as I saw Ed's skidoo dip into a depression ahead of me. Momentarily I thought he must have broken through the ice, but as I slowed to get a closer look I realised it must have been a pool of water recently formed in a depression in the surface of the ice, deformed by the pressure either side of it.

We slowed down to walking pace. 'Shit, it's a bit dodgy out here,' shouted Ed. I agreed, anxious to keep moving, the shore seeming a long, long way off. Again we accelerated up to 50, heading for the far side. Not twenty seconds later Ed was suddenly airborne. Unable to react in time, so was I a split second later. For just a moment we were both airborne almost in slow motion, until with a crash we both hit the surface of the ice at speed, accelerating again as the caterpillar track of the skidoo got purchase. Shiiiit! We stopped to take stock of our situation, although that was perhaps the least sensible thing to do. The ice appeared solid – and if it hadn't broken under that impact, let's face it, it probably was. Now it became a game as we took the camel bumps at speed, landing just long enough to accelerate before hitting the next one.

We ascended the brow of a hill on the far side of the bay and looked back at Barentsburg, dwarfed by the Arctic landscape in which it sat. Ahead of us in the distance we could now see the blotchy patchwork of dark ocean and sea ice and a distant tower that evidently marked the weather station.

Twenty minutes of hard throttle and we pulled up outside the station. We were stiff with the cold, and it was good to give the ears a rest after half an hour of raucous ear-splitting noise. You weren't going to sneak up on any wildlife on a skidoo, that's for sure. Before we had the chance to knock on the heavy wooden door of the weather station it creaked open and there standing before us was a small figure.

'Hi, we've come from "Longyear" and were hoping we could have a look round the weather station,' I offered, looking down at the dwarf before us. The figure took a few seconds to respond and, as usual for Scandinavians, did so in perfect English.

'Sure, come on in.' We entered the station, removing boots and clothing layers to adjust for the warmth. It was old and atmospheric with whitewashed walls, and reminded me of light-houses in Scotland I'd been to as a kid. Within a few minutes we were acquainted. Eric was a dwarf, but in stature only. He was from Tromso on the Norwegian mainland and manning the station single-handedly for a few days and although not lonely was happy for the company.

He invited us to stay for dinner just as the prospect of expe-dition provisions loomed. Soon we were tucking into a hearty reindeer stew and a few beers and chatting away enthusiastically.

'Why'd you do it?' Eric asked. Ed and I explained our reasons and once again, when asked the question directly, the answers sounded bland. I heard myself saying words like 'challenge' and 'life is short', but the deeper reasons related to wanting to live up to my potential and find out something about my place in the scheme of things. Eric seemed satisfied with our answers. I don't think he was worried one way or the other. 'I'd be unable to do that kind of thing anyway,' he laughed. 'Not exactly the build for pulling heavy loads.' We all laughed.

'Let's go and see my old friend Igor at the reservoir,' sug-gested Eric. 'I haven't seen him for a while.' Intrigued, we agreed, and donned our gear. Eric appeared a couple of minutes later transformed, wearing cold weather gear, a big bowie knife and Magnum pistol round his waist, with a bottle of vodka and some biscuits under his arm. 'Follow me!' he shouted, blasting off east towards Barentsburg on a beast of a machine. Ed and I floored our skidoos, having to work to keep up with Eric's small frame on his more powerful machine.

Soon we began climbing ever more steeply, cutting clean swathes through the snow as we powered upwards, until eventually we reached the head of a pass. There we stopped and looked down on an amazing scene. Just below us was a frozen lake tucked in between two mountains with a small hut next to it, smoke coming from its chimney. Way below on the far side of the valley was Barentsburg.

We descended towards the hut and were met by a couple of vicious-looking, barking huskies. Eric knew them and shouted something so that they immediately shut up. In the doorway of the ramshackle hut a huge figure appeared – the opposite of our experience of only a few hours earlier at the weather station. On the face of it, he was more of a deterrent than the dogs: at 6 feet 4 inches, wearing tight-fitting thermal underwear that left little to the imagination, fluffy slippers and sporting a wild orange beard, he was quite a sight.

Eric spoke a few words of Russian to him and he invited us in. Inside was warm and in one of the inner rooms we were introduced to another guy who sat intently watching TV. Of all things it was the Eurovision Song Contest – just the kind of thing you come to a place like Spitsbergen to escape. We half-watched it to take the pressure off the stilted conversation we were having that relied on Eric's 100 words of Russian to continue. It was a surreal scene. Two Englishmen who'd just manhauled across Spitsbergen, in the company of a Norwegian dwarf and two Russian reservoir operators watching the Greek entry in the Eurovision Song Contest, on a TV in Arctic Norway.

It wasn't long before our bottle of vodka, plus one of theirs that had been standing on a shelf (presumably waiting for just such an occasion) had both been polished off. The conversation now flowed easily and the Russians suggested going to the top of a nearby mountain to afford a view of the west coast.

One guy remained and Igor, Ed, Eric and I blasted up a steep mountainside on the skidoos, leaning heavily into the slope to stop the skidoo rolling over a long menacing-looking drop below us. I wasn't sure how safe it all was but with a few drinks inside me and no pedestrians or other motorists to watch out for I wasn't too bothered. Above me Eric flew up the mountain until I saw the brake light of his skidoo go on. I slowed down myself, and just as well I did as we appeared on the flat summit which was little bigger than a golf green. Had I been going fast I could easily have flown up and over the precipitous edge and dropped seven or eight hundred metres.

There were sheer drops on all sides other than the one we'd just come up and 360-degree views of the frozen pack-ice, angular peaks, and vast snow fields glistening in the sun. It was an incredible scene. We turned the skidoos round, physically having to lift them and point them back in the direction from whence we'd come as there wasn't room for a turning circle up on the summit, and started our treacherous descent.

As we headed back to the weather station, the sheer scale of nature, the brutal honesty of the environment and the pristine beauty of the place left a lasting impression. The trip had been amazing, with the camaraderie between Ed and me being a real highlight. I knew that it would not be the last experience I would have in the polar regions; I would have to come back for more.

5

Great southern land

Still no sensation in my right hand – Christ, that wasn't normal. I fumbled around for the zip on the sleeping bag and managed to get it undone. The hard-won warmth haemorrhaged out into the frigid interior of the tent where the now familiar ice crystals had already begun to form. I remember tents being inviting places as a kid – but not here where once your body heat was sealed up in your sleeping bag the cold quickly reclaimed the tent turning it into an icy tomb several times colder than your fridge freezer.

I seldom took off my innermost glove layer – not even in my sleeping bag – due to the cold, but now I needed to, to assess the damage. My hands were shaking, and I felt a rising wave of nausea with the anticipation of what I might find. I tentatively peeled off the glove and was shocked by what I saw. The fingers and thumb on my right hand from the knuckles upward were frozen solid and had assumed the colour and glassy sheen of ivory, with the tips already starting to turn black. Instinctively I hit them on the side of the pot next to me to get aural confirmation of what my eyes were telling me. Sure enough, I heard a dull metallic thud and felt nothing – the flesh was solid and lifeless. Although I'd prepared myself for this I was scared as

I knew how quickly the tissue can turn gangrenous once the circulation is cut off. Severe frostbite can spell permanent loss of sensation at best and the loss of fingers and potentially fatal blood-poisoning at worst. I lay there in the light of the midnight sun, with my world seeming like a very dark place. My fingers and right thumb had probably been without blood supply for six or seven hours and that was not good.

My co-expeditioner Peter was asleep and I felt a wave of emotion well up inside me as my mind started racing. It was a combination of fear of what could happen, and knowing that if this turn of events did not stop me, it could still mean the loss of my right thumb and my living with a severe handicap once this was all over. I hated this place for being so unforgiving – taking all you had to give and then some. I again questioned my reasons for subjecting myself to such intense physical and mental punishment. I repeated the rhetoric I had so confidently told well-wishers and journalists like a mantra before I left: 'I want to test myself and see what I'm capable of.' 'I want to push my personal envelope and learn something about myself.' The words seemed hollow now, but they were all I had to hold on to. I lay there and told myself that to reach the Pole meant enduring this kind of hardship and that I would have felt disappointed if it had been easy. Right now though, 'easy' would have been just fine.

I set to work bringing myself back on an even keel. If I could just get this situation under control I'd be able to keep going. Only twelve days to go to the South Pole and we would have accomplished the fastest ever unsupported journey to it. That would be more than my wildest dreams and then some. Beyond the Pole was something to be thought about later.

The panic began to subside, replaced with a veneer of resolve. We'd been doing it tough for over a month and the strain was beginning to tell both physically and mentally. I'd had to dig deep into my reserves of energy and now I had to overcome this setback on top of the assault on the body and mind to which Antarctica was going to subject me tomorrow. I sat up and started the stove to warm some water to try to thaw out my hand and snap me out of my despondent frame of mind. Peter woke and asked what I was doing and I showed him my hand. 'Shit, that's not good,' he managed, but offered little else. I felt lonely but the roar of the burners and wave of heat as the stove burst into life at least gave some comfort. It was day 35, and I knew that for another 55 days I would expose my body to conditions just like those that had caused my frostbite. It was a daunting prospect.

^ ^ ^

Only two months earlier, my partner Andrea and I were sitting at Peter's place in Sydney planning the final aspects of the trip. We'd met when she had been my rowing coach in Adelaide and although she'd supported me with most things she'd been against my trying this right from the start. She couldn't understand the reasons why I wanted to do it, didn't like the danger associated with it, and most of all I think she feared the physical and mental condition I would come back in, if in fact I came back. I understood her fears but found some of the sentiment strange coming from her. She was pretty single-minded about her rowing and certainly expected others, me included, to fit in with her plans.

Trying to explain my reasons to her at least helped me distil my thoughts on why I was going to attempt the journey. I suppose I've always been someone who resists convention and has had a questioning mind. One of the things I have always had a problem with is the way in which people seem to create an artificial divide between our working lives and what we do the rest of the time. To my mind it's all just life – nothing else. Still, society persists in ordering our time, giving it an artificial structure – nine to five, Monday to

Friday, financial years, daylight savings, going for Sunday drives. We live and function by the rules that are imposed upon us, or that we passively accept. To not have them would undoubtedly cause mayhem, but to steadfastly and unquestioningly live by them means that you may just miss the bigger picture. To my mind there's so much more you can discover about yourself, and about the world in which we all live, if you try different things and try to live life more on your terms. This is central to the reason why I enjoy challenging journeys. They help you to transcend this temporal and societal structure that we give life, such that you see it stripped back to its basic elements – raw and powerful, occasionally harsh but ultimately quite beautiful. Planning and undertaking journeys becomes a heady experience and quite empowering. The excitement of trying something different is like a drug. You are going into uncharted territory where you are in charge of your destiny and, often, your very survival. The only dimensions are those of your own creation.

To me the idea of trying to cross Antarctica was the very embodiment of these ideas. It was all about the excitement of waking up one day and saying, 'Today I am going to embark upon a journey to try to reach the end of the earth,' and wondering at every point along the way what was going to happen and whether I could make it. It wasn't just the allure of going to a place like Antarctica, but as much the fact that it represented a place described by experts as one 'least suited to human habitation' – a place where I would push myself to my physical and mental limits and probably reset all of my horizons. It was a big adventure and life is too short to not have at least one or two of those while you can.

Like many dreams, if you're not careful they seem to slip away as your time and energy are dissipated and robbed by so many of the other things that we clog our lives with. What I was sure of was that I didn't want to have a conversation with someone a few years down the track and have them say, 'Whatever happened to that idea of yours to trek across Antarctica?' and for me to say, 'Oh, that trip – unfortunately I never got round to it.'

∧ ∧ ∧

I've always been a sociable person. That perhaps is the irony of attempting polar journeys, which tend to be very lonely pursuits. I never set out to do things on my own in life, but when you come to the realisation that there are few others who share your particular goals, things just end up that way. Having said that, I knew that I didn't want to attempt Antarctica alone. I wanted to be able to share the experience with someone. Plus, the trip was as extreme as you could possibly get and so going alone wasn't a realistic option.

Crossing Antarctica unsupported is arguably the biggest land-based challenge on the face of the earth. This is not only because of the distance, the effects of altitude, and the extremely low temperatures, but a combination of this and the effort required to pull a massively heavy sled laden with all the food and equipment you need to survive such conditions. The stats for the journey say it all.

The South Pole sits on a plateau at almost 3000 metres high and parts of the journey are up over 4000 metres where the air is even thinner and more difficult to breathe. The high altitude means the atmosphere contains less oxygen, and temperatures as low as –40°C, or some five times colder than your domestic freezer, make the air even more rarefied. The incessant wind of Antarctica – the windiest continent in the world – lowers temperatures even further. Perhaps the Canadians best describe the effects of these conditions on the human body. Their 30 Rule states that at –30°C in 30-mile-an-hour wind, exposed skin will be frostbitten in 30 seconds.

In order to survive a journey of over 2700 km on foot across Antarctica you need to drag some 220 kg or 500 lb of food, fuel and equipment behind you in a sled. In the words of the famous British explorer Ranulph Fiennes (regarded by many as the world's greatest living explorer), trying to pull such a weight is 'like trying to pull a bath tub with three grown men in through sand'. It was little wonder that no-one had ever managed the journey unassisted before.

Choosing someone to accompany me for such a trip wasn't going to be easy, but strangely we didn't choose one another as much as circumstances chose us.

I'd arrived in Australia in February 1997 to take up a job as an environmental scientist in Adelaide. Funnily enough, that job had to a certain extent found me too. After a couple of years in Chester, I'd decided I needed new challenges and applied speculatively to a series of environmental organisations in the Asia–Pacific region. With my desire to do more meaningful work in the environmental and overseas aid fields, and wanting to get back to where I'd spent most of my childhood, Asia felt like the place to be. Of the 30 or so organisations I'd applied to, the first one to step forward was a firm in Adelaide, and so three months later I was there.

I hadn't known what to expect when I arrived as I'd never met anyone from Adelaide before. Despite all my years of travelling I had silly images of men wearing long socks, desert boots and cork hats in a city of dusty streets with wooden verandahs. On arrival I was pleasantly surprised to discover a beautifully laid out city with gardens, churches and water fountains and lovely sandstone buildings from the Victorian era. Coincidentally, of all the places I could have ended up in Australasia, Adelaide was the place most steeped in the legacy of exploration, and in particular polar exploration. In the nineteenth century Sturt, Stuart, and McKinlay had left from Adelaide to 'discover' large tracts of Australia, and their legacy had been continued into modern times. The likes of Len Beadell who had built roads through some of Australia's most remote areas, Warren

Bonython who had explored many of South Australia's vast salt lakes and biologist Tim Flannery, who had explored Papua New Guinea and parts of Australia's interior during his extensive field surveys, all called Adelaide home.

As far as polar exploration went, I discovered that Adelaide was also home to two of Australia's leading polar explorers – Hubert Wilkins and, of course, Sir Douglas Mawson. Wilkins and Mawson were each very different men in many respects, but both achieved much in the field of polar exploration and set the bar pretty high.

Hubert Wilkins was born in rural South Australia in 1888, the thirteenth child of a South Australian sheep-farming family and as such wasn't an obvious candidate for polar explorer. Nevertheless he had a pioneering spirit and a passion for adventure and over the years this resulted in his becoming one of the foremost pioneers in polar air travel, pulling off some amazing solo flights over the polar ice caps.

Somewhere high over the ice of the North Pole in his little plane he hatched a crazy plan to take a submarine beneath the ice of the North Pole. To carry out the journey he bought a surplus World War I sub for one dollar from the US Navy. He called it *Nautilus*, recruited a crew and in 1931 set sail from the US on the long ocean journey across the Atlantic. As soon as they encountered pack-ice Wilkins delivered a rousing speech to his men and told all hands to prepare to dive. The sub, however, had been damaged, apparently deliberately by one of the crew. Wilkins was devastated by this turn of events but still determined to prove that submarine travel under the ice was possible. With what little control remained in the sub's diving planes and by distributing the ballast to the front of the boat to make it nose-heavy he rammed into the ice, and the sub continued under the ice for some kilometres before turning back.

Mawson on the other hand is remembered for his incredible journey of survival in Antarctica in 1912. He and two colleagues, Ninnis and Mertz, set off from the South Magnetic Pole to explore the uncharted coastline of Antarctica. They trekked across heavily crevassed glaciers, and were hampered by terrible weather, including blizzards with wind speeds of over 100 km/h. One fateful day, Mawson and Mertz stopped to rest, turning to see where Ninnis was. Ninnis, the sledge and his dog team were, however, nowhere to be seen. Retracing their steps they came to the edge of a gaping crevasse and there on a ridge some 45 metres below was a dog, whining, its back apparently broken. Mertz and Mawson called into the depths for over three hours, but their rope could not even reach as far as the dog.

They were in serious trouble as Ninnis's sledge, pulled by the six fittest dogs, had carried most of the indispensable supplies, including the tent, most of the food and the spare clothing. Saddened, they continued on, forced to consume the dogs as they went. Still 250 km from Main Base, Mertz died inexplicably in convulsions in Mawson's arms (as it transpires, from toxic levels of vitamin A present in the dogs' livers that he had eaten). Mawson battled on alone with virtually no food save the parts of the dogs they had not yet consumed, including their paws. Despite almost indescribable odds he finally collapsed through the door of the hut at Main Base. He was on his last legs with injuries, malnutrition and frostbite so bad that the first words uttered by his men were, 'Which one are you?' He was virtually unrecognisable after his ordeal.

Both stories were inspiring ones and both men had been regarded as world players in polar exploration terms. Interestingly, in addition to Adelaide's polar legacy, the surgeon to whom I had been referred following my knee injury two years before, Greg Keane, was also based in Adelaide. Although I didn't get my knee operated on further, these were interesting coincidences, or perhaps invisible forces were at work. Either way, circumstances seemed to be conspiring towards my attempting another polar journey.

South Australia was a breath of fresh air literally and metaphorically, from its pristine beaches and rugged coastline to the massive expanse of outback and its ancient mountain ranges. I had discovered a new place to explore, complete with new challenges and had soon involved myself in a whole range of activities. By the end of 1997 I had cycled across the Simpson Desert, four-wheel driven through several others, and become a member of Adelaide University's Men's Rowing 8, training for the hotly contested Inter Varsity (IV) Championships.

Knowing of my ergo victory of the previous year, local coaches stuck me in a rowing boat expecting great things, physically. I was probably the strongest in the crew, but despite securing a seat in the IV 8, I knew it would be a while before my technique was as polished as that of the other guys, many of whom had rowed since they were kids. The irony of rowing is that although it requires massive power output it also requires precision, with one person in a crew of nine able to upset the whole boat – especially someone of my size. I loved the rowing and the camaraderie of the Men's 8, but I craved something less technical that I could throw strength into. Someone at the rowing club jokingly suggested I should try surfboat rowing.

I say 'jokingly' as it's a case of never the twain shall meet as far as surfboat and river boat rowing are concerned. Surfboats have been largely replaced by lightweight inflatable boats with outboards for patrol and surf rescue duties, but a huge national competition racing these old boats remains. River boat rowing is all about finesse, balance and the controlled application of power. Surfboat rowing is radical, gut-wrenching and dangerous, involving punching through whatever the ocean throws at you. Big, robust and stable though, surfboats offered a good prospect for my 'style' of rowing, especially as I was living down at Adelaide's main metropolitan beach, Glenelg, anyway. I got an introduction down at the club and based on strength alone joined the men's 'A' crew unaware of what I was getting myself into.

The team consisted of the nuggety captain Mick – a motor-bike cop when he wasn't surfboat rowing; Doug, a former State-level river boat rower; Wade, who had won bronze in river boat rowing at the junior world championships five years before; and myself. We were the engine room, and our sweep or helmsman was 'Breaky', a cunning grey-haired bearded campaigner who had an uncanny ability to read the surf. After a few weeks of practising in calm ocean conditions we started to become a pretty useful unit, managing to time our strokes well. I was enjoying it and felt I was beginning to get the hang of things until Mick casually announced we were off to Sydney to contest three of the toughest surf 'carnivals' at the Manly, Narrabeen and Freshwater beaches in a few weeks' time. That gave us the next three weekends to practise my as yet untrialled race technique. I began to feel the gradient of a steep learning curve approaching fast. That sensation at least was familiar to me even if surfboat rowing wasn't.

We headed down to Adelaide's south coast the next weekend. The sea was violent and fizzing with energy, with large waves crashing in rapid succession onto the shallows before even reaching the beach. It was cold and grey, and the whole scene was raw and uncompromising. We dragged all 300 kg of the boat into the water, put the oars in and paddled out into the inferno to practise.

The first wave engulfed us, filling the boat one-third full of water. It was cold and took my breath away, and it made the boat instantly heavy and unmanageable. Despite massive aerobic effort we seemed to be rowing on the spot, just maintaining our position against the force of the surf trying to throw us back onto the beach. Mick kicked on the electric bilge pump and the weight of the boat began to lighten slightly until the next roller crashed in, again immersing us in icy foam. The boat bucked wildly as we ploughed over or through the successive waves, each man trying to row in unison to send the boat forward.

Finally all was quiet as we reached the relative peace beyond the breaking waves.

Now we were on a rolling ocean of massive swells that swept menacingly beneath us en route to the beach to wreak the havoc we had just experienced. 'Time to head in,' said Breaky. I was now rowing with my back to the shore and could see the waves rising up behind us; fat grey walls of water that were above Breaky's head. I wondered what the hell was in store for us.

'Okay, this one!' he shouted. Everyone began to row like crazy as if their life depended on it, including me. Suddenly the boat was weightless and I couldn't row fast or hard enough to get a purchase on the water beneath us. We were on the back of a massive breaker that had picked up the boat and the 450 kg of its passengers and was hurtling us back towards the shore. 'Trail oars!' shouted Breaky. Everyone took one final stroke and ducked beneath their oar, rushing back up the boat to sit around Breaky. I followed suit, breathing heavily with the effort and coursing adrenaline.

Breaky worked hard to keep us pointing straight into the shore on the back of our wave with his 'sweep' oar. If we veered off course, the wave would tip us over and pound us into the surf. Ten seconds later we came to a stop on the beach and all jumped out whooping with excitement.

'And that's surfboat rowing, mate,' said Doug smiling broadly.

'Bloody good! I shouted, the prospect of five races in today's carnival already in the back of my mind.

Just a few weeks later, we stood ankle-deep in the water in a line of a dozen boats across Manly beach, waves rolling in at regular intervals. The gun went and we sprang from the shallows into the boat, leaning back on our oars, easing into our seats to take our first stroke. As we did, a large wave hit, lifting the boat to near vertical and throwing me out of my seat and onto the floor. I recovered quickly, jumping back into the seat to continue rowing, looking down at my oar handle to make sure my hands were correctly placed. There was something wrong with my right hand though. My index finger was snapped outwards at a crazy angle at the knuckle.

'Can you row on?' shouted Mick.

'Err, no . . . don't think so,' I replied.

After a visit to a local GP, the bad dislocation in my finger was popped back in, though it now looked distinctly like a snake that had swallowed an egg. I strapped the injured finger to those either side of it and felt sure I could compete the next day. Out of the Manly carnival now, I sat on the beach, half-watching, half-reading the paper, soaking up the sun and the atmosphere.

I flicked casually through the paper and did a double take. There staring out at me was an article about the exploits of 'Australia's leading polar explorer'. His name was Peter Treseder and he was a Sydneysider who'd just returned from Antarctica. I couldn't believe my eyes. Here I was sitting on Manly beach in my bathers, nursing a badly dislocated finger and reading an article about Antarctic exploration. Again I felt that unseen forces were at work. I decided to call the number at the bottom of the article to try to speak to this guy, unsure of exactly what I was going to say.

The voice at the other end of the phone was from a charity nominated by the expedition team, but after I described myself as a polar explorer from the UK they were prepared to give me Peter's number.

'Is that Peter Treseder?'

'Speaking.'

'Hi, I'm Tim Jarvis.' I described my Spitsbergen epic and then to my surprise found myself saying that I was planning a trip to Antarctica. I got the distinct impression that the voice on the other end of the phone was now listening intently to what I had to say and I found myself in dangerous territory as I didn't really have a plan.

'Which side would you go from, the Ross or the Ronne?' I guessed he was referring to the Ross Ice Shelf, from where Scott had set off back in the early 1900s, and I suggested that the Ross sounded good.

'Interesting,' replied the voice. 'How do you intend to get there? Have you managed to sort something out with the Americans at McMurdo?'

I wasn't even sure it was the Americans who ran the McMurdo Base on the coast of Antarctica nearest to New Zealand. 'Not yet, no,' I replied.

Peter cut the conversation short. 'Listen I only got back from Antarctica a week or so ago so I'm a bit tired. Why don't we talk in a few weeks' time?'

Well, that's the end of that, I thought after we'd said our goodbyes. I was sure I'd sounded pretty half-arsed and was annoyed with myself.

∧ ∧ ∧

Three weeks went by. Then a friend of mine, Bruce Macky, called me up and asked if I wanted to go to a lecture on Antarctica that a friend of his was giving in Adelaide in a couple of weeks' time. Bruce was something of an adventurer himself. He had been my support driver in the race I'd taken part in across the Simpson Desert and was a good guy.

'Who's giving it?' I asked.

'A guy called Peter Treseder,' he replied. 'Heard of him?' I couldn't believe my ears. Another coincidence.

After the lecture, I went up and spoke to Peter. A number of audience members were loitering with intent so we agreed to continue the conversation over dinner the next day at Bruce's place. Interestingly, now that we'd met face to face, Peter seemed keen to talk.

Sitting round the table at Bruce's the next night we sized one another up. Peter was bespectacled with intense blue eyes and a full beard, but surprisingly was slightly built at 5 feet 11 inches and didn't look like your 'typical' explorer. Despite this, he had an amazing CV of achievements in the outdoor field and at 41 years of age was touted by many as Australia's leading explorer. At his lecture he had spoken very confidently and with great authority about his previous polar journey, and as Bruce poured out the red wine in customary fashion, the conversation soon turned to Antarctica and my plans.

I explained that I had started off considering the possibility of trying to retrace the journey of Douglas Mawson, but had changed my mind and now thought I'd go for broke and aim higher. 'Basically, now I'm interested in trying to cross the whole thing.'

'Why?' asked Peter.

'It's of greater interest to me and I think the public and sponsors will get behind it as well. You've got to try and break new ground and this is breaking new ground.' I waited anxiously for his reaction.

'It'll be breaking new ground all right. I've been thinking along similar lines. I liked the idea of the Mawson journey when you first suggested it to me, but this appeals far more. It's got to be the biggest journey that anyone could attempt and I reckon it's achievable if we can get all the elements right. There are a lot of obstacles we'd need to overcome to make a journey like that work, not least of all finding the money to do it.'

I headed home with in-principle agreement from Peter that we would try to pull together a proposal and take it from there. That night I felt excited in the pit of my stomach. I knew this situation – the honeymoon period you get when the wonderful simplicity of a good idea forms in your mind, before the hard work of trying to make it reality bites. I lay in bed that night amazed that we had got to this stage in only a couple of meetings and felt like I'd pulled off a real coup getting someone of Peter's calibre interested. Agreeing to work together to get such a big trip off the ground when we were both still pretty much unknowns to each other did seem strange, though. I discovered a year later that Peter had actually done a lot of asking round about me since we'd first spoken and was instrumental in our meeting via Bruce that day. By the end of two years' planning we would know one another just fine.

Peter and I had a mutual interest in the journeys of Sir Ernest Shackleton and in particular his incredible journey of survival in Antarctica. Shackleton had decided to attempt the holy grail of polar exploration – the crossing of the Antarctic continent via the South Pole (as the North and South Poles had recently been reached by the explorers Peary and Amundsen respectively). But things went from bad to worse as Shackleton's ship, the *Endurance*, en route to Antarctica first became entombed in the ice of the Weddell Sea for over a year, and was finally crushed and sank before they ever reached Antarctica.

What followed was a script that even Hollywood couldn't have come up with. Shackleton managed to rescue his men from certain death, leading them to safety by first dragging the *Endurance*'s heavy wooden lifeboats across the frozen ice of the ocean to a deserted barren Antarctic island, Elephant Island. Shackleton and four men then embarked on a seemingly suicidal journey across almost 1300 km of furious open ocean in one of the boats, to raise the alarm at a remote whaling station on the island of South Georgia. The journey has gone down in the annals of exploration as one of the most heroic ever, but it left unfinished business in the form of the original intention of the expedition – the unsupported crossing of Antarctica.

To a point Peter, like me, wanted to attempt the crossing simply because he knew it hadn't been done and the temptation to be the first to do it was too great to pass up. As Ranulph Fiennes once put it, 'Life is too short to waste time on second-class ambitions. Go for the big ones, even if that means a higher failure rate.' I felt that with an Arctic trip under my belt and with

Peter having already undertaken an Antarctic expedition, we could give it a good shot. In fact it would have been 'rude' not to try it. I felt Shackleton would have approved.

Peter and I were, however, very different characters in many respects. He was an intense and fairly serious personality at heart, with an obsession for undertaking challenges one after another leaving little time in life for anything else. He moved from one to the next with almost limitless energy, as if were he to stop he would never again find the momentum to get moving. Some saw his efforts as born of an obsession in building up his outdoor CV, and from a desire for acclaim. Others saw him as a hero figure, tackling one insurmountable challenge after another, donating all of the proceeds from the inevitable media attention to charitable causes.

Some of these reasons formed part of why I attempt such journeys, but for me it was to do with my finding out a bit more about the world and my place in it. Building up a list of outdoor achievements was never the goal; rather, I wanted to try one or two big challenges in life to see what it felt like and to know what I was really capable of.

Regardless of motives, the key to success in attempting something as major as this is having a common goal and objectives. In this respect we were like-minded. We both firmly agreed on two key points. First, the fact that the journey should be unsupported and second, that in order to do it properly we needed to start it from the coast of Antarctica.

'Unsupported' meant manhauling everything we would need for the journey. Our journey would therefore use none of the techniques favoured by modern polar adventurers, such as sails to harness the wind, motorised transport, food caches or any other aids. Even though the early explorers had some of these techniques at their disposal, such as animals to help pull the sleds and food drops set out by support crews to lighten their loads, these were used only to shorten the almost insurmountable odds the explorers faced, rather than make their journey easier per se. And so by way of recreating some of the spirit and intense hardship of those early expeditions we decided our journey should be an unsupported manhaul.

We would start from the edge of the permanent ice as the explorers of old had done, quite simply because they could go no further in their boats. Antarctica's vast coastline is actually made up of a combination of solid rock and permanent ice shelves many hundreds of metres thick, much of the latter having been there for tens of thousands of years. If the icy mantle was removed it would reveal a very different situation. The peaks of the Transantarctic Mountains would form islands, and the continent itself would be split into several parts separated by ocean.

To start at the edge of Antarctica proper, we therefore needed to commence at the Antarctic coastline as formed by the edge of the permanent ice, even though this added over 1000 kilometres to our journey. The early explorers didn't have the luxury of flying to the edge of solid land hundreds of kilometres inland, further south and nearer the Pole and so neither would we. We were reminded of the importance of this distinction by the fact that it was on one such ice shelf – the Ross – that Scott and his remaining men died in 1912. At the very least we owed it to them to start from the edge of the permanent ice.

6

Planning the improbable

Despite psyching myself up for it, when Peter called me early one morning to tell me what the final price tag was it knocked the wind out of me. 'I've just spoken with Kevin – basically we're looking at about two hundred grand.' I had an instant sinking feeling in my stomach. Two hundred thousand Australian seemed a huge figure to have to find. There was a pause at Peter's end before he spoke again. 'U.S.' 'Two hundred thousand US$!? – Christ almighty, that can't be right, surely?'

'It is,' replied Peter, 'they won't fly down there for less, it's just too risky.'

I couldn't believe how outrageous the amount seemed. 'How the hell are we going to get $400 000 Australian?'

'I don't know, let's go away and think about it,' said Peter. I agreed. There was no point continuing the conversation now when neither of us had anything positive to say about it.

That night it felt as though my dream had just evaporated right before my eyes and I went to bed feeling despondent and directionless. We'd already been planning for a couple of months and momentum had begun to build to such an extent that I was beginning to think that it alone would carry the day.

The following morning I rallied and called Peter to discuss things properly. Peter explained the list of risks that had been reeled off to him by the flight company. ANI or Adventure Network International were quite simply the only private company able to fly to Antarctica. Their costs included insurance against loss of aircraft and personnel, time delays due to bad weather, injuries, accidents, wear and tear, the cost of ferrying in drums of fuel to Antarctica for operations down there, and of course danger money for the pilots. All in all it was the proverbial high-risk venture for them, and apparently they made only a modest profit out of it in the end. I began to appreciate the magnitude of the task.

Nearly 90 per cent of this figure was the cost of actually getting in and out of Antarctica by plane. This is because there isn't exactly what you'd call a scheduled service down there, particularly not where we were headed, and so we needed to arrange our own flight. ANI ran a limited flight service using an old Hercules aircraft from the southern Chilean town of Punta Arenas to take climbers to a place called Patriot Hills in Antarctica. ('Patriot' has a natural ice runway and is near Antarctica's highest mountain, Mount Vinson.) For $20 000 US each we could get on ANI's flight to Patriot, which was a start, but we needed to book our place immediately to guarantee a seat for the following year. We could only do it by spending all that we currently had in the budget plus some, which we did, but it left us to the tune of $10 000 in the red and meant I had to cancel my Gold Coast break and cut back on Friday nights for a while. The irony was I felt like I needed them more than ever with the stress of organising the trip.

The cost of the first leg of our journey down to Patriot wasn't the expensive bit. It was the second leg, which involved us having to track down an aircraft capable of landing out in the middle of nowhere on the ice at a grid reference of our choosing, that caused problems. It was something the Herc couldn't do as its wheeled undercarriage couldn't land on the snow. We needed pilots of the highest calibre and a good aircraft with enough range to do the job, able to take off from a conventional runway and yet land on the ice down at Patriot Hills to meet us and then fly us to some deserted location on the Antarctic ice cap. This narrowed the field somewhat. After months of searching, a solution was found. Their names were Kevin and Dave and they were madcap Canadians who flew a Twin Otter aircraft in the Canadian wilderness making 'deliveries'. They never told me what exactly they delivered and I had images of them flying around consignments of caribou pelts or crates of whisky. I didn't ask too many questions; I just had it on good authority that they were the best and that's what we needed. They assured me their Otter would be up to the task as it was a twin-propeller plane that could carry about ten people. In our case it was going to be us, two heavily laden sleds and a couple of hundred gallons of fuel.

The deal was that they would fly the Otter all the way from northern Canada to Punta. They would then equip it with 'wheel-skis' which allowed take-off from a conventional runway and a landing on snow by retracting the wheels. They would spend a few weeks ferrying fuel from Punta to Patriot and that would give us the range to make the final journey from Patriot to our start point on the edge of Antarctica some 500 km from there.

It seemed straightforward enough – just fly across the fuel you need and then go for it – but as we were to find out, it wasn't quite that simple.

A few weeks earlier, on a wave of enthusiasm Peter and I had loftily mentioned to a journalist that we were going to try to use the trip and any media coverage we got from it to raise money for the New Children's Hospital at Westmead in Sydney, one of the main transplant hospitals for kids in Australia. Now I felt really bad. I couldn't see how on earth we were going to get four hundred grand to make the trip happen, let alone leverage a charity on the back of it, and in addition raise money for them. We began to feel naive and stupid for having thought this was going to be easy and guilty for having raised their hopes.

Westmead was chosen as we both felt that we wanted to use the trip and any media attention we got from it to do some good and children's health was as good a cause as you could get. We felt too that there were parallels between our own massive physical challenge and the challenges faced on a daily basis by many youngsters with serious illnesses at Westmead. As far as I was concerned I wanted to put something back into Australian society, having only recently been made a citizen. Westmead were a great crowd to work with, but in hindsight we should have waited until we were certain that the trip was a goer, as knowing they were expecting big things from us added a lot of friendly pressure.

We weren't the first to have money worries. The history of polar exploration is littered with stories of explorers sneaking off under cover of darkness owing money. Expeditions are normally extremely expensive and that can make money the limiting factor as much as the nature of the trip. Our reality was that we now needed about half a million Australian dollars or some 50 times more than the cost of the Spitsbergen expedition or we weren't even getting on the plane.

Peter had an OAM (a Medal of the Order of Australia) from a distinguished career in exploration and the outdoors and had secured the support of Prime Minister John Howard as patron for a previous trip. He decided he would approach him again to see if he would support us and Westmead as a good cause. His patronage would add credibility to the expedition and our ability to raise funds. In just two weeks Peter called to tell me that John Howard had agreed to be patron. It was the first major break we needed.

Spirits were buoyed by our success in getting John Howard's support. Peter then suggested out of the blue that, based on my being a former British citizen, I ask the British Prime Minister Tony Blair if he would like to be joint patron to honour the legacy of joint British and Australian polar expeditions over the years. I fired off a speculative letter to 10 Downing Street in London, explaining our project and providing a copy of John Howard's letter of support, and received a reply back saying my proposal was being considered.

A week or so later Peter informed me to expect a cc'd letter from John Howard's office that had just been sent to Tony Blair providing a reference for me! The letter which started, 'My dearest Tony . . .' suggested that we were a worthy cause and that he support the project. I was incredibly flattered. I had never had a reference from a prime minister before – normally it was difficult enough getting one from an ex-boss.

A month or so later an official-looking letter arrived at my house from 10 Downing Street and I opened it with nervous anticipation. 'Dear Tim, I would be delighted to perform the role of joint patron in what sounds like an incredible journey of discovery . . .' the letter read. Tony Blair had not only agreed – in fact he wholeheartedly supported us and even asked me to send his regards to the 'people of Adelaide', having spent a few memorable years there as a kid.

The patronage from the two prime ministers buoyed our confidence hugely and we remain truly indebted to them for their support. It made us feel that anything was possible almost as much as it helped our fundraising cause and our self-belief that we could make this whole thing happen. We got to work using our joint patrons' letters to good effect, photo-copying them and adding them to what was now becoming a pretty weighty proposal document that we mailed, faxed and took personally to potential sponsors. After six months we had lots of irons in lots of fires. In the final analysis, however, we had only managed to raise $30 000 from the Australian Geo-graphic Society courtesy of Dick Smith, and the Youth Hostels

Association, towards the journey. The total price tag was a massive Australian $530 000 – that left us $500 000 short, assuming the US dollar, ANI's specified currency, didn't strengthen further. That possibility alone added or subtracted as much as A$20 000 of the total cost of the trip. Some days we went backwards. It was bloody depressing.

Then John Leece got involved. John is an altruist and a millionaire accountant to boot – something of an oxymoron under normal circumstances. A genuine philanthropist, he provides his time and support to a range of worthy causes. One of these was involvement with the Australian Scouts where he performed the role of treasurer and from where he knew Peter who was a spokesman for the movement. John added us to his list of worthy causes and from that point on we never looked back.

To say John was well connected in Sydney is something of an understatement. He counted some of Sydney's most influential people as friends and many others as clients of his firm. One such person was Chris Roberts, then on the board of Telstra. Chris loved what we were trying to do and the parallels between the trip and Westmead. He wasn't sure whether Telstra could be involved, but felt sure that he knew other people who would want to be part of it all.

In the meantime John and Peter had managed to get a copy of our proposal in front of Lachlan Murdoch at News Ltd. Incredibly, Peter got a call from Lachlan Murdoch's secretary, asking us to come and meet him in his Sydney office to discuss our proposal a few weeks later. News Ltd had already indicated that they would be interested in covering the expedition as it unfolded, but we wondered what Lachlan Murdoch was going to say. I scraped together my Frequent Flyer points and got a flight over to Sydney.

Peter and I stood outside his office like kids waiting to see the headmaster, nervous with anticipation about the meeting. The door opened and we were invited in. Lachlan stood up from behind a large desk, leant over and shook hands with us. He was a young fit-looking guy with a friendly smile and demeanour and a distinctly American accent betraying the fact that he'd spent much of his childhood in the US. We sat down and he did most of the talking. He explained that prior to taking over part of the Murdoch news empire he had spent a year off climbing and trekking, and knew where we were coming from with the motivation for attempting the journey. He also indicated that the trip would provide a good ongoing news piece and that News would like to be involved in helping out Westmead via the coverage from the weekly articles. The only condition was that we needed to be able to update a News journalist every week with something newsworthy from down on the ice. We agreed, explaining we had a satellite phone and that updates would be straightforward. Twenty minutes later Lachlan seemed satisfied, stood up, extended his hand to us and the meeting was over.

We shook hands and got up to leave, feeling it had gone very well but not wanting to push our luck by broaching the subject of money.

'I was thinking along the lines of A\$100 000 as being News's contribution,' Lachlan said as we neared the door to his office. We nodded in agreement, as if we too had had that kind of figure in mind. The reality was we hadn't really got a clue what our story would be worth and would have taken whatever he'd given us. 'I'll get someone here to draw up a contract then,' Lachlan said.

'Great, look forward to receiving it, and thanks for your time and your help,' Peter and I spoke pretty much in unison, managing to keep the smiles off our faces until the lift doors shut. We punched the air. 'You bloody beauty – we're in business!' And we were.

Now our proposal document had international patronage and a letter from News Ltd effectively guaranteeing weekly media coverage in all of their Australian Sunday papers – a total of over seven million readers. Lachlan also told us to spend what we needed from the money, knowing we had some up-front costs we needed to meet, even though the trip was still far from a certainty. 'News wants this thing to happen,' he had said in his soft American accent. 'We can talk about it some other time if for some reason things don't work out.' We owed a lot to him for that and it couldn't have come at a better time. A few weeks later we got a call from the company in Germany who were building our sleds and from ANI. Both needed hefty deposits 'yesterday', and so no sooner had the money come in than it was all spent.

^ ^ ^

My eyes were tired of looking at the maps that covered Peter's lounge floor – and they only covered the first half of our journey to the Pole itself. What made it even more difficult to concentrate was the fact that there were no assurances that all this planning would amount to anything unless we got another $400 000. Regardless, I knew the planning needed to be done – and done well, or it could spell disaster. I went out onto the verandah to get some fresh air and looked at the beautiful copse of mature trees at the bottom of Peter's garden. His garden in suburban Sydney contained more greenery than exists in the whole of Antarctica. Christ, what a prospect.

Peter and I had divvied up the planning tasks equally. He looked at communications, medical supplies and clothing, and I sorted out navigation, route planning, food and equipment. Both of us were responsible for sponsorship.

Getting maps of Antarctica was our starting point for planning the trip, but they'd proven to be an interesting commodity, as much of Antarctica is made up of a large ice cap that is moving and changing. This, plus the harshness of the place and the treaty protecting Antarctica against exploitation makes the continent of little use from an economic point of view (a good thing). It isn't therefore the subject of much in the way of recent mapping. Our maps dated from the 1960s and even they were pretty sketchy on detail in some areas.

I recalled my conversation with the Australian Antarctic Division in Tasmania when trying to get my hands on maps a few months before. I'd been given a frank but enlightening response from a guy down there. 'Have you got a photocopier in your office?' I'd replied that I had. 'Well, open it up and take out about twenty blank sheets of A3.'

'Why?'

'Because they'll be about as much bloody use as the maps that exist for much of your route.' Although he was blunt, he seemed to have a good sense of humour and we'd chewed the fat for a while. 'It'll be an absolute bastard of a trip,' he said, clearly sceptical of my ability to pull it off and probably of my sanity.

He had a point though, particularly about the maps. There was no way we were going to be carrying a heavy map roll containing 40 or 50 maps across Antarctica, especially as we were even planning to cut our toothbrushes in half and pull labels out of jackets to save weight. Thus for 2300 km out of a total of 2735 km, we would rely on GPS grid references. The only places we would take maps for were bits we knew we needed to get right, like the mountains and glaciers that provided access to the polar plateau and where there would be crevasses and risk of falling. We would later come to realise how incredibly exciting it was when the GPS told us we had reappeared on a map after hundreds of kilometres alone in the vast emptiness of Antarctica. Looking at the map reassured us of what the GPS and our tired bodies were telling us – that we were creeping ever closer to the South Pole.

The next major issue facing us was what clothing to use to survive a journey like this one. Peter and I had a good idea from our previous trips but decided it was worth getting in touch with as many people for advice as possible. In fact I'm convinced that's a key aspect of expedition planning – never thinking you know more than you do and never being too proud to ask for basic advice from as many people as possible. With this in mind I managed to get the contact details for Ranulph Fiennes in the UK. He is something of a legendary figure and someone who had undertaken an incredible journey in Antarctica in the early 1990s.

Ran's book gave an interesting account of how he and his colleague Mike Stroud finally ran out of food and were dramatically rescued. Interestingly, Ran seemed to rate trust in a partner's abilities above friendship. I agreed. Working well together and being able to trust the other person with your life is most important. If you can find all that in a person you like, that's simply a bonus.

A deep, slightly suspicious aristocratic voice answered the phone. I told him I was interested in talking about Antarctica and the tone changed immediately. The conversation with Ran confirmed what I already knew, which was reassuring. For attempting to survive on an unsupported journey in the polar regions you need to dress reasonably light, start cold and keep warm through working. If you dress too warmly you overheat, dehydrate and your sweat freezes into your clothing. The ice then sits next to the skin, making you colder and more susceptible to frostbite in the long run.

Ran mentioned that Antarctica would be far colder than Spitsbergen, due to the wind and the fact that the polar plateau is up to 4000 metres high. 'Survival up there is tough,' he mentioned casually. 'A couple of sets of thermals and a breathable jacket is okay, but you'll need to keep moving to generate warmth and safeguard yourself against frostbite.' I knew from experience that a whisper of wind on a –20°C day and your extremities go numb inside six or seven minutes. It varies from person to person but if you leave it longer it can take a while to get them back. If you leave it too long you won't get them back. Circulation will stop, flesh will turn first white, then black, and then you're in deep shit.

Ran thanked me for my call, referring me to his polar partner, Mike Stroud, a doctor in the British army, for advice on nutrition. I thanked him for his time and was about to sign off when he made a final offering. 'Do you have a foreskin?' It was an unusual comment, so unusual I didn't have time to think about what he was driving at. Perhaps it was the phone equivalent of the Freemason's lifting of the trouser leg and I was being initiated into some polar club.

'Yes, I do,' I replied. 'Is that a problem?'

'No, no, quite the contrary. Protects the old fella from the cold. We were born with 'em and I think they're great protection.' His voice trailed off. 'All the best, anyway.'

∧ ∧ ∧

Let's face it, Australia isn't the ideal place to buy cold weather clothing. That's a problem with specialised gear – you can't just buy it off the shelf, you need to test it out first. On the off-chance I was flicking through the Yellow Pages one day and to my surprise I spotted that the Norwegian manufacturer Helly Hansen had an office in Melbourne. They had a very high profile for cold weather gear in the Northern Hemisphere, but were apparently more renowned for sailing and snowboarding gear in Australia. I gave them a speculative call then and there to see if they could help and was put through to their Product Manager, Craig Cobbin.

Craig was something of an outdoor enthusiast himself and the trip appealed to him on both a personal and professional level as an opportunity for Helly's to get some profile. He had been looking for quite a while for a vehicle like our trip to promote their extreme weather clothing range in Australia. 'It may just be your lucky day,' Craig had said at the end of our first conversation. Within two weeks, Helly's had said yes to supporting us with all the clothing we needed. It had been just pure luck that my timing had been right. It felt like a good omen.

I gave Craig my wishlist of critical properties that our clothing would need to possess. It would need to be breathable, yet capable of protecting us against winds of up to 80 km/h; durable and warm, but not too warm; and, of course, lightweight. Craig recommended an outer layer consisting of a Hellytech jacket and pants, and then either two or three thin thermal tops and leggings underneath – not much when you look at what conditions we were about to throw ourselves into.

Planning our journey threw up a whole series of interesting issues and Peter and I got to work trying to think through every conceivable aspect of the trip. Things like how easily we could put up the tent should the weather get nasty (which it often did). This was critical as the tent represented our only sure means of survival if the weather really deteriorated. If it became too windy to put the tent up the consequences of being stuck outside in extreme weather would have been dire. In the lead-up to the trip I took the tent out in some of the squalliest weather I could find to see how I coped and came up with a good rule of thumb at around 40 knots. Beyond that and you were grappling hopelessly with flapping fabric. Down south that could mean death.

With about fifteen months to go I began seriously training for the trip in the decidedly un-polar environment of Adelaide. Adelaidians are quick to inform you that Adelaide is the driest city in the driest state on the driest continent in the world. This isn't exactly accurate. Adelaide had a 37-day period with no rain a couple of years ago and people started reaching for the record books. In some parts of Antarctica there has been no precipitation, either snow or rain, for 250 000 years.

As that was where the similarities ended I decided I needed to find some way of simulating what it would be like to pull a heavy sled around in snow. When planning the Spitsbergen trip I had heard that dragging a heavy tractor tyre around was a good way to build up the fitness required. I knew there was a Bridgestone tyre dealership in downtown Adelaide and the next day I wandered in to make a few enquiries. A salesman appeared and asked me what I wanted. I told him I was looking for some old tractor tyres.

'For what?'

'To pull along.'

'To pull what along? What vehicle are you actually going to put them on?' he asked, now confused.

'On a rope attached to my waist,' I replied. I expanded. 'I'm after some old tyres to pull around for training for a trip I'm planning to Antarctica, to simulate pulling a heavy sled.'

'You're shitting me.'

'No, I'm serious.' Five minutes later I was fielding questions from him and the regional manager about the trip and they were keen to help.

'We've got a heap of old tyres out the back and you're welcome to whatever you want – we'll even deliver them to you – it's the least we can do. Just let us know how the trip goes.'

The next day, much to my elderly neighbour Connie's amusement, a pair of worn tractor tyres weighing some 60 kg turned up outside my house. Connie kept an eye out for parcel deliveries when I was at work and she knew to expect the unexpected. The previous week some ice-axes had turned up and I had warned her that I was also expecting a bulk consignment of woollen socks to arrive any time. She found it all a bit strange, but I think she liked the excitement really. Andrea was a little less happy with all of the expedition equipment that was starting to accumulate as it served as a constant reminder that this thing was beginning to gain momentum.

That weekend I lugged the tyres into the car and took them out for a 'training run' down one of Adelaide's metropolitan beaches – Henley Beach. I felt absolutely ridiculous as I bounced them out of the car onto the ground, rolled them down to the sand and attached them to my waist. A couple of elderly early morning walkers strolled past and looked at me very strangely and I smiled feebly back at them. They were going my way along the beach, and I decided to try to catch them. After fifteen minutes they had comfortably receded into the distance, despite my working tirelessly (excuse the pun) to catch them. They were probably experienced walkers, I told myself, and no doubt keen to put as much distance as possible between themselves and a sweaty, heavy-breathing nutter like me.

I finished my first session exhausted after about an hour. I had covered about 3 kilometres, had conversations with eight people about what I was doing and smiled goofily at quite a few others. It was a real worry that it had been so bloody difficult to pull two 30-kg tyres down a sandy beach. I imagined it was what dragging a body through the sand would've been like. I just hoped like hell that pulling a 220-kg sled through snow would be easier. The thought worried me all the way home. What if we got down to Antarctica and could cover only a fraction of the distance we were aiming for? That would leave us a long way short in terms of food, and you don't want that in a place like Antarctica. I pushed the thought to the back of my mind as for now there were more pressing issues like raising money, but it would haunt me until I got down there and took my first steps.

Training with tyres was a great idea in principle, but people's natural curiosity always prompted them to stop me and ask what I was doing. After a few more runs I decided that unless I intended to be stopping regularly to chat with people down in Antarctica it wasn't a representative way of getting fit for the journey. I used them a few more times after that but most of my training became long bike rides, runs in the Adelaide hills, rowing and weight training sessions – all fitted in around the gruelling regime of planning and organising the logistics of the trip.

Along with acquiring our unusual skills set for the journey, our endless round of trying to get sponsorship continued. We had described the trip as the last great land-based journey in the world and came out with some rather large claims as to media coverage we were going to get. It quite simply represented the best possible sponsorship opportunity for a company to become involved in.

We soon became pretty adept at talking up the details of the trip, depending on who we were talking to. To the media it was a hugely dangerous trip with the likelihood of plenty of exciting events and the possibility of death, that would make for either great viewing numbers or readership levels. As far as insurance companies were concerned, it was really just a glorified long-distance cross-country ski trip and we conjured up images of family holidays spent skiing from one log cabin to the next with virtually no danger at all. As for my mum, each time we would have a long-distance phone conversation, she would say, 'You will be careful, won't you?'

'Yes, Mum, don't worry, you know me.'

'Yes, I do, Timothy,' she would reply knowingly. That was precisely what she was worried about, as she knew that since I was a kid I'd always been inclined to bite off more than I could chew, and had just become accustomed to chewing faster to get through things. I loved my mum and understood her concerns. I also made a mental note to tell her not to refer to me as 'Timothy' if she ever spoke to the media.

The reality was we weren't really that sure of what the chances of death or serious injury from the trip were, although we discussed it many times when trying to plan contingencies for all the risks we would face. The funny thing with a trip like this is that people assume you are an expert in the field, even though in my case I'd never even been to Antarctica.

'What do you reckon?' Peter had asked me one day as we sat around his pool taking a break from things.

'About what?'

'You know, dying out there – what do you reckon?'

'I guess the cold, falling in a crevasse, getting lost, or losing one another are the big-ticket ones,' I replied. He agreed. As far as losing one another went, we planned to try as best we could to ensure that each of us had the equipment required to stay alive, like a stove, GPS, food and fuel in each of our sleds. That was fine for those items that we had two of, but certain items like the satellite phone and tent we only had one of. If you were the one who got lost without the tent, then you would be lucky to make it through a day and a night. Climbing into your sled would be your only possible option. That or digging a snow cave and hoping for the best. There were no real answers to this problem – we just had to ensure we didn't lose one another.

Crevasses were also going to be a problem. They formed chasms in the ice sometimes hundreds of metres deep and often invisible from the surface, lurking where the ice sheet changed slope or direction. We practised 'rescuing' one another from a crevasse down at the local climbing wall, by lifting one another up the wall while wearing heavy rucksacks full of weights. It was an exercise in futility for us to lift one another and we quickly realised that the chance of one of us being able to pull the other one out of a real crevasse with a 200-kg sled attached to him was pretty much zero. For weight saving we also only had 20 metres of rope, so if either of us had fallen into anything deeper, sled or no sled it would have been game over.

Peter continued with his train of thought. 'What about how far we push ourselves from a risk point of view?'

Suddenly I knew where he was coming from. 'You mean do I think it's worth risking our lives for?' I thought for a moment and then realised that of course it wasn't. 'I want to push myself as far as I can without overstepping the line,' I replied. It wasn't much of an answer but Peter nodded in agreement. As far as I was concerned I just hoped we would know when a risk became too great when we got down there. The problem, of course, is that it doesn't come down to those kinds of rational decisions, and often you don't know what the risks are to be able to make a decent judgment. Instead death is more likely to sneak up on you in the guise of something we'd done a hundred times before, or something we couldn't control, like a once-a-year storm that could simply blow our tent off the face of the earth.

From the warmth of Australia we looked at the prospect of death in Antarctica pretty philosophically – either that or we just didn't take the risk of it seriously. We knew, though, that we would have to wait and see what Antarctica threw at us before really being able to find out whether it was all just bravado. With that, we agreed that if either one of us had been unable to go on, or worse, became a fatality, the other would remain with him and ensure that they got back home no matter what, and that the expedition would be over for both of us if one of us had to stop.

The burden of organising the expedition weighed heavily. We had raised everyone's expectations including our own, arranged flights, food, equipment and logistics, as well as spending $100 000 of News Limited's money and yet were a long way from making the trip a reality. Still we pushed on, confidently telling everyone that the trip would happen, and most of the time I managed to convince myself it was.

With seven months to go we still hadn't managed to land any major sponsors since News's kind offer, despite having irons in various fires and lots of positive noises. When we spoke to potential sponsors, it was as though we only needed their money to ensure the trip went ahead. The reality was that we needed all of them to say yes to get us over the line, and the strain was considerable.

In early February we finally got the big break we needed. Arnott's Biscuits had been considering our proposal for them to hold naming rights for the trip. Peter and I readied ourselves and went down to see them at their HQ in Sydney. Before the meeting had even got under way, they said yes! We were stunned. 'Arnott's has a line called Arnott's Adventures, aimed at the Scouts, kids, youth and so on, and we feel that the trip is a perfect vehicle for it,' said Alec Waugh, their Intellectual Property Manager. (I later jokingly asked Alec what the intellectual property of a biscuit was but then wasn't the time to ask.) They were prepared to pay $250 000 in sponsorship, on a series of conditions, one of which was that the journey had to be called the 'Arnott's TransAntarctic Expedition'! We were so happy you could have changed Peter's name to 'Tam' and called the thing 'Tim and Tam go south' for all we cared, and we said yes to all of their requests.

We were still $150 000 short with about eight weeks to go when the final piece of the sponsorship jigsaw turned up. Our saviour was a company called Virtual Communities – an internet services provider.

We were ecstatic. A few weeks later and all the money we needed had been transferred into the expedition bank account. By our final reckoning, the way the budget was travelling, in addition to donating money to Westmead via paid talks and articles on our return, we in fact had a small surplus of about $20 000 that we would be able to give to them as soon as it was all over. It was funny, but we had signed away our lives in contracts with our sponsors where we were bound to give them media coverage and a whole series of other things for their investment in us, and they had free rein to use our image in perpetuity. That, however, was nothing compared with the toil and stress of raising the money and the pressure we felt to do the right thing by Westmead. That night I celebrated with a few friends in Adelaide and it must have been the cheapest night's drinking I'd ever had, with the heady combination of the alcohol and the lifting of the massive burden from my shoulders. I woke feeling seedy the next day, but as soon as the brain clicked into gear I remembered that we had done it; we were going to head south and nothing could now stop us.

Even with the high of securing the remainder of our sponsorship, my energy levels and confidence still ebbed and flowed during the final stages of planning and I would often wake at night, get up and frantically write down a list of things I needed to do the following day. The human mind can be intensely frustrating. Something good happens and it is all too easily erased or forgotten as you move straight on to the next thing on your never-ending list. Some nights I would just wake and lie there wondering what I was setting myself up for. The doubts and concerns that come to visit us all in the early hours were compounded for me by the wealth of literary material about the achievements of the polar heroes we sought to emulate and I found myself worrying about my ability to pull the trip off. I had to dig deep to remind myself that there was going to be only one way to find out where the truth lay and that was by going and giving it a try.

∧ ∧ ∧

After reliability, the number one consideration with every item for the expedition was weight. Weight is the biggest killer on these trips, which is what makes unsupported trips like ours so difficult. In particular food weight. You need a massive amount of energy to sustain yourself in the extreme cold and rarefied air of Antarctica and when you're engaged in the massive effort of pulling a heavy sled. In fact, in order to sustain yourself you need as much food as it is humanly possible for the body to metabolise each day. That's all well and good, but it means you've got to carry it, which in turn has huge implications for the weight of your load and your energy expenditure. At some point, the curve of additional food is cancelled out by the extra effort of having to carry it and we didn't know where that was. When the bodies of Scott and his remaining men were discovered the summer after they died, they were only 17 km from the safety of their food depot, their sled containing amongst other things some 30 kg of rock samples.

At the suggestion of the Australian Antarctic Division I got in touch with the Australian Defence Nutrition people for advice on food and certain aspects of equipment. They were happy to help but recommended I first get in touch with an army doctor in the UK called Mike Stroud. Of course, I knew Mike's name as he had accompanied Ran Fiennes to Antarctica back in the early 1990s.

I mentioned what Ran had said to me and Mike chuckled. He was a friendly guy and his advice as both a doctor and a polar expeditioner was topnotch. Mike was frank. 'It's an awful place to try to keep mind and particularly body together on one of these trips, Tim, especially when you're manhauling. It didn't seem to matter how much Ran and I ate down in Antarctica, we just couldn't keep the weight on as our bodies seemed incapable of absorbing the calories. Basically your body's deteriorating fast in such conditions.' By Mike's reckoning we'd need to be eating somewhere in the region of 6500 calories or roughly 22 Mars Bars' worth of food a day and he kindly offered to fax over information on a good polar diet.

Mike's faxed list contained lots of useful insights, including that it was best to consume your biggest meal of the day at night to allow the body maximum chance to absorb the calories. He also stressed the importance of eating lots of fat. Fat is best as it is the lightest of the three main food types in relation to the amount of calories it provides (ahead of protein and carbohydrate). He also recommended pemmican as a good source of fat, the principal ingredient basically being lard or boiled-down animal fat. Pemmican, a cake made of dried meat, fat and dried fruits, had fuelled a whole generation of explorers from the 'heroic era' including the likes of Scott, Mawson and Shackleton.

The massive food consumption was designed to slow the loss

of body muscle through the combined effects of extreme exertion and extreme cold, where you can easily burn over 8000 calories each day – the equivalent of three marathons a day. It was a truly worrying prospect thinking about what condition we would end up in, remembering how much weight Ed and I had lost in Spitsbergen where both the sleds and length of the journey were less than one-third of what we now faced.

Now we devoted all of our time to trying to devise the highest calorie, lowest weight diet we could, trying to translate Mike's scientifically devised expedition calorie chart into something we could actually buy from the supermarket and eat. Actually, organising the food was good fun. The overriding principle was doing the opposite of everything that dieticians and nutritionists tell you to do. The diet needed to be full of fat. That meant nuts, chocolate, and olive oil in huge amounts with no fruit or vegetables. I chuckled to myself, recalling friends who live on that kind of diet anyway and who have no intention of going anywhere near the South Pole.

I went into the supermarket to get some idea of what was around and find out who manufactured what we needed. Packet noodles, fat content 10 g per serving – not enough; dehydrated mashed potato, fat per serving 8 g – not enough. An hour and a half later I left with a list of potential food sponsors running to several pages and not a single thing in the trolley. Almost all that we approached came to our aid, with Arnott's being particularly helpful.

In addition to their sponsorship money they made an off-the-cuff comment about an unlimited supply of Tim Tams in the lead-up to the trip. We of course held them to this, and the following week, true to their word, they duly turned up at Peter's place in Sydney. I flew to Sydney to Peter's partly out of curiosity to see what a garage full of Tim Tams looked like and to sample a few for quality purposes. We opened the garage and were almost crushed by falling biscuit boxes as they toppled out of the door. As a polar explorer you accept that what you do is extremely dangerous, but being crushed to death by boxes of Tim Tams in suburban Sydney wasn't quite the headline I had in mind.

I'm not what you'd call a culinary expert but after my trawl around the supermarkets and a few international phone calls to my mother, I managed to put together a 'menu' that actually sounded pretty good. No eating dogs for us. We had three different evening meal types. There was beef bourguignon, chicken curry and a pasta dish – essentially all the same meal, supplemented with nuts, a healthy dollop of olive oil that we took instead of pemmican, and served up with high carbo staples like rice or pasta. Breakfast would be a muesli type thing, with nuts, chocolate and of course olive oil. As long as we got the required calories into us as efficiently as possible it didn't really matter.

We opted for olive oil instead of pemmican or lard particularly after trying the latter for a couple of days. It was bloody disgusting, looking and tasting too much like the stuff they squeeze out of the arteries of the heart attack victim on the TV ad. Olive oil sounded a bit New Age man and poofy, but if it gave us the same calories then that's what we'd take. By way of getting used to consuming 150 ml a day each, we weaned ourself on to an olive oil rich diet before we left. We couldn't afford to be having stomach upsets when we got down on the ice, that's for sure. I can still remember that first morning I poured it onto my cornflakes and milk. It tasted like warm spew, or at the very least diesel oil rather than olive oil and I had to force it all down. Within a week I was 'used to it' – sort of.

∧ ∧ ∧

And that's what it was like for most days during the two years of planning it took to make the trip a reality. The trip came before everything else and even when it didn't it was always on your mind. It reminded me of revising for exams where there's always more you can do until the exam day arrives and then you wing it. There was always training, checking up on something, chasing sponsorship opportunities or practising how to use the equipment that might mean the difference between life and death when on the ice. With odds like those it was difficult to relax and it became an exercise in motivation to wake each day and try to get a few simple things on your long list accomplished before your energy ran out. I'd normally start with easier ones first up and progress to tackling the big issues later in the day.

The planning of the trip took a toll on my relationship with Andrea also. Some days she could look at it philosophically, others she couldn't. It was a hard time as sometimes I felt that I was just being self-indulgent putting people close to me through all the stress, uncertainty and danger of the trip without them being able to share in actually doing it. I gave her reassurances about the fact that I would return from the journey and that everything would be fine without having any real idea myself and it added to the burden that the trip placed on both me and everyone close to me. Cancelling our trip to the Gold Coast to reserve my flight to Patriot would not sit well with most partners. Andrea was no exception, and it was a relief for both of us when she headed off on her own to see her folks up in Brisbane.

Christmas 1998 came and went and I could now no longer think of the journey as something in the distant future. On the one hand this was good because it was a sign that I wouldn't be planning this thing forever, on the other it meant we didn't have long until September 1999 by which time we needed to have left for Antarctica. Despite not yet having the money to make the trip happen, as the months went by I still needed to be learning the skills required for the journey. I called on favours left, right and centre, soaking up knowledge from everyone from explorers, scientists and doctors, to nutritionists, dentists and podiatrists.

Luckily there was some light relief along the way. With a polar manhauling journey it is important to try to put on weight before you go, because the extreme cold and heavy workload during the trip are such that you can't eat enough food to equal what your body needs. In order to survive you need fat reserves to stop your body consuming muscle for energy. You can therefore eat whatever you want in virtually whatever quantity you want, without feeling any guilt. In fact you positively have to do it and this can be great fun. The aim was therefore to put on about 10 kg if possible, which surprisingly wasn't easy when training each day and under stress much of the time. It was tough, but I rose to the challenge.

In actual fact it's just as well as you scarcely have enough time to think about healthy eating during the lead-up to the trip. So in this respect it's a marriage of convenience. Buckets of fried chicken, followed by chocolate and ice cream, all washed down with a few beers now became a good balanced meal and I wasn't complaining.

The sponsors too were good to us. Arnott's in particular couldn't have been better as principal sponsors, with many of their staff really getting behind the trip. One day I received a call from their product development people who told me they had made a product for the trip that they wanted me to trial. It was basically Tim Tam chocolate moulded into ultra thin slabs, designed to stop you breaking your teeth on normal thickness chocolate that turns into concrete at −30°C. It was just a throwaway comment I had made and I never asked them to do it, they just decided to help.

About a month before we were due to go, Alec Waugh from Arnott's asked us if there was anything we needed last-minute. I suggested that I needed backup gloves, some spares for the stoves and some additional thermals. The four of us met up in Sydney to go shopping – myself, Peter, Alec and Alec's credit card. Alec had said that he'd read an article about single-handed ocean sailors using music to lift their moods when they were down, almost like a psychological crutch. 'You've got to have music,' he said. An hour later Peter and I emerged from Sony, grinning, with a mini disc player each. When we got down there, however, we were to find that Antarctica robbed you of this pleasure, the howl of the wind drowning out even 'Ride of the Valkyrie' at full volume.

In the few weeks before we were to head off we began the last bits of physical preparation for the trip and I began toughening up the feet with alcohol to safeguard against blisters. Saying we were going to do the trip had become increasingly easy throughout the planning of the journey, as had the belief that we were already some way towards achieving the crossing with each media appearance we made – I think it's called believing your own rhetoric and is a dangerous mindset to get into. When we actually touched down on the ice and stepped out of the warmth of our small aircraft into the freezing white expanse of the Antarctic for the first time, that illusion vanished immediately, never to return.

Our final week before leaving was a hectic round of TV and radio appearances in Sydney arranged by Arnott's PR company, culminating in a press conference at Sydney airport just before flying out. It was a heady time with the PR company faxing over a list of radio, TV and press appearances, we were to make each day with casual reminders as to how we could get in a mention of sponsors' names casually in conversation. If asked what we were going to eat we would reply, 'Well, Arnott's prepared these biscuits . . .' If asked what we were going to wear it would be, 'Well, Helly Hansen have this breathable fabric . . .'

I'd never appreciated what PR people did for their money until now. It was full-on. The first radio interview with a regional radio program in Brisbane would be at 7.35 am. The next would be at 8.15 am with a radio show in Melbourne. Then we would head into town and be recorded live on Sky

News. Then back to more radio interviews. Then lunch with a journalist. We even had an interview with the *Australian Women's Weekly* asking about how our partners felt about the trip. That was a tricky one as I knew Andrea was now getting less and less keen on the whole thing as our departure date approached and now regretted her decision to join me in Sydney where the trip was in your face constantly. From *Women's Weekly*'s point of view this is just what they wanted and they interviewed us with relish on Peter's front lawn. It was fascinating to hear Andrea's thoughts on the whole thing as she spoke calmly about how selfish she felt I was about the journey. At the end of the day I would challenge anyone to organise something of the magnitude of this trip without a degree of 'selfishness'.

Something of a highlight of the whole week was our appearance on Channel 9's *Today* program with Tracy Grimshaw and Steve Liebmann. I'd seen people being interviewed on the program before and wondered what it would be like. Wired up, we sat in the famous chairs and the camera rolled. Peter and I answered the now familiar questions with aplomb and I found myself waffling on about how I was going to handle problems that hadn't even happened to me yet and how I was likely to be feeling after two months on the ice. It was fun talking to the media and being in the spotlight, but in my quiet moments all the big talk made me nervous. It was definitely time to get on with things.

7

Two against the ice

After two years' planning we finally arrived at Sydney airport to be confronted by a mass of journalists and well-wishers. We fielded the final questions, battled our way through the baggage check-in complete with ice-axes, cold weather gear and crampons and said our goodbyes. It was a warm muggy day in Sydney and all of the gear seemed totally out of place. Finally we boarded the plane and were off – bound for Punta Arenas, our jumping-off point for Antarctica and another milestone towards the achievement of the dream. I sat back on the aircraft, knackered from all the effort.

I woke to the sound of the pilot's voice booming over the PA system. 'We are now over the coast of South America, and you will start to see the Andes mountains below us.' I looked out the window and sure enough there they were, spectacular jagged peaks of snow and ice. I must have watched them pass beneath us for over an hour as we flew east towards Buenos Aires, right over their spine. It brought home to me what we were about to do. I felt excited with a mixture of anticipation and adrenaline. If we could have started the journey right then and there I would have.

We spent a day in Buenos Aires and had a quick look round.

I had always wanted to go there, but now felt detached and remote and could think of little else but the trip. At least it gave me the chance to brush up on my Spanish that I knew I would need for our eight days in Punta Arenas. The next day we headed for the airport, stopping at Eva Peron's grave – former first lady of Argentina. It immediately struck me that for a woman who had been larger than life, her little tomb was insignificant – a small concrete pigeonhole containing her ashes. It was a salutary reminder of how transitory life is. Whatever you do in your lifetime you must do for your own reasons and not for the passing admiration of others.

We flew south along the length of the Andes, arriving in Punta Arenas (or 'Sandy Point' as it translates into English) at the southern tip of the mighty South American continent. 'Punta' is majestically hailed as the southernmost city in the world, and boasts the highest number of prostitutes per head of population if you're that way inclined. To us it looked like a pretty uninspiring, scruffy little place. From the treeless concrete harbour front, we watched the wind whip up the ocean into whitecaps and as we turned to walk back into town, the view was a ramshackle collection of old and new buildings, clinging to the steep hills. It had little to commend it other than its spectacular position at the southern tip of South America where the mighty Pacific and Atlantic Oceans meet. The tip of the Antarctic Peninsula was only 1000 km or so from here, so it was where we needed to be.

All the pieces of the jigsaw needed to come together in these salubrious surroundings in the next eight days. We were to meet the South Africans who were going to fly us from Punta to Patriot, Kevin and Dave our Canadian pilots, and a guy from Germany who had built our sleds and who was bringing them out to Punta personally as he didn't trust Chilean Customs. All this plus our freighted equipment sent several weeks earlier from Australia. All concerned had been given our hotel details in Punta – the 'Condor'.

It was with some relief that we found messages from all of them waiting for us at reception. The Condor was a neat little place with a jovial chain-smoking manager who spoke no English. We moved in to a small, musty room with beds that were about a foot too short and within minutes we had turned our room into something that resembled an outdoor shop during a stocktake. There was equipment littered everywhere – fuel containers, stoves, clothing, tent poles, boots and skis. On first impression one could have been forgiven for thinking it was the stuff of normal camping trips, until other items gave the game away: ice-axes and crampons for climbing, a rope for rescuing one another from the many crevasses that lay ahead of us, and communications equipment.

After two years of planning, $500 000 worth of sponsorship, training and research we were about to meet a group of people who were quite literally going to hold our lives in their hands. We did what any self-respecting person would do in the same situation – we went to the pub.

Nowhere is far from the sea in Punta, but the pub must have been right next to it – the smell of fish, and old seaweed heavy in the air. We pushed open the door and in the dark amongst the smoke haze instantly spotted, or should I say heard, the South Africans. They were about a foot taller than everyone else and laughing and talking loudly. They'd obviously been there a while and we shook hands and exchanged names and another round of drinks was ordered.

The beer began to flow, as did the bullshit as we exchanged tall tales. They told us that when they weren't flying to places like Antarctica, they were on dangerous missions airlifting food aid in to war-torn parts of Africa and coming under fire in the Middle East. They reckoned that on one occasion they had taken off with almost 250 refugees on board – well over the plane's maximum payload, rescuing them from certain death at the hands of Eritrean rebels. They were a tough, fit-looking group of guys who knew how to handle themselves and instilled confidence. Their part in the Antarctic drama was going to be a cakewalk.

Half an hour or so later two guys who looked even less Chilean than we did appeared at the bar. Kevin was a large jocular Canadian Inuit and Dave a small, wiry moustached Canadian from Nova Scotia. They didn't exactly fit the stereotypical body shape or appearance of rugged polar pilots. I'd kind of expected tall, muscular characters like I'd seen in the Jack Daniel's 'Jack Lives Here' whisky adverts. They were pretty laid back, but when the topic turned to wilderness flying you could see their demeanour change as they focused on answering every question we had.

I woke feeling seedy the next morning. All around me were packing boxes full of clothing and equipment, kitchen scales and plastic bags for weighing and decanting food and the remains of a half-eaten packet of biscuits in my bed. Peter as a teetotaller was disturbingly fresh and making a lot of noise, presumably to wake me up.

We intended to be in Punta for about a week and pretty soon got into a routine of sorting through expedition gear during the day, going for a walk or run, eating a large meal at night, and occasionally meeting the pilots at the local bar to 'unwind', all interspersed with healthy amounts of Tim Tams and coffee. It would soon be time to leave and we went through the equipment, food and personal items with a fine-tooth comb trying to think of ways we could save weight. Finally after almost five days of weighing and re-evaluating our possessions we were reasonably satisfied we'd done as much as we could.

'Shall we take three or four pairs of thermal underpants for the trip, Tim?' asked Peter.

'Well, it's a three-month trip, so I guess we'd better go for a pair a month,' I replied.

'Sounds good,' said Peter. Three pairs it was.

Some of our equipment and food assessment antics were definitely psychological, that's for sure – partly to convince ourselves we had done all we could to reduce weight, and partly to take our minds off thinking about the trip all the time. But some of the process was definitely worthwhile. Take soups for example, where with each packet we repackaged we saved about 10 grams. When you multiplied this by the number of packets two people were going to consume over 90 days it made a difference of over 2.5 kg! That's a lot of packaging to carry around for no good reason.

And so it went. Toothbrushes were cut in half, labels were removed from clothing, and packets of soup were decanted into lighter weight bags. Our hotel room began to smell pretty bad. It was an odd aroma – a mixture of foot and body odour, glue from the skins on the bases of our skis, with a hint of chicken and leek soup, chocolate powder and powdered milk that had been ground into the carpet. The weight saving all seemed a bit pointless beyond where we were now at and I had had enough by about day 4. Peter, however, could always keep going, and it was certainly an irritating characteristic that he could not stop fiddling, weighing and checking things. His motivation was understandable though, partly because it's in his nature to be thorough, but partly because I knew he was really concerned about being able to pull the weight. At the time, I thought, Christ what's it going to be like living in a tent with this guy for three months, where we can't get away from one another?

It dawned on me that we really didn't know one another that well. I had based my belief in him and he in me on the fact that we had a couple of mutual friends in the outdoor fraternity. We knew each other's history, but that was it, other than having of course gone through the emotional highs and lows of pulling the trip together. I just hoped that it would be enough to cement us into a winning team.

It was now the day before we were due to depart and we were buzzing with anticipation and nerves. We were finally to embark on the biggest journey of our lives. Each hour found my mood fluctuating wildly, from accepting that it was going to happen and feeling ready for it to being temporarily distracted by something and then feeling almost in a state of denial about the prospect of the trip when I thought about it again. I slept fitfully that night, but finally drifted off in the early hours.

We were to have a weather report in the morning. I walked up to ANI's headquarters in a small house near the hotel to find out whether we were going or not. 'Not today, mate,' said Mike the South African captain as I came through the door. 'Maybe tomorrow.' There was a body blow of disappointment – followed soon after by a strange sensation of relief, although I didn't let on. I trundled back down the hill to the Condor and the next instalment of my Latin American soap on TV.

The following day the weather was again bad. This was repeated the next day, and the next, until six days had passed due to bad weather and we had begun to wear a well-trodden path between the Condor and the weather hut. I now realised that the most immediate challenge was going to be getting out of Punta. In order to do this the weather had to be okay where we were, good en route and absolutely bloody marvellous where we were going, and that rarely happened.

Punta must be the second windiest place in the world after Antarctica. It actually has fixed ropes along the pavements to stop people being blown over. A local told me proudly that once he had seen a dog get blown down the street such was the strength of the wind. On another occasion I met a Dutch couple who were intending to cycle the length of South America and had made several attempts to get out of town. They had been defeated by the wind on each occasion, trying to cycle north into the teeth of it, unable to reach the next town. And so they along with Peter, myself, the Canadians and South Africans all sat in Punta waiting for a break in the weather.

It was a roller-coaster ride mentally as each day we had two weather updates to determine whether we were flying or not.

Each weather update held our fate in its hands quite literally. If it was bad weather we would have a shower, eat another burger and continue with the gradual osmosis of learning Spanish via watching lowbrow Latin TV. If it was good we were off on the biggest adventure of our lives.

By the second week, repeated false alarms had made us complacent and in the habit of not even bothering to turn up to hear the weather reports. It seemed crazy to have such a lull after all that had gone before, but there was nothing we could do. Worst of all was the fact that our window of time was now getting smaller by the day. In order to make the crossing we needed every available day of the Antarctic summer, as once the 'colder' weather started the journey would become increasingly difficult. It felt that someone up there was beginning to mess with our minds just to see how long it would be before we broke.

It was to Punta Arenas that Shackleton had returned after his amazing rescue journey across the Southern Ocean in his small rowing boat, the *James Caird*. He had delivered a rousing speech to the wealthy graziers of Punta Arenas and managed to finance a rescue mission for his men. I had decided to try to find out where Shackleton had stayed whilst here but, after a day and a half trawling round museums and the library, was disappointed to hear that the 'Hotel Cosmos' no longer existed.

Our comms guy for the expedition was a tubby, balding Scot called Neil – technically gifted but with a nervous and slightly scatty manner that did little to instil confidence as our sole contact with the outside world. That night a few of us went out for a meal and Neil somehow managed to lose his Iridium satellite phone which was to be our principal means of contact during the expedition. Luckily there were several spares, but the fact that he had been absent-minded enough to lose a $3000 phone was concerning.

I agreed I'd head down to the police station with him to act as translator. The process involved a lot of form-filling and waiting around, but the police guys were keen to chat, having read about the trip in the local paper. I mentioned that no-one had ever crossed Antarctica before and that it was the explorer Shackleton who had attempted it first. Their eyes lit up on hearing his name and they asked me if I wanted to see where he had stayed, pointing upwards.

The building was old but smelt of paint from recent refurbishment with computers and new desks looking conspicuous in the surroundings. Despite that, there was certainly an atmosphere to it, especially upstairs. They unlocked a door and I found myself standing in the room that had apparently been Shackleton's bedroom when the building had been the Cosmos Hotel. It was a truly amazing coincidence, the significance of which wasn't lost on me. A superstitious person would have felt that forces had conspired to lead us here. Completing the formalities of reporting the lost phone, we thanked the police guys for the tour and made to leave. 'The building is haunted, you know,' the captain added.

'By whom?' I asked.

'No-one knows and no-one has seen anything, but we often hear someone moving around up there late at night when the building is locked up.' Just for a moment I had an image of Shackleton pacing around the room, unable to sleep, concerned for the safety of his remaining men still stranded down on Elephant Island.

The following day was our seventeenth in Punta. I awoke as usual to the prospect of a day in the hotel spent variously trying to remember and forget that we were off on the biggest challenge of our lives, when the phone rang – it was Kevin. 'Get your gear together, we've got a green light. Be ready in 45 minutes.' I heard the words and the adrenaline flooded my body – this was it – after all the planning, waiting and anticipation, we were going. The prospect was daunting and now it felt like we were rushing. The sled had lain packed with all of my food and equipment for over a week and I had put two years into planning precisely what to put into it. Still there was a niggling doubt that I had forgotten something.

A few minutes later, a truck pulled up outside, complete with several guys to help us manhandle the sleds. Six of us had to work hard to lift each of the sleds onto the truck. As we drove to the airport there were questioning looks from some of the men. How were we even going to be able to move these things, and even if we could – why try? Peter and I looked at one another and saw the same questions going through each other's minds.

With both of us and the sleds safely on board the Hercules, the crew worked fast to get us moving. After a series of checks, the propellers finally whirred into life and we were airborne. When the loading ramp opened next we would step out into the ice.

Peter and I sat alone with our thoughts, which was just as well as it was too noisy to speak over the engine noise anyway. It was only an hour before the first iceberg loomed into sight – a lone berg, brilliant white against the dark of the ocean. Soon an ill-fitting jigsaw of pack-ice began to appear and finally in the distance the jagged snowy peaks of the Antarctic mountains.

Six hours later the plane thumped down, making a bumpy landing on a natural runway of blue ice, and we emerged into the bitter cold and glare of the Antarctic 'night'. As the loading ramp was lowered, the dry cold air took your breath away, sucking the warmth from your body despite the multiple clothing layers. Patriot Hills is a location where government agencies maintain emergency fuel supplies buried in the ice, but there are no permanent buildings, just a small makeshift base of a dozen or so tents that appears in the summer. The same ferocious winds that keep the 'runway' clear of snow mean that tents would never survive the winter here. It is a spectacular place. Patriot's so-called 'hills' were certainly an understatement for what we beheld – a vast icy plain ringed by angular mountains

– the first of many underestimations of the scale and grandeur of Antarctica.

With numb hands we hastily put up the tent and crawled inside, lying in our sleeping bags in the freezer that was to be our home for the next three months. Our thermometer went down to –30°C and the mercury stubbornly sat near the bottom of it. In the morning ANI staff would feed us while we waited for the Twin Otter to follow us over – a perilous journey for a small aircraft. I settled into a fitful sleep with the sound of the wind buffeting the tent, unable to get warm, knowing that now I had to make staying alive a part of each day's routine.

The following morning the sound of the wind and the flapping fabric of the tent was broken by the faint drone of a distant engine. Ten minutes later the Twin Otter appeared as a glint on the horizon, and then, dwarfed by the surrounding mountains, landed on the snow and taxied over to our small camp. Kevin and Dave jumped out, transformed now by multiple clothing layers and goggles. We retreated into the mess tent, which was set up with a heater, removed our goggles and balaclavas and welcomed them to Patriot. It was good to see them and despite the fact that we were paying them handsomely for their time I felt grateful that they were here.

After some rest we sat down and discussed the weather between Patriot and our start point on Berkner Island some 500 km away. The forecast unfortunately wasn't good, with strong winds and poor visibility en route, according to satellite images. We wouldn't be flying today or, more than likely, tomorrow either. Disappointed we got back in our sleeping bags and tried to sleep. It was miserable. There was nothing to do and nowhere to go, other than the mess tent that had been erected. It was frustrating. We'd done so much getting this far and now we were waiting again.

On day 4 a shadow fell on the side of the tent and Kevin's voice broke the silence. 'C'mon guys, let's go – now.' He had spoken to the weather station at the British Antarctic base Rothera and the weather looked good enough to give it a try. After two days of lying motionless in the tent, another burst of frenetic activity saw us loaded up and ready to go.

We bounced over the uneven icy ground, making very heavy going of taking off with our payload of four people, a 220-litre drum of spare fuel and two massive sleds on board. It was what I imagine it would be like in a horse-drawn carriage falling into metre-deep potholes. Finally we bounced off the back of a large sculpted wave of ice and, after crashing down again once more, bunny-hopped into the air like a duck with lead gonads.

I looked out of the windows of the plane as we gained altitude slowly and for the first time could really appreciate the vastness of Antarctica. To the horizon in all directions was the vast frozen Antarctic ice cap, and directly below us as we banked at a crazy angle was the knife-edge ridge of the mountains of Patriot Hills. On the distant horizon you could see mountains poking through the ice, and I wondered how high they actually were, knowing that the mantle of ice that cloaks Antarctica is more than 2 km thick on average. If the 28 million cubic kilometres of the Antarctic ice cap were to melt it would raise global sea levels by some 70 metres. It was an awesome sight to behold.

Two hours into the flight Dave unbuckled his seatbelt and clambered back over the sleds to where we were. Over the loud drone of the engine his face was the picture of worry, although I could barely hear his words. He pointed out at the right wing, mouthing concern about the state of the undercarriage after our heavy take-off. You didn't have to be Einstein to realise we'd given the undercarriage a bloody good hammering. He crawled back to the co-pilot's seat shouting the words, 'No good' as he went past. They spoke for a while and then turned to us, gesturing a circle in the air indicating we were turning back. The plane banked heavily and finally the mountains of Patriot again came into view. Peter and I analysed the pilots' body language, wondering what was yet to come. Dave crawled back to us again and gestured that we should assume the brace position, shouting that we were to make an 'active landing'. An active landing is basically a crash-landing and I put a brave face on our predicament, taking solace from the fact that Peter was not fond of small aircraft at the best of times. For him this would be even worse.

We approached the ground and I put my head between my knees as instructed, wishing I'd paid attention to the safety videos on the many flights I'd been on. We touched the ground and bounced into the air off the waves of sastrugi, the many small ridges formed by the high winds that ravage the Antarctic continent in the winter months. I can only recall the violent shaking and crashing of the plane as it ploughed across the ground while I stared at the floor of the plane. Finally we came to an abrupt standstill.

We jumped out and assessed the damage. The right wheel ski was crumpled and we were lucky that it hadn't collapsed altogether. Dave explained that it would have been too dangerous to have landed in the middle of nowhere with the damaged wheel ski, for fear of not being able to get airborne again or worse. With that we got to work replacing the wheel ski with a stronger snow-ski. We again set up our tent to wait things out, getting back into the sleeping bags. It was too late to fly today and so another night on the ice at Patriot was in store – our fifth, and 25 days since we left Australia. Doubts crept into my mind about whether or not this was meant to be. We still had 90 days in Antarctica ahead of us. I was tired, cold, irritable and stressed, and we hadn't even started yet.

Mercifully, the weather held and with the snow-skis fitted we managed a smoother take-off following the path that we had bull-dozed through the waves of snow and ice on our first attempt. I switched on my GPS unit and watched as we moved towards our start point. After three hours my GPS told me we should be somewhere over the Ronne Ice Shelf – a massive bay of ice the size of Victoria. As I looked down I saw the shadows and creases that indicated the presence of crevassing. It went on for miles and miles and I realised that this must be the dreaded 'hinge zone' – the point where the Ronne deforms and splinters with the movement of the ice as it rises and falls with the tide and collides with the Antarctic continent. The sight was awe-inspiring.

I strained to see open ocean beyond the Ronne somewhere to the north, but to the horizon was ice. My GPS indicated we had only 90 km to our chosen start point on the northernmost tip of Berkner Island – a supposedly stable place to land the plane adjacent to the northern edge of the Ronne that marks Antarctica's coastline. With only 60 km to go, Kevin turned round to us and signalled down, making a smooth landing on the ice of the shelf compared to our earlier one in Patriot. The props came to a stop and he informed us that the weather at our grid reference had packed out. 'Sorry, guys, I don't like doing this but we're going to have to put down here on the ice shelf and hope it clears tomorrow.'

Disappointed we spent yet another night in the tent – this time somewhere on the Ronne Ice Shelf. Light relief was provided by watching Kevin trying to get the cumbersome aircraft battery into his sleeping bag to keep it warm on what was the coldest night I had ever experienced in my life. I couldn't get warm and I wondered whether our equipment was going to be up to the task. Again I had to work hard to convince myself that we knew the beginning of the trip was going to be coldest. Summer was just beginning and the temperature would creep up a bit. It needed to.

Finally the weather again broke, giving us just enough time to fly to our start point on Berkner Island. It seemed almost whimsical that I had worked out this position from maps back in Australia and was now telling these two experienced wilderness pilots where to put down.

Berkner felt almost familiar to me after the amount of time I had pored over maps of the place, and I had images in my mind of what it would be like. When Kevin leaned round to me and said we were at the grid reference I had given him I had difficulty believing it. Below us was a vast and featureless expanse of foreboding white. And that's what Berkner is – a 300-kilometre island locked into the permanent ice of the vast Ronne Ice Shelf. My illusions of familiarity were shattered – the names and map coordinates had all led me to expect something other than what I now beheld – an endless horizon of ice with not a rock or mountain anywhere. We circled and again landed smoothly.

With only four of us to lift them, the sleds dropped awkwardly with a crunch onto the snow from the door of the plane, and we worried that their lightweight Kevlar construction might break with the 225 kg of food and equipment in them. Still, they had been rigorously tested and designed to handle impacts such as those from the chaotic surface of wind-blown sastrugi, which we had been warned to expect, particularly up on the polar plateau.

Before we had time to comprehend the significance of the moment, the Otter was above us and dipping its wings in farewell as it receded into the distance. As the sound of the engine was lost in the wind, it hit me just how unbelievably isolated we were. I stood there for a moment staring towards the vast horizon, before the cold forced me to move. I checked the GPS which was still warm from being in the plane, strapped on the chest-mounted compass, put on my harness and stepped into my skis.

The plane had been gone less than ten minutes and already the feeling of utter isolation was overpowering. The key now was to get moving to generate some warmth and take my mind off the enormity of the challenge we faced. We were ready for this and I was pleased to just be getting on with things. I would worry about reaching the end of Berkner Island, some 300 km away, another day. As far as the Pole went that didn't even figure in my mind. It was a whole world away. Delays had cost us over two weeks and our tight window of time was now down to the bare minimum. Summer in Antarctica only lasts about 100 days and in order to make the crossing we were going to need over 90 of them.

Leaning into my harness, I felt the weight of the sled for the first time and it was desperately heavy – like pulling a piano. The realisation of just how heavy it was and the fact that we had 2735 km to go left me depressed as I battled on for what seemed like a mile. I looked at my watch. I'd pulled for just over four minutes and had probably only moved 200 metres – maybe less. I felt sorry for myself at the prospect of what I was about to subject my body to, and a mild form of panic about the magnitude of the task facing us. I tried to think through the situation.

I was coming off a few weeks of inactivity and stress and was bound to feel physically and mentally lacklustre. The sleds were at their heaviest and the weather at its coldest, reducing our physical performance and reducing the glide of the sleds over the snow. A heavy sled works on the principle that the pressure exerted on the snow causes it to melt at the interface with the runners, enabling the sled to glide. The snow in much of Antarctica is, however, renowned for being extremely dry, reducing the lubricating effect and hence the glide you experience, and this effect is heightened when temperatures are very low. I told myself it wouldn't all be as bad as this. Would it? If it was, we would be in real strife.

My legs burned with the exertion and I worked hard just to proceed forward slowly. I kept on plodding, but by the end of a reduced first day I had little genuine conviction that we were going to be able to make it. We decided to make camp early and start afresh in the morning. That night we checked the GPS to see how far we'd come, hoping to be pleasantly surprised. After over four hours' pulling we had covered only 6 km. We both harboured thoughts of how the hell we were going to physically and mentally make it to the other side of the continent, but kept them to ourselves and fell into an uneasy sleep.

I woke after a bitterly cold night where I had to move every half an hour or so just to prevent my feet becoming numb, determined to get on with the task at hand. Today couldn't be as bad as the day before. We had slept, had survived our first night and now at least knew what to face. My watch said 4 am but the sun already shone brightly. After taking over two hours to melt snow for the day's drinking water we broke camp.

The temperature was below the −30°C range of our thermometer, my hands were numb and the horizon looked completely unchanged from the day before. I stuffed my warm down jacket into the sled and felt the instant cut of the wind through my thin working layers burning my skin. I had chosen to come here and try this to find out more about myself and what I was capable of and now it was time to get on with things. I put the compass round my neck and pushed off. The sled inched forward reluctantly and I stopped 50 metres later to adjust my clothing, disappointed that the sled felt no easier to pull. I had no choice but to try to put it out of my mind and push through it.

Today we would go for six hours and the goal was to try to pull for more than 10 kilometres. I had decided I would divide my first hour into four fifteen-minute blocks with a short rest of 30 seconds punctuating each block. After my first block I glanced over my shoulder to see Peter moving extremely slowly despite following my broken trail or 'lead' through the deep snow, such that he had already dropped over 100 metres behind. I kept going, understanding now something of how Scott and his men must have felt when they too were managing less than 10 km a day of hard pulling. By my second fifteen-minute block I was feeling tired and having increasing difficulty remembering my motivation for being here. After a total of less than five hours' pulling I was having to dig deep, which really worried me, already reduced to breaking down the journey into small manageable increments. I had anticipated doing this, but not so soon and such small pieces. Trips like this are not about 90 days, but thousands of small blocks of time that you are able to find the resolve to motivate yourself through.

I realised just how much Peter was struggling when, having reached the end of my first hour, I heard a voice shouting over the sound of the wind. Still strapped into my harness I looked round and shouted a response. 'What's wrong?' Peter was some few hundred metres behind and down on his haunches. He shouted a response which was lost in the wind. I undid my harness and stepped out of my skis, sinking up to my knees in the deep snow. Breathing heavily and swearing I put my skis back on and skied back to him. His hands were clasped around his left ankle.

'What's up?' I asked, concerned.

'Feels like I've torn my calf muscle!' He dropped to his haunches, massaging his leg.

'What do you think?' I asked.

'I don't know, I'll keep going and see what happens.' With that he took the strain and shuffled slowly away from me, drawing level with my sled. I skied behind him, determined that never again would I ski without the sled as it was demoralising feeling how easy it was without all that weight.

We agreed I would break trail for the rest of the day to make his going easier. We had a drink of water and pushed off again to start our second hour. That hour was much like the first except that I now had the worry of wondering whether Peter would be okay and the prospect of leading for the rest of the day staring at the vast featureless horizon of ice.

We regrouped again after the second hour and sat on the sleds to rest. 'It feels pretty bad, Tim – if it stays like this I'm not sure what's going to happen,' Peter said, the sound of defeat in his voice. After a couple of minutes I broke the silence. 'Let's get on with it, eh? We'll freeze if we sit here much longer.' Peter nodded in agreement and we moved off again.

I strained for a piece of snow or ice in line with our compass bearing that I could head towards. I knew now that I had to keep taking one step after another to maintain our momentum and help us keep this expedition on the rails, especially with all of the weight of personal and public expectation on us. Surely after all that we had gone through we couldn't stop now – so many people had helped us to get to where we were.

Leading was exhausting. It required constant vigilance to keep on course and to watch out for crevasses, quite apart from the fact that breaking trail through the deep snow was much harder work both mentally and physically. Worst of all, psychologically you were responsible for the speed of the team's progress and that weighed heavy on the mind. I longed to be able to switch off and follow Peter, but it wouldn't be today.

That night we fell into the tent knackered after digging snow blocks to melt in the pot and securing the tent with the ice-axes. In the sleeping bags and with a hot tea in my gloved hand, half an hour later things felt much better. I warmed the GPS between my legs inside my sleeping bag to render it usable. I needed to do this otherwise the liquid crystal display was sluggish and completely unreadable. We had covered 9 km. Disappointment again, although at least it was better than 6. Tomorrow we needed to focus again on getting into double figures.

We awoke and the tent was again an icy cavern, with moisture from our frozen breath hanging from the roof like stalactites. Sitting up in my sleeping bag I surveyed the scene. My boots lay frozen near my feet, and the moisture in my thermal top felt cold against my skin. The jacket I had used as my pillow creaked as I unfolded it and put it on to have breakfast. The temperature in the tent was –20°C – some three times colder than your domestic freezer – and Peter's leg was extremely sore. It was a wretched place to be. I forced down as much of the muesli breakfast as I could, finding it hard to eat the layer of olive oil scum that had congealed half an inch thick on the surface of the muesli in the cold. It was day 3.

I led again and resolved to not think about distance any more – just time. I would go as best I could and whatever distance we did, we'd live with. Ultimately we only had to get to 3 kilometres an hour and do that for ten hours a day. 'Only' – what a joke that word was in the context of everything about this place, except the cold.

I plodded on for my first hour and waited for Peter again, the only sound in the emptiness and silence being my breathing and the steady creak of my ski bindings as I moved onwards. The silence was broken by Peter's voice beside me. 'I can't go on like this, Tim.' His voice sounded desperate. The sleds were terribly heavy and his leg injury was slowing him badly. I agreed something had to be done or I would be leading for the rest of the journey and I couldn't handle the prospect of that. When he did lead he would also need to go fast enough to enable both of us to work at a pace where we could generate body heat. That meant the kind of speed I was managing when leading. With his injury he couldn't even keep up when following. At worst he might not even make it. We agreed that he couldn't continue with the sled weight as it was; some items would need to be discarded. He had two spare food bags, a fleece and a small amount of spare fuel. We settled on the food and fleece, deciding that to discard the fuel would be too risky, especially as we would likely require more to boil the stove when higher up on the polar plateau.

We buried the food and fleece and moved off again with no noticeable difference in Peter's speed, despite removing the 5 kg of items. Time would tell. At the second break I agreed to take one of his food bags and his crampons, removing a further 4 kg from his sled. That was the best we could do. Now we had nowhere to go. The sleds were as light as they were going to get until time passed and we consumed food and fuel, reducing each man's load by about 2.5 kg every second day.

I broke trail for the whole of what was a seven-hour day, and that night we had managed 11 km. It was a week before Peter's leg was well enough to handle the extra strain of leading through the deep snow, and the physical and mental strain on both of us was intense as we pushed on, unsure of whether his leg would recover.

Slowly we moved through the vast, never-ending expanse of Berkner Island, evidence of progress provided only by our daily GPS reading as the daily distances we managed to cover crept up into the teens. It was day 8 and I was still leading – trudging along in a world of my own, zoned out to my surroundings, just occasionally checking the spherical compass to find a suitable piece of ice on the horizon to aim towards to keep us on course. That was Antarctica for you. When you woke in the morning, all you wanted to do was get moving and get warm, and often after starting moving all you wanted to do was stop and rest. It was still 200 km to the end of Berkner Island.

The atmosphere was so crystal-clear when the weather was good that you could see infinitely further than on any other continent, even further than on those vibrant, blue-sky days in Australia. When combined with the painfully slow progress of pulling such a heavy weight in such a vast place it often tricked you into thinking that you were in fact not moving at all. We needed the GPS like a psychological crutch to confirm to us that we had actually made progress.

Midway through the following day the ground beneath me suddenly fell away. Momentarily I felt a strange weightless sensation as my knees bent to absorb the impact, and I was sure I was headed down into a crevasse. I couldn't tell what the hell was happening as I had no point of reference to gauge things by. The sudden drop was accompanied by a thunderous roar like a distant jet engine and a whoosh as snow and ice collapsed beneath me and in a radius of hundreds of metres all around. 'Christ, what the hell was that!' I shouted to Peter and anyone else who happened to be listening, my pulse racing. It was like an earthquake and must have been triggered by the weight of us travelling over an unstable area of snow. Beyond that I wasn't sure what it was. It gave me food for thought for the rest of the day – and it was the kind of experience that made doing this kind of thing worthwhile – Antarctica offering up its strange secrets to us.

Each day from now on for some reason was punctuated by these strange 'snow quakes'. We never really knew exactly what caused them and they gave you a distinctly uneasy feeling, thinking about what might lurk beneath the snow and ice you walked across. They seemed to vary in size from small drops of only a foot or two, to a lurching sensation as you dropped a couple of metres with a raft of snow and ice seemingly a few square kilometres in size. Each time they occurred you hoped that you would stop a split second later and that you weren't bound for the bottom of a crevasse.

Peter was now sharing the leading and we were travelling for up to nine hours a day. This had got us up to covering almost 20 km, and I was beginning to feel more optimistic about things, even though the workload was still gruelling and I had no idea for how long we could sustain it. Our sleds were 10 kg lighter, though this seemed to make little difference and I still dared not think of anywhere beyond the end of Berkner.

It was strange following someone. Watching their sled as it moved away from you served to pull you along, as if a rope connected your sled with theirs. I can't explain it but this trick of the mind at least equalled the undoubted physical benefit of following a compacted path of snow where all the navigation and danger assessment had been done for you. When the wind allowed, I would hear the sound of my bindings creak and the syncopated rhythm of little sounds made by my sled and ski stocks and it would send me to another place.

Our latest issue was the satellite phone, which was unfortunately causing problems. Despite a few days of bright sunlight with the solar panel strapped to the top of Peter's sled the phone battery hadn't charged one bit. We were at a loss to work out why and it meant we would be without any phone contact for the remainder of the trip if we couldn't fix it. Peter was great at improvising and set himself to try to work out the answer to the problem. After taking the recharger unit to pieces in the tent, warming his hands inside the sleeping bag every five minutes to manage the dexterity, he decided there was nothing wrong with it and that it could only be the cold that was preventing the battery taking any charge.

The next night as we slept, the sun as usual wheeled around above us but this time the solar panel sat fastened to the sled outside and the wire passed up through the zipped floor of the tent and into Peter's sleeping bag where he slept with the phone keeping it warm. The following day the battery recorded full charge. We whooped with joy. It was a major success and we fed off the confidence it gave us for the remainder of the day.

The temperature was still bitterly cold, seldom above −30°C due to our early start date. I could feel that I had burnt off my layer of fat. Now it was just the food consumed each day that would sustain us and slow the deterioration of our bodies in the extreme cold. Each day as we moved across Berkner's vast and unchanging landscape I played mind games that had me turn shadows and slight slopes into valleys and distant mountains as I zoned out to make it through the day.

The wind constantly blew in Antarctica. When it was occasionally still and the sun shone, amazingly it could be tolerable in −20 degrees. As soon as there was a whisper of wind it cut through you like a knife, whipping away your body heat before you could enjoy it, and certainly before your body felt it had enough left-over heat to bother sending any to your extremities.

After two weeks I began to get the feeling that we were

descending slowly. Our Casio watches had altimeters and they indicated we had dropped slightly, but the landscape was so vast and the drop so slight that I couldn't be entirely sure. It certainly made no obvious difference to the weight of the sled which as usual seemed to need to be dragged with great reluctance through Berkner's deep snow.

It was day 15 when I spotted a gaping hole some distance ahead of me, visible first as a dark strip that got wider as I approached. From 20 or so metres away, I could see it was the mouth of a gaping crevasse, with menacing icy walls just visible from where I stood. I gave it a wide berth and guessed that to have such a large crevasse meant that we must be approaching the hinge zone.

The hinge zone is notorious for crevasses, being the point where the stable ice of Berkner meets the unstable ice of the Ronne. The Ronne, despite its vast size and thickness (up to 800 metres thick) floats on the icy water of the Weddell Sea, rising and falling with the tide. Not only that but the movement of ice off the vast Antarctic ice cap pushes the ice of the Ronne northward past Berkner. All in all it is a place where vast forces come together and is a dangerous place for people to be. It is an amazing feeling to think of something of this scale moving up and down and is just another example of the mind-boggling scale of things in Antarctica.

We roped together and moved off. I put my foot through a weak snow bridge to reveal a gaping hole beneath me, but luckily with the rope attached went no further. Two hours later, we guessed we were beyond the crevasse danger.

Reaching the end of Berkner felt almost like reaching the Pole itself; it had been our goal for so long. Its achievement served to convince us we had actually gone somewhere. Day 16 felt like a great day. We were now down on the ice of the mighty Ronne Ice Shelf, clear of the awful monotony of Berkner – and we were still here.

Reaching the Ronne meant we were about to drop off our map of Berkner, to reappear on our second map only when we reached the mountains another 200 km distant. Now, though, we could put the Berkner chapter behind us and concentrate on getting across the shelf and finally seeing the mountains.

The workload was not easing as I had told myself it would, however. Gradually reducing sled weights and the eternal hope of firmer snow to ease the awful strain of pulling the sleds never seemed to come and we were getting more and more tired. Each morning I woke in our icy cavern wondering if today might be the day when my resolve or physical strength gave out. Anticipating the Ronne had at least offered the promise of an improvement from Berkner

After two days we were well and truly down on the Ronne and disappointingly it hadn't got any firmer or easier. On day 18 my diary finally read, 'Given up on prospect of better pulling. Know it will never come.' And so the gruelling routine continued. Breaking each day into something manageable in whatever way you could – numbers of steps, amounts of time, pieces of ice on the horizon – was the name of the game, and a real exercise in concentration. Halfway across the shelf we were putting Peter's injury woes behind us and scanning the horizon for the first signs of the mountains that would provide our route up onto the polar plateau, when the first of our big storms hit.

The weather on the Ronne had been quite good, but when the storm approached ominously on the horizon we followed our drill of closing ranks to ensure that we didn't get separated in deteriorating visibility. As the wind steadily increased we made the judgment to pitch the tent and prepare ourselves for the onslaught – and onslaught it was, with winds blasting around us. Dry ice whipped across the snow, the whole surface alive with movement. Every guy line was straining under the pressure of the wind. I remembered the storm on the Lomonosov

Ice Cap and hoped, like I had then, that the storm would break before the tent did.

It was an amazing feeling though to be lying here with the wind howling all around and the sound of snow and ice peppering the side of the tent. The harshness of the Antarctic was on the other side of a thin piece of tent fabric whilst we were warm inside our bags around the stove. But there were other noises too when the wind abated before gusting again: the sound of the guy lines whining in the wind, the sound of my pulse beating ever faster as I lay in my bag hoping all would be well, and crunching noises of snow being compressed that sounded like footfalls in the snow. With a bit of imagination it could almost be the spirits of the early explorers come to see who had ventured down to visit them in this wild and desolate place. Up in the Arctic I would have sworn it was a bear.

Spitsbergen had taught me a few important lessons about surviving storms in such places. In storms the wind is so strong it reduces visibility to zero and can freeze you to death in no time as the wind whips away your body heat in minutes. Polar exploration is littered with stories of people who have died or had close calls stranded within arm's reach of their tent. The biggest danger, apart from the tent being swept away by the sheer force of the wind, is therefore the need to venture outside. We'd taken to cooking inside for this reason and to provide us with heat from the stove, sweeping out the frozen condensation using an old decorator's brush. It seemed to work well and each night we would sweep out the frost from the previous night as part of our routine of setting up camp.

We'd modified the tent too, such that the floor unzipped to provide access to the snow beneath for filling the pot or – without putting too fine a point on it – for defecating. As long as you didn't take the snow for the pot from the same area you were safe. The proverbial 'don't eat yellow snow' – or snow of any colour other than white – was the order of the day. For all other ablutions there was of course the most important piece of equipment for any polar journey: the piss bottle. It was a wide-rimmed screw-top bottle that allowed you to relieve yourself without having to leave your sleeping bag. Critical in conserving body heat and important for safety.

The following morning the wind still raged, visibility was zero, and the contents of the piss bottle had frozen into a solid block. Our tent may as well have been pitched up in the clouds for all we could see outside. There was no choice but to stay put, as the windchill factor made the outside temperature life-threateningly low, and even the sleds 2 metres or so from the front door of the tent were invisible with the turmoil going on outside. If we'd moved there would have been a high risk of either losing one another or falling into a crevasse. We stayed put, slumbering in the bags, our tired bodies grateful of our enforced rest day. I got the stove going to make hot chocolate and watched lazily as the frozen urine in the bottle melted on top of the stove, so that I could pour it away and use the bottle again.

The following day we emerged from the tent stiff and cold, almost 40 hours after getting in. The strong winds had blown themselves out, but 'white-out' conditions remained. White-out is a frustrating, hazardous, and unfortunately pretty common weather condition in Antarctica, where in mist or blizzard, sky and ground appear as one. It was like travelling in a seamless white room, where you have no idea of the lie of the ground, or which way is up. Travel in such conditions is slow and completely reliant on following your compass as you stumble drunkenly into, or through whatever is in front of you. We knew, however, that time was against us and after some deliberation decided that we needed to push on.

Loss of vision represented the final nail in the coffin of sensory deprivation that Antarctica submits you to. Even under normal circumstances there is no smell, or sound other than the constant wind in your ears and no darkness as the sun spins above you for 24 hours a day, imparting little in the way of warmth. There is also nothing in the way of animal or plant life – not even algae on rocks, nor birds in the sky – the vast majority of Antarctica is a high-altitude frozen desert – completely inhospitable and devoid of all life. Each day I longed to see something other than snow and ice.

We plodded along, keeping close to one another, the leader turning regularly to check the man following and stopping if he didn't feel the tap tap of ski tips of the man behind on the back of his sled for more than a few minutes. Now Peter moved fast, ensuring that he didn't drop back, and the two of us moved almost as one. Mentally it was gruelling. We went on for what seemed like an eternity as I fought to find things to think of. I was amazed to realise how much of my daily routine relied on keeping my mind occupied by aiming for various pieces of ice on the horizon.

Today I had nothing to look at or to occupy the senses and so had to pick a topic to think about. Ambitiously, I chose my life, to see if I could come up with any meaningful conclusions from the people I'd met and all the situations I'd found myself in. After a couple of hours it was too hard to contemplate and I switched to thinking about house renovation, designing a whole new plan in my head by the end of the day. More often than not I would spend large amounts of time breaking the journey into manageable parts that I could motivate myself through as the enormity of the task was simply too overwhelming to consider. And then just fleetingly, I would realise why I was here and what it meant to me to be doing what I was doing and I would feel an upsurge of energy and conviction, although try as I might I could never hold the thought.

And that was normal – thinking about anything from the profound to the inane as long as it kept you putting one foot after the other. By camp that night the GPS told us that incredibly we had stumbled almost 20 kilometres south.

8

Terra firma

The following morning I casually looked out in the direction we were headed and felt the hairs on my neck stand on end – there, barely discernible on the distant horizon, I thought I saw a small collection of dark triangles. Excited, I grabbed the compass and sure enough they appeared to be in line with the bearing. They might be the Transantarctic Mountains, although I couldn't be sure as to concentrate on them too directly seemed to make them vanish before my eyes. We shouldn't have been able to see them this soon either. They should still have been some 70 kilometres away.

Enthused at the prospect of reaching the mountains that marked the gateway to the solid geology of Antarctica I pushed off on our compass bearing, the sled protesting as usual behind me. Even the bitter cold could not contain my excitement as I began my routine of forcing blood into my numb hands, stopping to shake them every 50 metres or so while staring longingly into the distance. After twenty minutes sensation returned to my hands in a series of painful but reassuring waves. Reassuring, as it meant the flesh was still alive and functioning. Now I could relax until my next break when I would have to repeat the process, with numbness setting in after seven or eight minutes of inactivity.

Like the end of Berkner, the mountains told me that we were on course and making progress in a more tangible way than a hundred GPS readouts could ever do. By the end of that day though, the peaks had vanished, and I even wondered whether I had been seeing things – a mirage of sorts. I remembered reading accounts of early explorers seeing things beyond the horizon as light was refracted by an interaction of air layers and ice particles to render distant objects visible when they should not be. I looked forward to the next day when I might find out for sure.

The following day disappointed as visibility was bad. I moved off as usual but found myself edging into a depressed frame of mind, tipped over the edge by a silly paranoia about whether or not I had actually seen the mountains, and a sullen, childlike annoyance that the weather was preventing me from finding out one way or the other.

These mood swings were more or less daily occurrences during the course of the trip – triggered by the smallest of things but unfortunately requiring a huge amount of energy to turn around. A frequent cause was our periodic contact with the outside world via the satellite phone, which was certainly a double-edged sword. On the one hand it provided welcome food for thought and news, but it certainly had downsides. It made you miss friends and family terribly, disrupted your concentration on the task at hand, and anything less than good news tended to put you in a depressed frame of mind. It had such a surprisingly profound effect on me, in fact, that early on I briefed Andrea and my parents to keep back problems.

The next day my mood was high again. Visibility had improved and my questionable sighting of the Transantarctic Mountains only two days before was confirmed as they appeared majestically out of the mist right in front of us. Still a day off, they looked like what they were – the entrance to a lost world – a formidable barrier of jagged granite; sentinels guarding access to the polar plateau. Dark and brooding with clouds amassed around their peaks, they seemed to watch our slow progress as we inched towards them across the snow. The only breaks in this massive wall of rock were steep passes of turquoise blue ice and brilliant white snow offering us treacherous routes up onto the polar plateau.

Back in Sydney we had picked one of these as a point to aim for, and it was unbelievably exciting that with our GPS, limited maps and a chart of magnetic variation we could get ourselves accurately to this spot under our own steam across such a vast featureless place. We had covered about 450 km and although I felt tired I was genuinely thrilled, as I was when we passed the milestone of the end of Berkner.

The geographical top and bottom of the earth ('true north and south') are of course not the same points as the sources of the earth's magnetism. Maps therefore have both a true geographical north and a magnetic north (to which our compass needles are drawn). As all compasses are magnetised to be attracted to the earth's North Magnetic Pole, magnetic variation is the difference between geographic North Pole and this northern source of the earth's magnetism. As the name implies, magnetic variation is dependent on where you are on the earth relative to these points. People tend to view the position of the geographic and magnetic poles as being in more or less the same place. The reality could not be more different. When you get there you realise just how far apart they are.

Caused by the movement of swirling masses of molten rock in the earth's core, the magnetic poles are still not fully understood, and the magnetic north and south poles are constantly on the move. The South Magnetic Pole is more than 1000 km from the South Pole and in fact isn't even situated on the Antarctic continent any more, having moved offshore some 40 or so years ago. To get to the magnetic pole these days you need a boat, as it sits out in the Southern Ocean 75 kilometres offshore. Even more amazing, it is moving and moving fast – heading north fantastically quickly – not at the geological snail's pace we are accustomed to, but at the unbelievable rate of some 5 km a year! In just a few hundred years, who knows, it could end up in South Australia, next to its number one son, Sir Douglas Mawson.

The North Magnetic Pole, on the other hand, has been moving increasingly rapidly in recent years, such that by 2002, it was moving almost 40 km a year, almost seven times faster than its average of 6 km a year since the 1830s.

Our route was designed to take us to Wujek Ridge, named by the Americans who surveyed it back in the mid-1960s. I just hoped like hell we were going to be able to get a heavily laden sled up it. It had sheer granite sides and climbed from a height of 400 m to almost 1200 m in its 4 or so kilometres in a series of steps, starting gently and becoming very steep towards the top. It would be a serious proposition with or without a sled, but it was a pretty direct route up onto the polar plateau. The pass at Wujek was a massive landmark on our journey south. Successfully negotiating it would mean we were successfully across the Ronne.

Wujek is in a part of the Transantarctic Mountains called the Dufek Massif – a discrete collection of peaks that are tall enough to poke through the thick mantle of ice of the Antarctic ice cap. We had chosen Dufek for precisely this reason – its mountains stabilised the ice cap, locking it into position and preventing it from moving like the great rivers of ice either side of it. Rivers like the vast Support Force Glacier needed to be avoided at all costs. A staggering 30 kilometres wide, hundreds and hundreds of metres thick and likely bristling with terrifying deep crevasses, it was awesome but would have been grim to try to negotiate. Ice that isn't moving is at least less prone to cracking and deforming and forming crevasses and for that reason we were confident our route through the mountains would be the safer

option. Secondly and significantly Dufek was only a slight devi-
ation off a straight line from Berkner to the Pole and had been
recommended to Peter by the Norwegian explorer Borge
Ousland.

Dufek paradoxically was not that big a target to aim for – only
a kilometre in width itself. From our start point on Berkner
450 km away, each step we had taken had been aimed at reaching this small oasis of stability.

As we approached we were dwarfed by the scale of the landscape around us, and it was staggering to think of the forces at
work. Thousands of cubic kilometres of ice pouring off the
largest ice sheet in the world containing almost 70 per cent of
the world's fresh water. The only thing capable of standing up
to these impossible forces was the granite of the mountains we
aimed to thread our way through. One day I knew even these
dark peaks would finally be worn down.

The names I had seen on the maps when planning our route
gave a sense of familiarity to the place. As with Berkner, that
ended abruptly when we actually came face to face with what
they represented in reality. It seemed arbitrary to give names to
such spectacular places, especially when the names bore no real
relationship or significance to them. Dufek and Wujek were
named after US military leaders, and the survey party were
Americans. The Support Force was a group of US personnel
providing, as the name implies, support to the main survey
party. None of the names did anything to impart the grandeur
or scale of the place.

Once at the base of Wujek, as with Patriot Hills we encountered clean polished ice – the result of wind that continuously
blows down from the mountains keeping the adjacent area clear
of snow. We donned our crampons and started to ascend, conscious of the clouds gathering ominously some 1500 metres
above us at the top. The sled moved easily for the first time, skittering across the clear, flat ice at the base of the pass. As we

crossed it, I could see boulders trapped within the ice, some a metre or so beneath the surface. They would have crashed down the mountainside to here and then, warmed by the sun, gradually melted down into the ice over the years. I looked carefully for any sign of life on those rocks on the surface I passed close to, but there was none. No insects, no lichen, no algae, no nothing.

The easiest pulling of the trip on the lower slopes of the pass was soon replaced by the requirement for massive effort to pull the sled up the increasingly steep and exposed sections. With virtually no snow on the slope for the sled runners to cut into, there was no choice but to go straight up the fall line, as any attempt to traverse sideways had the sled drop below you like a plumb-bob, pulling you off balance.

It was perhaps the most gut-wrenching physical effort I had ever subjected myself to. Twenty steps at a time, followed by stopping to draw deep lungfuls of air was the best I could muster, as I leant forward, my nose about a foot from the surface of the ice trying to counter the weight of the sled as it threatened to pull me down. My heart was racing and adrenaline pumping, and I was sweating copiously even with −25°C temperatures and the cold blast of the wind pouring down from the mountains above. My calves and ankles burned with the effort of being overstretched as I tried to hold the weight of my body and sled with only the points of my crampons adhering me to the ice. I peered upwards, straining my neck back to see how far the pass went on, but it was like trying to look into a third-floor window from the pavement below and I simply didn't have the angle to see anything.

I was getting hot with the high workload, but strangely my hands became cold as all the blood was being sent to my legs. Weighing on my mind now was the fact that I had seen a wind-sculpted ice cliff with a drop of 70 or 80 metres to my right at the beginning of the climb. Now, some steepening of the ice directly above me was slowly but surely making me head right and I was conscious that the cliffs probably lay somewhere directly below me. A fall from my current position would likely have sent me over the edge. A bloody-minded determination combined with the prospect of that drop kept me going. Despite my tiredness, I wasn't going to fall, nor could I afford to.

At one of my many 'recovery stops' to catch my breath, I looked back down the pass at the figure of Peter some 200 metres below me and to my left, steadily climbing. As if in slow motion I saw him stumble and his crampons fail to bite. Before I could even shout down to him, he fell and the sled pulled him down. I watched helplessly as he careered down the slope still attached to his sled, until he came to rest 30 or so seconds later.

I stood motionless to try to hear something from below as I couldn't turn around properly to see what was going on. All I could hear was the roar of the wind in my ears. My mind started racing as I thought of ways to somehow attach the sled to the ice and climb back down to effect some kind of rescue. He was quite a way to my left when he'd fallen, and was lucky. Had he been where I was, he would have fallen over the ice cliff for sure.

The irony was that for the first time on the journey I was in no position to help. The only thing I could do was keep going, reach the top, leave the sled and climb back down to try to help him. With every ounce of energy I now pushed onwards; twenty paces, rest, twenty paces, rest, driving for the top, reaching a succession of false summits before the slope finally flattened out. After a gruelling climb, for the first time in over two hours I was able to unshackle myself from the sled and stand upright. I looked back down the pass and could see Peter coming back up.

I climbed part of the way back down and met him. He was smiling, probably out of relief as much as anything. 'What a ride,' he managed between breaths. I was smiling too, just because he was okay. I've had a few nasty moments in my life in the outdoors, but the prospect of sitting in the tent making a call to tell Peter's wife Beth bad news would have been the pits.

It was only then that I realised how strong the camaraderie between us had become after eighteen days on the ice. You decide to throw yourselves into a challenge such as this and become not only dependent on one another but also feel quite protective. It's partly because that's how you genuinely feel but also because your own self-preservation relies on their being okay. Peter was badly shaken and bruised. He'd seen the cliff at close hand as he'd tumbled down the slope but had been powerless to do anything about it and was lucky to have avoided it. Lucky too that he was a tough campaigner and able to laugh about the whole thing only minutes afterwards.

We stopped to rest and eat some chocolate at the head of the pass, and decided to make some distance between us and Wujek. 'Let's get away from anything we can fall down,' said Peter half-jokingly, and we pushed on again for another hour until well above the pass. Despite being cold and inhospitable much of the time, the tent at the end of a hard day blocked out Antarctica and allowed you to forget its savagery for a while. Tonight we were particularly grateful to zip up the tent and were excited to have Wujek behind us and the mountains to look at for the next week or so until we reached the plateau.

I had mixed emotions about the mountains. On the one hand there were some spectacular peaks that afforded something interesting to look at. In addition they provided us with something to navigate towards instead of endless pieces of ice as on the ice shelf and Berkner. On the other hand, the time saved from not having to constantly hunch over the chest compass to follow our bearing now gave us time to see just how slow our movement through this vast landscape was – something that doesn't happen when there are no landmarks to gauge your speed by.

The following day our tiny convoy trekked out across the vast snowy plain between the two parallel ridges of the Dufek Massif. Sure enough, there were no crevasses anywhere in sight across the plain although the surface was definitely beginning to change. Now it was becoming more uneven, and we started to see the first signs of the sastrugi, the chaotic wind-eroded surface of ice that we had been told to expect up on the plateau. Now it consisted of small wind-sculpted scoops of ice 10–20 centimetres high and we moved across it without too much problem. Occasionally the sled would snag behind some obstacle, but a solid thrust with the hips would normally bulldoze it over or through the obstruction. That night we camped right in the middle of the plain with mountains all around in what must have been one of the most spectacular campsites in the world.

Our routine at least was by now well developed and involved instilling a structured sense of urgency to each day. Following our digital watches, we would work for a solid eight and a half hours, having decided this was the optimum daily schedule, adding on time whenever we had a mechanical problem or needed a toilet stop. Of these kind of impromptu stops there would be many, but we truthfully added on time every time we stopped to adjust a ski or eat something. By at least deciding how long we would work and rest for each day, we retained our sanity and some sense of control over our lives. Failure to do this would leave us faced with the enormity of our task and the vast isolation of Antarctica.

I would start each day with a solid two-hour lead, making use of the energy from our olive oil laced carbo breakfast, before a short rest. This would be followed by an hour going as fast as I could go. There is an event in world cycling where competitors try to see how far they can go in an hour. I approached this hour's lead the same way, finishing with a 'sprint' as the seconds ticked down, as if a finishing line was just ahead of me and the world record distance was within reach. I would throw myself into that hour, blasting forwards, imagining that someone was holding up a stopwatch and saying, 'He's going to do it, he's on course to break the record.' I switched off completely when following Peter for his three hours, each day picking up from where I had left off the day before with a particular topic to analyse, almost as you would a book. It was my best private time to think and I would consider all manner of topics.

My hour and a quarter after Peter's three hours I would look on as the all-important session where I got the chance to get us ahead of what we had done the day before. It was all subterfuge really, of course, as each minute of every session contributed to our total, but it was amazing how I managed to convince myself that all that mattered was this session. The rest of the day had been getting the basics done. This session was the make or break that separated the average from the exceptional and I never let myself off the hook. Each day I would tell myself that the time had come to prove myself, to my parents, to my friends, the kids at Westmead, the PMs and to myself. This was the time. If I didn't do it now there would be no other. Life is short and this was a once-in-a-lifetime thing I was doing. I was making history, pitting myself against perhaps the most extreme environment in the world and I was going to win. This hour and a quarter was my time and I was going to take it.

By contrast Peter would lead the final session of the day and most days I would just hang on, watching the back of his sled in front of me, imagining that he was pulling me along too. I found it best to watch the sled, as it completed the deception that I was somehow getting a free ride. If I looked up at Peter bent forward, shoulders straining, breathing hard like a beast of burden it reminded me I was doing the same. And so each day was a series of small battles won. Battles that you could get to grips with, rather than face the enormity of the whole campaign.

Once or twice if I had the energy I would let Peter get a fair way off and then try to catch him. On one occasion he obviously felt I'd dropped a fair way back as he kindly took the time to draw a large yellow directional arrow pointing south. I was suitably impressed with his creativity and bladder control.

Along the way there were some wonderful spires of granite poking through the ice cap, many of which will likely remain unclimbed. Occasionally too we would catch glimpses of unnamed mountains away to the side of our route, looking like ships cast adrift in a vast white sea – distant and mysterious, but sadly too far away for us to concern ourselves with as we toiled on. I took the opportunity to name a few to pass the time, thinking back to some of the names that Australia's early explorers had given the mountains they had discovered in Australia's interior. They'd given a clue as to the way they were feeling at the time – Mount Hopeless, Mount Desolation, Mount Abrupt. There didn't seem to be many 'Mount Easy' or 'Mount Doddle', that's for sure and I understood the sentiment.

After a week I finally started to lose patience with the mountains – ever present and omnipotent – and I longed to reach the polar plateau proper that would signal we were on the final leg into the Pole. What never ceased to impress was that the small rocky outcrops or 'nunataks' we passed were in fact the tops of vast mountains buried in the 3-kilometre-thick ice present in this part of Antarctica. It was an eerie feeling that made you feel even smaller and more insignificant, if that was possible.

I looked up expectantly at the rocky ledges and crannies of the nunataks as we passed by, hoping at any moment to hear the screech of birds. Even a solitary one would do, showing us we weren't alone in this place. Instead all was silent, save for the creaking of my skis, the thumping of my sled as it rumbled over the sastrugi and the sound of the wind in my ears. No wonder humans have never settled Antarctica – nothing lives here. The only people in the interior of this vast place were us and those at the small Russian and American scientific bases of Vostok and Amundsen-Scott. The chances of bumping into any living thing were pretty much zero. The sensory deprivation of 24-hour light, seeing nothing alive, and hearing and smelling nothing save the odour of fuel and bodies in the tent was another dimension to the assault on the senses that Antarctica subjects you to.

On day 23 I could see no more nunataks beyond the one a couple of kilometres ahead of me. Slowly we drew level with it and finally edged past it and the mountains gradually receded into the distance. From now on there would be no more peaks on our route, just the cold lonely windswept polar plateau, and finally the Pole itself. The Transantarctic Mountains do, of course, continue on for another 2000 km to the far side of Antarctica, but none of them along our route were big enough to pierce through the thick mantle of the Antarctic ice cap. If we passed any from now on it would be as we skied right over their summits.

Leaving the mountains coincided with Peter's birthday even though he didn't know I knew. I had a special treat for him that I'd brought along with me – a small packet of marshmallows. As I walked along that day, though, I'd already decided to give him something extra – a few sheets of my precious toilet paper. I did this because I'd been astounded by the fact that Peter hadn't brought along any with him in a bid to save weight. And so each morning he would, without putting too fine a point on it, wipe his arse with snow. It seemed a particularly unpleasant way of finishing what was already a pretty unpleasant activity, all to save the weight of carrying a bog roll weighing 300 grams. My gift was gratefully received, but was a double-edged sword, making him realise what he'd been missing out on all this time.

The area in the lee of the mountains was a disappointment: a vast never-ending bowl of powder that we toiled in for two whole days – like a giant sandpit. Looking back I could still just see the mountains behind us on the horizon and longed to lose sight of them so I could satisfy myself that we were up on the plateau proper. The going was tougher than normal as we struggled to move the sleds through the soft snow. Sometime that afternoon we crossed 83° south and I had a horrible sense of foreboding that the plateau was all going to be like this. I was annoyed with myself for thinking negatively, knowing full well that things could change just as quickly as they had started. These conditions had to be the result of the wind shadow of the mountains causing them to drop their cargo of snow in a thick bank behind them. Once a bit further away from the mountains we would leave this soft stuff behind and the going would get easier. It needed to as the effort of pulling a sled that still weighed over 170 kg was desperately hard. We were less than halfway to the Pole and each day I willed myself to get up and keep pushing on.

My moods still swung through 180 degrees in a mater of minutes, depending on how bearable the conditions were. In the deep soft snow beyond the mountains I could only manage to grind out twenty minutes before a brief stop for a minute or so to catch my breath, legs burning with lactic acid from the effort.

I had no way of verifying it, but I knew I was losing weight fast now. I could feel my clothes getting looser and in the sleeping bag at night could also feel my legs and stomach were thinner. In fact there wasn't an ounce of fat anywhere on my body. I just hoped our diet would slow our bodies' consumption of muscle as it fuelled its heavy workload, knowing that we were burning more each day than we could even absorb. This heavy snow wouldn't help, and nor would the thinner air up on the plateau.

Our altimeters put us at about 2200 metres high and, with the weight of the sleds, even slightly thinner air made a difference. The temperature too appeared to be getting colder as we climbed, at about the same rate as the 'warmer' summer weather came on. In fact we had timed it to get up onto the plateau only after the warmer summer weather made it more tolerable. Getting up here too early would have been too inhospitable.

I was woken from my mental struggle as a huge raft of snow and ice that I happened to be on dropped several metres. Heart racing, I looked back at Peter and he was standing with his arms up in the air questioningly – he too had felt it several hundred metres behind me. It was the biggest snow quake we had experienced and the raft of snow seemed to stretch to the horizon. The sound of the quake echoed around the mountains in a wild primeval roar for almost two minutes. It was an awesome feeling thinking that we had caused such a major event, almost as if Antarctica, despite its size, was really a sensitive giant that could be affected by even our presence passing quietly over its surface. I screamed out with the excitement of the whole experience and listened to my voice echo around behind us.

Slowly but surely now we began ascending and the air correspondingly seemed to get thinner and the temperatures colder with each successive day, making each day harder than the one before. Even a cough or a burp would find you having to stop and catch your breath again and a wave of lactic acid would sweep through your legs. I remembered planning all this months before, thinking that the extra effort caused by the altitude of the plateau would be compensated by our sled weights coming down by almost 1.5 kg a day as we consumed our food and fuel. Worryingly though, the workload never seemed to get any easier. In fact quite the reverse. I sat on my sled trying to force some food into my mouth through the frozen opening of my balaclava. Next session I decided to concentrate on trying to remember my reasons for being here as at the moment those reasons seemed hard to find.

The terrain now was also becoming increasingly rough and I realised that we were moving into the dreaded sastrugi belt that stretches from 84 degrees across the high part of the polar plateau. Over the next two days the sastrugi continued to grow, such that on that second day I passed the whole of my three-hour lead without my skis touching the surface of the snow, moving instead from one frozen wave crest to the next in an endless procession.

By our third day in the sastrugi, what had begun as small waves a foot or so high had become an obstructive landscape of tightly packed ice sculptures that needed to be negotiated. The sled was now a liability more than ever before as it regularly snagged behind features that looked as though they were designed for precisely that job.

By the time we crossed 85° south, the sastrugi had become so large and difficult to negotiate that we regularly lost sight of one another in amongst it. It was like being in an ocean of whitecaps snapped frozen, with waves and troughs of ice metres high that needed to be negotiated. As we progressed, they seemed to get larger and larger, and each day, completely spent, we would search for an area flat enough to pitch the tent in amongst the confusion. Each of us had now become involved in his own private battle against the sastrugi, trying whatever combination of brute force and psychology worked, heading for some icy feature on the horizon and working towards it through the frozen labyrinth via whatever route we could find.

The sense of isolation up here was complete. The light was clear but ethereal, the air thin, and the landscape a strange collection of features sculpted imaginatively by the wind. We were as isolated as it was possible to be and that feeling was affirming and exciting. It was the way it would have been for the early explorers and rather than find it intimidating I found it good to know there were still places like this left in the world that humankind has not subjugated with technology.

We continued with our sat phone hook-ups every few days, but now knew there was no chance of rescue even if we wanted it, with scarcely enough flat ground for a tennis court, let alone for a plane to land. I remembered the story of Rob Hall in John Krakauer's book *Into Thin Air* on the sat phone to his wife from Everest's summit, needing help but knowing it would never come and tragically dying.

^ ^ ^

Day 30 was much anticipated as it signalled the first change of underpants. I had three pairs for the trip, a pair a month, and midway through each month I would turn each pair inside out so that slightly less soiled fabric sat next to the skin. It was a tricky manoeuvre doing all of this inside my sleeping bag but I managed it and burnt my old ones with a few drops of fuel from the stove. Strangely these little gestures made me feel like I was pampering myself, rather than the reality which was quite the opposite as I stressed my body to breaking point on a daily basis.

Each night our chicken broth of noodles, rice, nuts and olive oil was more gratefully received by our tired bodies than the day before as we greedily soaked up the calories. After a hot meal we felt at our most relaxed and we would discuss all manner of things while the yellow rays of the sun even generated some warmth in the tent. Often we talked about things we would do when this was over. In this way we were reminded that the trip was finite and that one day the need for constant vigilance and mental and physical effort would be over.

Some days when moving along I felt really positive about things – we were getting through this place despite its harshness. The sense of pride that we were still here and managing to survive was elating, and the Antarctic, although often malevolent and not always fair, was so real and stunningly beautiful compared to our cluttered city lives.

Annoyingly, though, it was difficult to hold onto these positive thoughts, and I knew that the following morning would probably find me less upbeat. The tent was a desperately miserable place in which to wake, especially when you knew exactly what physical and mental angst and hardship awaited you each day.

The day began not as one might imagine when you started

sledding, rather when you unzipped your sleeping bag and lost all of your valuable body heat within the space of a few seconds. Not only did you have to lift your fatigued body, warm and damp from its cocoon into icy temperatures you would experience in a meat locker, but your lost body heat melted the ice on the roof of the tent, so that it almost immediately began dripping down on you, soaking your sleeping bag. Some days it seemed we were in a dank, dripping cavern rather than a tent. This moisture would then freeze into our clothes and sleeping bag as soon as we stepped outside. At least the unpleasant environment of the tent each morning made it less difficult to face the world outside.

I unzipped the tent and peered out at the jagged surface that lay ahead of us. We finished the slops of the olive oil and muesli breakfast, put on our stiff boots, and crawled out of the tent to start putting our equipment in the sleds, moving as quickly as possible to keep warm and try to slow the creeping loss of circulation in our hands. Within two minutes they had as usual become gluey and slow. I hurriedly put the compass bracket round my neck, picked the bearing to follow and, with tired muscles, leaned into my work.

The sled reluctantly began moving, regularly snagging behind sastrugi, before freeing itself and throwing me off balance as it came lurching forwards, causing the chest compass to spin out of control and requiring a few seconds' wait until it settled again. It was demoralising, energy-sapping work and I began sweating even in the bitter cold. By mid-morning the wind was slamming into us as we battled to follow our compass bearing south. It had a ferocity surpassed only by the storm and had come on so quickly that we had no choice but to push on and hope it abated by the end of the day. To try to pitch the tent in these conditions would have been nigh on impossible.

Howling around us, the wind stripped any snow not firmly frozen to the icy surface, and sent it racing across the ground, giving the impression that the whole surface was moving. Luckily, for some reason, visibility remained good and we could still see 500 metres or so ahead of us. The force of the wind blew my sled out at an angle behind me despite its weighing over 160 kg, and the wind and cold combined to produce a terrible windchill that easily whipped away any body heat generated through working. Even though I felt no warmth from my efforts and my hands felt numb, I knew that working hard was the only thing that was keeping me going. To have stopped in such conditions without the shelter of the tent would have been suicide.

I worked hard to keep the momentum I had going. Antarctica now seemed to be throwing everything it had to offer at us and I zipped up all of the clothing layers, put my woollen hat on over my balaclava and put on my extra mitts. Several minutes later, without warning I was wrenched violently backwards, coming to an abrupt halt. I peered over my shoulder through the small window of visibility afforded by my iced-up goggles and saw that the sled had become wedged behind a large piece of sastrugi. I swore at my luck but was used to it by now and clumsily backed up in my skis before throwing all my weight forward to try to bulldoze it through the obstruction. 'C'mon you bastard,' I screamed – the words pushed back down my throat by the force of the wind. The front of the sled buried itself in deeper. I tried again and again, and then I felt something give, and careered forwards into a wall of ice.

I steadied myself, disorientated by my efforts, and scanned the icy maze until I spotted Peter appearing on top of a mound before again descending into a trough. He was a few hundred metres away and I leaned forward to follow him. But the sled holding me back felt different. Sure enough, when I looked around I could see that one of the two buckles that attached my harness to the sled had broken and the sled still sat stubbornly behind the obstruction. I stared at it in a mixture of disgust and disbelief. I unclipped the other buckle and stepped backwards awkwardly in my skis to the sled, the backs of my skis digging into the sastrugi causing me to stumble. Peter was still plodding away into the distance and I shouted to tell him to stop, but my shouts were lost in the wind. I sat there for a minute, miserable beyond belief. It was a hellish place – cold and unforgiving, and the terrain cruelly obstructive. I was tired and cold and now had to concentrate to fix this thing or I would be in trouble.

I cursed out loud at the ice, myself, and Peter too for good measure. It was day 35 though and we had become complacent. I was usually faster than Peter, and during his leads he tended to be confident I would be right there behind him.

'Stupid bastard,' I muttered, aiming my comment at the world, and removed three of my four glove layers to try to fix the harness so that I could get moving again. I worked as fast as I could with my thin wool base-layer gloves providing scant protection from the bitter cold. The harness was going to be tricky to fix and I knew I had to be fast as every second of exposure was time for the cold and wind to eat into my hands, freezing the blood and tissue. As I worked to re-attach the harness using wire and rope from my spares bag, the sensation started to go in my fingers. It was a downward spiral. As my fingers slowed, so the repair took longer, which in turn made my hands worse.

My mind was frantic, contrasting with the speed of my hands which had slowed to the point where they scarcely obeyed what I was telling them to do. Beginning to panic I continued trying to repair the old buckle with wire, intent on tying this round the belt of my harness with some rope. It was a catch-22 situation. If I left the sled I could catch Peter and get him to help me with the repair, but I risked losing the sled in amongst the sastrugi as our tracks were being obliterated almost as quickly as we were making them. If I did not fix the harness properly it would break again and cause me more problems. Yet if we lost one another it would be disaster. In addition, I was fast losing the use of my hands. I had no choice but to keep on with the repair. In desperation I looped the rope through the repaired buckle and tied a clumsy knot around the waist belt, hoping it would hold. It would have to do, as any further work with my anaesthetised hands was no longer possible.

Hurriedly, I put on my down jacket over my Hellytech and, unable to do it up, threaded my numb arms through the shoulder straps of my harness. With hands sitting limply in the loops of my ski poles, unable to grip, I hastily moved to catch Peter. I was shocked by the state I was in. Normally tolerant of the cold, my arms from the elbows down now felt like hunks of meat and completely numb, as if I had fallen asleep on them during the night and cut off the circulation. I knew though that only hard work and body heat would force blood back into them.

Fear now drove me on. I had to get warm as fast as possible and Peter was a long way ahead. For an hour I pursued him like a madman, banging and crashing through the sastrugi with scant regard for myself, my sled or the repair I had just made. Still there was no sensation. I had never experienced such total deep tissue numbness and after an hour although sensation in my forearms and hands had painfully returned, my fingers were still dead. I had no more cards to play. The only way I could get warm was to work and so I did, worried whether it would be enough.

Then I felt the sickening lurching sensation again. The harness slumped for a second time and I knew my knot had come loose. I had only slight sensation in some of my fingers yet I had to find the strength to overcome the situation. Even as it was happening I knew it was one of those defining moments in life where I needed to summon all of my resolve and strength to get through it. As I worked I could hear people back home saying, 'Was it worth it?' as I showed them my frostbitten, damaged hands. I resisted the strong temptation to give up and rest and busied myself with a second repair. I managed to get my harness off and kneeling on the snow, wind howling around me, pulled off my outer gloves to expose my thinly gloved hands to the very conditions that had hobbled them so effectively. I slowly tied granny knot on top of granny knot, hoping they would collectively hold the strain, barely able to do more. The numbness was terrible and I yearned for the awful pain of circulation returning. All I wanted to do was stop and rest, but I couldn't afford to.

I got up to move again and cursed loudly. Peter was still a long way off and again I rushed to catch him. I pushed on and on, but still there was no sensation in a number of my fingers and in the thumb on my right hand. Finally I got within a few hundred metres of him and mercifully saw him stop and plant his ski poles firmly in the ground – it was the end of his 2.5 hour lead and he was stopping for a drink.

I felt intense relief as I knew now I would not lose him. As I got within earshot I started abusing Peter for not keeping an eye on me. He was surprised at the ferocity of my verbal attack but it was short-lived such was my elation at my ordeal being over. Although I was glad to catch him and wanted more than ever to talk about the trauma of the last two hours, I now dared not stop to rest. He put the compass around my neck and after some chocolate and water I pushed off again. Over the next hour or so the excruciating pain of circulation gradually returned to my hands and most of my fingers, although my right thumb remained worryingly numb.

Me (back row, third from the left) aged 8 at Alice Smith School, Kuala Lumpur – always planning something, even for a class photo.

In preparation for the North Pole trek, Peter and I dragged carts 1100 km across the Great Victoria Desert. My cart weighed some 220 kg, similar to the weight dragged down south.

The snow 'shadow' cast by our tent and snow wall following the storm we endured on Lomonosov Ice Cap on the Arctic island of Spitsbergen. The snow wall was surprisingly robust despite the furious winds.

One o'clock in the morning on Spitsbergen, looking across at the valley we needed to traverse the next day, nestled between two spectacular mountains.

An unwelcome and unscheduled stop in minus 35 degrees, somewhere on the Ronne Ice Shelf en route to Berkner Island, Antarctica.

Peter and sled in the early part of our South Pole trek. Little did we know that far worse was to come in the thin air and tumultuous terrain of the Sastrugi up on the polar plateau.

The typical buildup of frozen breath and sweat encrusts my balaclava. At the end of each day, pulling the balaclava from a beard was hell. The beard gave the ice purchase, holding it next to your face and increasing the chance of frostbite.

Olive oil on cereal – disgusting but it provided valuable calories.

Wujek Ridge (to the left of picture) in the Transantarctic Mountains – our chosen pass up onto the polar plateau. It was unbelievably hard work to ascend with a heavily laden sled in tow.

Campsite on top of the world – in Antarctica's Transantarctic Mountains approaching the polar plateau proper, showing how isolated we were.

Our tracks alongside the last 'nunatak' before the Pole, still 600 km distant. This small rocky outcrop was actually the summit of a mountain buried in 2.5 km thick ice. From this point on, no mountain was high enough to break through the icy mantle of the polar cap and we would ski right over their summits.

Repairing the compass bracket. At minus 20 degrees in the tent, manual dexterity ebbed away within a matter of minutes.

Peter in a serious moment. The strain and steady decline of our bodies showed on both our faces.

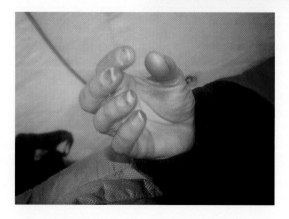

The blistering indicated the gradual recovery of my hand from frostbite.

Mirrorball marker at the South Pole. A fitting marker, originally designed to take panoramic pictures of the aurora australis (southern lights) before the invention of the fish-eye lens.

Day 47, leaving the South Pole with me leading and Peter behind, crossing vehicle tracks that led out to a point some kilometres from the base where global air quality measurements are made.

Standing beneath the photographs of Scott and Amundsen at the South Pole base of the same name after a week of recovery, and with the record fastest unsupported journey to the South Pole under our belt.

Peter and I at the press conference on our return from Antarctica.

Discussing the North Pole route with Zaz Shackleton, granddaughter of Sir Ernest Shackleton – a staunch supporter and good friend. Sir Ernest watches over us from the photo on the book shelf.

Roger Daynes showing how the two sleds attach together to form a stable platform for paddling across wide sections of open ocean or leads that form in the Arctic ice. The 1.5m wide sleds were hell to paddle through water clogged with brash ice.

Peter in our Khatanga hotel, contemplating the North Pole journey we were about to face.

Peter and the larger-than-life Victor Boyarsky testing the Iridium satellite phone in Khatanga. They seemed to work when they were next to one another!

No danger of hitching a lift to the Pole in this. With the Cold War over, the military base on Sredniy was abandoned with everything left behind.

The large military-issue Sikorsky helicopter getting ready to fly us to our starting point for the North Pole attempt.

The chaotic surface of pressure, North Pole. Obstructive and soul destroying to pull the sled through.

Pressure ridges formed by the constant movement of ice on the surface of the Arctic Ocean, buckling and contorting to form walls of rubble.

Preparing to bridge a small lead with the sled – nerve-racking at first but after a while we became practised at it.

9

Breaking new ground

The polished ivory white of frozen tissue was plain to see in two of my fingers on my right hand and my right thumb. I couldn't believe that within 400 km of the Pole a couple of simple mishaps could in the space of an afternoon totally alter things. The thin veneer of control we had established via strict attention to our routine was blown apart. Antarctica was harsh and unforgiving and it was a mistake to ever lose sight of that. Our vigilance kept us alive in this place, but disaster lurked just beneath the surface if we ever let our guard down.

My diary reads, 'That was the toughest day of my life' for each of those days in amongst the obstructive terrain, bitter cold and thin air of the sastrugi, with each day unbelievably seeming to eclipse the last. It was clear that the journey and constant workload were taking a toll on us. The frostbite caused by my harness breaking that day was bad and my body felt as though it was getting weaker at the same rate as my sled weight reduced. My neck and nose were covered in scabs from frostbite caused by the wind and cold that froze any exposed skin and my gums ached. Even though I had not set eyes on my body for six weeks beneath my clothing layers, I could feel as I lay in my sleeping bag that my body had long since begun feeding on my muscle to fuel my workload.

I'm not sure how I kept going through those days, but somehow I convinced myself that the conditions the next day would be better and that the sastrugi would get smaller. Each day I was disappointed, but somehow managed to look positively at my hardship, telling myself that I would have been in some way disappointed if the conditions had been easier. I played all sorts of positive and negative scenario mind games. 'These are the kinds of conditions that Scott and Mawson wrote of that I wanted to experience,' I told myself. 'I'm managing to get through what they did.' 'How would I ever forgive myself if I didn't keep going?' 'Just think of what it will be like to arrive at the Pole and hold up the flag and stand at the end of the world.' Beyond the Pole would be breaking new ground and a world record for unsupported travel. It's what I dreamt of and I used anything I could lay my hands on towards achieving that goal.

On day 37 we had a phone sched (our satellite phone link-up at a prearranged time) with ANI in Patriot. We reported my frostbite and our general condition and, with the formalities out of the way, Neil jumped in to tell us something.

'You are 310 kilometres from the Pole. If you can get there in less than 49 days, you will have the world record for the fastest unsupported journey to the Pole.' It was a mixed blessing. On the one hand I was pleased beyond belief at our progress, but on the other I knew that to cover 310 km in eleven days to get there in 48 days meant an average of just under 30 km a day. We had managed this for the past couple of weeks despite the sastrugi, but to put ourselves under the pressure of trying to maintain this was a horrible thought. I knew, though, that as soon as the words were uttered I wouldn't allow myself to shrink from the challenge.

I discovered things about myself during those days up on the plateau. I'd always been my own worst enemy – biting off more than I could chew ever since I was a kid and I was beginning to appreciate what this means in Antarctica. Never allowing myself to give up, and thinking of it as a weakness in some way if I did. In Antarctica this is a dangerous attitude, as it just takes and takes and then it takes some more until you're completely spent, and then treats your efforts with contempt and destroys you as soon as you lower your guard, or your body or equipment lets you down. Some days it felt downright malevolent, and for at least some part of every one of those seventeen days in the sastrugi I scared myself with how hard we were pushing ourselves trying to maintain our 30 km a day average. Each day I woke and wondered whether today would be the day when I would find I could no longer force myself on. Somehow, though, I kept going.

The early explorers had done some incredible things, yet they were only human. Thinking about them in those terms gave me a greater respect for them than I'd had thinking of them as superheroes. The reality is that you go to places like the Poles and do what you have to do to survive. If you manage to achieve what you set out to do it is because the place has allowed you to, not because you have got its measure. Bad weather or an accident and it will chew you up and spit you out, whoever you are and no matter how long your CV of previous trips.

I'd heard explorers recount tales of feeling as though they were in the presence of someone other than themselves, and I think I experienced this sensation up on the plateau. With vast fields of obstructive sastrugi, heavy sled weights, hacking coughs from the dry thin air, failing equipment and reduced strength we managed distances previously only achieved by dog teams. I wasn't familiar with the kind of person I'd become up on the plateau. It was almost as if my normal persona looked upon the achievements of my alter ego with pride and disbelief, and that the person I found accompanying me along the way was none other than another part of my own being, so different from my normal self that I almost believed it was someone else.

The reality was that although the Pole and the record were

'only' 300 kilometres away, most days it was too much to contemplate more than the metres that lay immediately ahead of
you as you strained to pull the sled through the desperate terrain
of the sastrugi. Most days still consisted of breaking down the
challenge ahead into a series of manageable portions that I could
motivate myself through – getting to the top of the next rise, or
to the next biscuit break, or piece of ice on the horizon. Our
journey to the Pole wasn't 1350 kilometres, it was thousands of
drags of the sled over shorter distances. Once at the Pole we
would think about the journey on from there.

∧ ∧ ∧

Eating is something I always enjoy, but other than the chocolate I grew tired of our food during the trip. The monotony of
the food and the requirement for it to be laced with hundreds
of millilitres of olive oil to provide enough calories to sustain
us each day was becoming tiresome. Olive oil in soup or with
noodles is one thing. Olive oil in large congealed lumps on
muesli first thing in the morning is quite another, and I don't
know what was worse – the prospect of this or leaving the tent
and feeling the icy blast of the wind for the first time.

Other than the à la carte stuff, you also needed to eat as you
went along, to give your body a chance to digest the large
amounts of calories you were forcing into it. 'Lunch on the go'
would be eaten on your sled with your back to the wind. Your
moist breath more often than not would have frozen your balaclava to your face, so that it assumed the properties of chain
mail, and not soft fleece as it had begun the day. Pulling it from
your face to eat would mean tearing out clumps of beard each
time you removed it. You would then wash down the food with
water that had been heated and put into thermoses, not to keep
it warm but simply to stop it from freezing.

After breakfast consisting largely of roughage and olive oil,
the next movement of the day was normally the 'movement of

the day', if you know what I mean. People always want to know how you do this in Antarctica and the answer I always give is, 'As quickly as possible' (and usually in the lee of the tent). It was quick and efficient and within two minutes you could have clubbed someone to death with it. As far as peeing went, this would also be done without hanging around as you stood with your back to the wind, sheltering your groin as best you could. I soon put my initial fears to rest that the old fella might fall off following exposure of more than a few seconds, and became quite imaginative with this activity. My pièce de résistance was a smiley face, requiring great bladder control.

The body though was by now beginning to deteriorate at an accelerated rate, and on day 40 as I sat on my sled eating a frozen biscuit I felt a distinct crunch and knew that it wasn't just the biscuit. Sure enough, I had managed to break a tooth, and spat several shards of it out into my gloved hand along with spittle and oatmeal crumbs.

The following day, to add insult to injury, I became aware of something loose in my mouth. It was a large molar, complete with metal filling rolling around like a gobstopper. The filling had dropped out as the metal had contracted in the extreme cold and become loose. It seemed like I had reached something of a threshold where teeth now decided they were going to start failing me. By the end of day 41, both were aching like hell and adding to my misery. One I would simply fill, but the broken tooth had shards still in the gum and these needed to be removed.

That night I rummaged through the medical kit and found our local anaesthetic and syringes, and wiped the leatherman pliers down with an antiseptic wipe (we'd discarded our metal dental instruments in Punta as part of our weight-saving purge). It was strange, but in amongst all the hardship and danger of Antarctica the thought of injecting myself scared the shit out of me. Going to the dentist is bad enough, but having to self-administer the pain was even worse.

I carefully melted the frozen vial of anaesthetic in between my legs and positioned our small mirror so I could see what I was doing. After an hour the anaesthetic was liquid and ready to administer. I filled the syringe, squirted some out to get rid of the bubbles and raised it to my mouth. I pierced the gum somewhere near the tooth, forced the needle in a good way and squeezed in its contents, falling back on my sleeping mat exhausted with the effort and pain. I let the anaesthetic take effect then pulled out the broken sections of the tooth with the pliers, mixed some dental putty we'd been given and filled the hole in the tooth and gum with a mixture of putty, blood and grit from the old tooth. Injecting the gum had been grim, but the tooth was now at least numb and filled. I decided to forgo the injection for the tooth with the missing filling and went straight to stages 2 and 3. I wasn't about to take up dentistry when I got home, that's for sure.

The broken tooth continued to ache on and off for the remainder of the trip as we were getting increasingly debilitated and the gums were now becoming prone to infections and swelling. To put a positive spin on it, at least it took my mind off my frostbitten fingers and thumb, which I now had to ritually immerse in hot water every evening to try to keep them alive.

Days went by in the sastrugi with constant theorising as to whether the waves of ice were getting larger or smaller in size as we reached the 200 kilometres to the South Pole mark. We'd done a slight dogleg around a suspected area of crevassing from my assessment of the maps of the ice cap and now I entered in the coordinates of the Pole for the first time. (That is to say, I entered 89°59'59"S, as the unit did not recognise 90° south.)

Strangely the GPS seemed to be telling us to head off on a bearing away to the right of the route we had been following for much of the last two weeks. Sure enough, our changed bearing meant that instead of following our shadows south at noon, our shadows sat out firmly to our side. Despite the fact that the sun could not possibly be wrong, I placed my confidence in the GPS and continued to stride out, buoyed by the thought that we were now honing in on the Pole itself. The sastrugi was particularly bad though and I found it hard to keep a straight course in amongst the turmoil.

We fell into the tent exhausted, relishing the opportunity to lie still inside the sleeping bags, warm without the need to move. It had been a very tough day, but I was sure we'd done a good distance. Once warmed up, I switched on the unit and sure enough we had covered 32 km, our best yet.

The happiness was short-lived. I checked to see what bearing we should follow the next day and the unit told me we should remain on our changed bearing, but that we still had over 190 km to go. That meant we'd only managed 13 km towards the Pole out of the 32 km covered. The routine of checking our position each night was a greatly anticipated event, and we were absolutely gutted by the realisation that we had gone so far awry. Not only had we wasted a lot of effort, but the self-imposed pressure of the record time to the Pole now loomed again. The unit couldn't be wrong, so what else could it be? As you get nearer to a destination, bearings vary by more if you become inaccurate with your navigation. Perhaps our dogleg was more pronounced than I had thought, and this bearing was correct. Today had been a bastard of a day and I convinced myself that our drift off course was due to failure to maintain a straight line in the sastrugi. That had never happened before though, and it troubled me. I slept poorly that night, keen to make up for the day's poor travel, but forced through necessity to rest.

We worked hard to keep ourselves focused the next day and I decided I would check our bearing after a few hours of travel – hopefully to put our minds at ease. This was an awkward exercise as to try to read the GPS outside the tent was difficult. The cold rendered the liquid crystal display almost unreadable and the batteries struggled to perform. Today I kept the GPS in my jacket so that I could keep it warm with my body heat, and the batteries in a pouch around my neck.

After three hours I removed my outer mitts and thick gloves and felt the cold on my damaged right hand as I keyed commands into the GPS. The bearing was the same as it had been at the beginning of the day and we had covered 12 kilometres, but only 5 of those were towards the Pole. Now I was really concerned. I stood staring at the horizon and was painfully aware of how vast this place was. Without the GPS we were lost, and lost is one thing you don't want to be in a place like this. It was a horrible feeling. It felt like another of those defining moments where your next move is one that is critical for your survival.

Peter pulled up alongside me. 'What's it say?'

'It's coming up with crap again. This fucking thing is telling us a bearing, but travel on that bearing is sending us sideways.' All around was the vast emptiness of the polar plateau and I knew that I had again become complacent. I had started to think that the Pole was more or less a foregone conclusion and that nothing would stop us reaching it – a big mistake to make.

The cold was creeping up on us again and a decision needed to be made. We decided to use the sun to navigate south. I knew that at 12 noon GMT the sun would be pointing directly south, as would our shadows. It was about 9 am GMT give or take, and I knew the sun moves through the full 360 degrees in 24 hours as the earth spins, and so 15 degrees an hour. Three hours is about 45 degrees, so our shadows should diagonally be out to our right at between one and two o'clock if we were heading south.

It was a worrying time, and I didn't know what we were ultimately going to do about our malfunctioning GPS. Now, though, it felt good to be heading in the right direction and it was exhilarating to think we were aiming for a dot at the bottom of the earth using our bodies as sundials to do it. My shadow gradually moved round beside me like an old friend until at 12 noon GMT it pointed south and I followed it for the rest of the day, allowing it to gradually drift round so that by 3 pm it sat out at between ten and eleven o'clock on our left-hand side. By that night we had travelled 24 km south and about 7 km west, most of the latter being due to our three hours on the wrong bearing at the beginning of the day. It had worked.

In the relative comfort of the tent I worked with the GPS and arrived at an apparent solution that involved giving the unit increasingly southerly grid points each day rather than using the coordinates of the Pole itself. This seemed to give us a similar bearing to the ones we'd been following before the problems. The following day we set off in nervous anticipation on a bearing taking us to a point 30 km south of our night's camp. Reassuringly at 12 noon the sun moved round to a position squarely at our backs.

I noticed that the wind too had returned to its normal orientation, blowing across us diagonally from left to right, and realised that, like the sun, it provided a good natural indicator of direction. It had blown from the same direction for weeks now and had undoubtedly contributed to the frostbite on my right hand. Unlike my left hand that was protected by the back of the mitt covering it, the clenched fist of my fingers on my right hand was exposed to the wind, the thumb in particular. The time spent repairing the harness had done it once and for all, but the wind had certainly weakened the right hand.

It was a huge relief to no longer be lost, but we still had our fair share of problems. The tips of the fingers on my right hand had now turned black and my thumb was a gunmetal grey. Two days of misdirection had moved us from 52° east to 57° west – well off course. The route to the Pole from hereon was now completely unknown, rendering obsolete all of the months spent route-planning to avoid possible crevasse fields. At least we were heading south again – we just hoped that the buildings of the Pole base would be visible the day we got there.

Problems became such an everyday part of our lives as we trekked along that we adopted a fairly philosophical attitude to them. This was necessary to retain sanity and to safeguard yourself against thinking that you were in some way being victimised by Antarctica. We overcame all that was thrown at us and hoped for good luck. Problems became opportunities to learn something and my frostbite became an opportunity to test my resolve more fully. Many of the accounts of the early explorers spoke of their suffering frostbite and so the fact that I had it and had to manage it meant that I was seeing and experiencing the place the way they would have seen it.

By day 44 we were only 100 or so kilometres from the Pole. The GPS for some reason didn't like the coordinates of the Pole itself and we were trying hard not to take this as an omen that we might never get there. Instead we continued to give the GPS increasingly southerly points to aim for along the 57 degree west line of longitude, based on the fact that all lines of longitude converge to one point at the Pole. To follow this one would inevitably take us there. It was a bit unnerving at first to have to go through this subterfuge to get us there after all the planning we'd done, but the logic was sound – it simply had to work.

Towards the end of day 44 we came upon a series of strange linear depressions running across our route and stretching into the distance in either direction. Each one was about 10 metres across, a metre deep and steep-sided like a canal and there appeared to be a succession of them further up the slope we were ascending. They were unlike anything we'd seen so far, and Peter unbuckled his harness, roped up and stepped down into the first of them gingerly. He crossed without a problem and I followed with the sleds, both of us struggling to pull them out on the far side.

Sure enough, a second, third and a fourth 'canal' appeared

ahead of us a few hundred metres apart. These we crossed without event and we were tempted to go without the rope until Peter, making his crossing of the fourth one, shouted, 'Take in,' referring to the fact that I should take in the slack in the rope, in preparation for his possibly falling. He crossed to the other side and I followed his path. 'See what I mean?' said Peter. And I did. There beneath a thin crust of snow was a vast icy void exposed by a solid thrust of Peter's ski stock. The features must have been large crevasses, although I had never heard of them having such wide mouths.

Our ski poles broke through the thin crust and plunged right down to the handle on a couple of occasions reminding us of the voids that lurked beneath the fragile surface of the snow. The field lasted for about 5 kilometres and it was with utter relief that we said goodbye to the last of it a few hours later. I marvelled at the fact that the Pole kept throwing up obstacles to stop us getting to it, making me even more determined to get through.

By now we were getting close to the mystical end of the earth and the excitement was palpable. In accordance with this, I made sure that I had Sir Douglas Mawson's balaclava to hand. It had been given to us by his family to take there, and while we deteriorated steadily and our equipment was being well and truly put through its paces, the famous garment sat safely tucked away in its plastic bag in my sled, awaiting its appointment with destiny. It was a family heirloom and immortalised in his image on an Australian postage stamp and banknote, and we weren't about to let anything happen to it.

At the end of a hard day's travel we knew we must be within 60 kilometres of the Pole. We set up camp and got out the GPS to check. The unit went about its normal process of 'initialising' or finding itself via triangulating off three satellites. It continued to gather satellite data but would not give us a fix. Instead it kept 'looking' for satellites, unable to find itself. The process normally took under two minutes but half an hour later it was still going. I switched the unit off in disgust. For some reason the proximity to the convergent lines of longitude at the Pole meant that the unit was confused and would not give us a bearing. Since our other trouble with the unit a few days earlier we had been on the same bearing for several days and decided to follow that the next day as carefully as possible – something made easier by the fact that the sastrugi had by now become quite a bit smaller.

We crossed a vast icy plain that day, and although I couldn't put my finger on the reason, we seemed to have a bigger horizon than normal. The vastness of the place with no points of reference always played tricks on the mind, but I imagined we were finally atop the dome that marks the position of the South Pole and this extra height gave a further impression of vastness in this already immense place.

That night we experienced a repeat performance from the GPS – no bearing but we guessed we had something like 30 kilometres to go to the Pole. We had been covering over 30 km a day for the past few weeks and knew we should be around the position of the Pole by the last hour of the next day. This was important to know as we had no bearing and so instead must keep a vigilant eye out for the small collection of buildings that make up the Amundsen-Scott base.

I didn't sleep much that night, anxious to wake and walk to the Pole and achieve a personal dream. Had we not still had a further 1400 kilometres to go to reach the far side we would have walked the remaining 30 km then and there, as night was the same as day as far as light went.

We woke at 3 am, a full hour earlier than normal, and looked outside. The weather was mercifully clear. Had it not been we would have had to stop early and wait until we had good visibility to ensure we didn't walk straight past, the base being only a small collection of buildings dwarfed by its surroundings. The sastrugi by now had reduced to small waves – like the chop you might get on a lake on a windy day. In order to beat the time set by a French military team by a whole two days we needed to get to the Pole sometime today. We still steadfastly followed our routine doing everything by our watches – not a second more or less time for each of our leads – our way of imposing our own framework on the otherwise dimensionless environment through which we travelled.

We knew that nine hours today should take us beyond the Pole if we could see it. We had agreed to make camp beyond it that night to maintain our focus and keep our routine. Our goal after the Pole would be Titan Dome – a high dome of ice 350 km or so beyond it. From there we would aim for the top of the Shackleton Glacier, another 350 km distant and then down it to the Ross Ice Shelf for the long 800 km trek to the coast.

We set off and I switched on our emergency beacon, setting it on an 'All OK' message so that it would record added proof of our having reached the Pole today, assuming we found it. I was the lead and began scanning the horizon for the buildings that make up the Amundsen-Scottt scientific base at the Pole. After three hours there was nothing. By the end of Peter's three-hour shift as lead, still Antarctica gave up nothing. I was beginning to get concerned. We must have done over 20 km and must surely now be less than 10 km away. Suddenly I wondered whether the two days we had in hand to beat the record would be enough. If we didn't find it today and then the weather packed in we could still be thwarted.

Suddenly, just away to the side of where my compass said the Pole should be, I spotted what I thought were some rocks on the horizon. Unbelievably, the penny didn't drop immediately. The cogs turned and I remembered that the ice of the polar cap is some 3 km deep here; there are no mountains that poke through it in this part of Antarctica. They had to be the buildings of the base!

I screamed wildly to Peter who was 50 metres or so behind me and then quickly adjusted my bearing to the base just in case it should disappear in a bank of mist. Peter raised his hands in triumph and we spent the next hour in conversation about life. I wondered how this would change it for us. Now that we had something tangible to aim for, I noticed how the base loomed in and out of view with the unevenness of the terrain. Finally after twenty minutes of being obscured, it appeared like Brigadoon right before our eyes as we emerged from a dip.

Now we could make out individual buildings and the gleaming silver geodesic dome that holds the main administrative buildings. I couldn't believe we were here after all of our hardship and I was utterly elated. Who would be there and what would they think? I was really excited at the prospect of seeing other people after 47 days on our own.

As we drew nearer, I saw movement. A group of people walking around outside. It was fascinating to watch them – the movement of other living things in this dead, cold place. Within 400 metres or so, I saw frenetic activity and arms pointing in our direction – we had been spotted. Soon the small group had become a dozen or so people and they were striding out forcefully towards us. My heart was racing as we closed to meet them, like people from different worlds meeting for the first time. Finally we stopped at arm's length from one another. Two groups of featureless humanoids looking at one another from behind face masks, reflective goggles and survival gear.

We lifted up our goggles and saw eye to eye, and I removed my four glove layers to shake hands with the guy at the head of the group. 'Welcome to South Pole,' he said in a broad American accent and smiling in disbelief at our appearance. To shake hands skin on skin was amazing and he looked down at my blackened fingers with a wince. For me, though, the relief was unbelievable. It was 15 December and we were here at the South Pole after 47 world-record-breaking days and would no longer have the self-imposed pressure of trying to keep up the pace to beat the record.

'They' were a group of American scientists and technicians. 'We heard someone was coming but didn't know when you were going to arrive,' a voice said. I smiled. If only they knew what we'd been through to get here. I tried to gauge from their reaction how we were looking. They were clad in warm down suits and heavy boots against the cold. We weren't. The cold was beginning to gnaw and we continued answering their questions as we went, skiing up to the Pole itself. Surprisingly the Pole was actually marked by a pole – a red and white one like a barber's pole with a smooth mirror-ball on the top of it.

Many years later on visiting the Antarctic Museum in Christchurch, I spotted a similar ball in the museum display. The information beneath it said that the 'sister' ball was situated at the South Pole and was used by scientists to photograph the aurora australis (southern lights) before the invention of the fish-eye lens. At the Pole, I had thought it was just a marker.

The base operates on New Zealand time as they are resupplied by aircraft from Christchurch. We were still on Chilean time, simply because there had been no reason to change our watches, and so we actually arrived in the middle of the night their time. Most of the base still slept, and by the time they woke, we would be gone. Time, of course, was in reality the same for all of us as we stood under the bright light of the Antarctic night at the point where all time zones converge. It was a surreal sensation.

Just as our arrival had surprised them, they were even more shocked when we took some photos at the Pole, rejoiced for a minute or two, and then adjusted our compass to its new bearing to take us on our onward journey. 'Aren't you stopping?' they said incredulously.

'No, sorry got to keep going to the coast,' I replied.

'The coast?!'

'Yes, the coast. Look, it was great to meet you, but we'd better keep moving.'

'Can't we do anything for you?' one of the scientists gasped as he walked alongside us as we pushed on through the small collection of surface buildings that form part of the US Amundsen-Scott base, heading for the wilderness of the plateau.

'Well, yes there is actually.' I stopped and fumbled around in my pocket and produced a couple of camera films. 'Could you post these to Australia?' He was sure the sheer eccentricity of my request was the dry humour for which Australians are renowned, but seeing I was serious agreed that of course he would.

With that we turned and started walking out in the direction of Titan Dome on a makeshift bearing. I must admit it was fun to have shaken their little world with our arrival. It was a real pity not to be able to cherish the moment at the Pole, having striven for it for so long, but we needed to keep focused and keep moving and couldn't accept assistance from anyone. When I stopped to adjust my harness some time later I looked back over my shoulder. A few of the figures were still standing there, probably wondering what the hell had just happened to them.

10

From the end
of the Earth

That night we made camp a few kilometres away from the
buildings of the Pole so that we would keep to our routine.
Our GPS was not working properly, as anticipated, and we
needed to again become focused on our task – difficult after seeing the warmth and safety of solid buildings and the company of
other people. Now our little tent seemed hopelessly inadequate
and we felt lonely even a few kilometres away from the Pole. We
had to force ourselves not to peep out of the tent back at the
buildings wondering what they would be doing in there tonight.

In order for the GPS to work again we guessed we would
need to get a good distance away from the convergent points of
longitude that mark the Pole and that meant heading off into
the vastness of Antarctica blind. Based on when the unit had
stopped working on the way in, we reckoned on it becoming
functional about 50 km past the Pole. It was a nerve-racking
prospect to be heading off into the enormity of Antarctica
without knowing where we were exactly and felt especially fool-
hardy given the safety we'd left behind.

I thought of Scott and Amundsen. When they and their parties
reached the Pole in 1913 and 1914 there was nothing here. They
were at the ends of the Earth and the furthest point from rescue.

Now, ironically, it was a small oasis of safety in this vast unforgiving place and to venture from it presented the biggest risk.

Going was good on the far side of the Pole – smaller sastrugi and reasonable snow, and we forged ahead, nervous but excited about the prospect of what lay ahead. It was nice to be free of the self-imposed pressure of trying to break the record time to the Pole, especially having achieved it. The next target was the Titan Dome – one of the highest parts of Antarctica with an altitude of almost 4000 metres, far away en route to the Shackleton Glacier. The Pole was not only an incredible prize to aim for but provided reassurance. I looked round at the end of one of my leads and it had disappeared over the horizon. I felt cheated that I had been pretty much forced to walk on past a place that has seen some of the bravest feats of human endeavour. I wanted to capture the moment but it seemed to be impossible to really grasp. Even years later the magnitude of having reached the Pole is still sinking in.

That night my thumb began to throb properly for the first time since I had damaged it. It was a good sign and, sure enough, on removing my inner glove I could see the thumb had ballooned to twice its size into what can best be described as a blister. I knew this was good news and that it was the body's way of healing itself. The thumb looked like it would survive although I had no real sensation in it. We were still here.

By the end of our first full day out from the Pole the GPS still hadn't begun to function properly, and we headed off again on the makeshift bearing I had worked out from the map. That night we phoned in to report our approximate position somewhere beyond the Pole and Neil was again excited. 'I've been told that no-one has ever gone beyond the Pole on foot and completely unsupported.' The only other people to go beyond the Pole were Ranulph Fiennes and Mike Stroud and even they used up-ski parachutes – the forebear of the modern kite sail – for part of their incredible journey.

We lay in the tent chatting for over an hour about our latest news. We had set out to reach the far side of Antarctica, and had broken the record for the fastest time to the Pole. Now we didn't even know where we were exactly. It was all too much to take in. I had now been to the Pole but had to put my elation aside, to be drawn on when things got really tough again – which I knew they would.

By the end of a second day's travel the GPS had thankfully started to function normally again and to our pleasant surprise we were only a degree off course for the Shackleton! I felt on top of the world, as if I had finally got the measure of the place. The reality was we were still so far away from it that we could have afforded to have followed the wrong line for a day or two and still remain more or less on course.

Now as we walked along, the horizon again seemed to be larger than normal, which meant we must be atop high ground. My mind wandered and again I became aware of what an amazing place this was – a huge high-altitude frozen sheet of ice. Antarctica defies description and the statistics associated with it are only paralleled by the facts and figures you hear about deep space, such is the scale of the place.

The following day, despite the achievement of the Pole in record time and being on our way again with minimum disruption, my mood had gone to the other extreme. I had been in a good mood bubble that had remained with me since our reaching the Pole, now it was deflating fast, perhaps with the enormity of what still lay ahead.

That night I decided to call my parents to bring my mood around a bit. Mum casually commented that phone reception sounded clear, and passed me over to my brother Dan who asked me what it was like. Bloody cold I replied. 'Yes, it's cold here too,' commented Dan casually, referring to the fact that it was December in the Cotswolds. I laughed to myself at the comparison.

I finished the call wondering whether anyone realised what we were really going through. I suppose they didn't, and I guess that's the point. The phone reception was good because its satellites are polar-orbiting, not because the weather was good. I wondered whether it would be worthwhile getting Peter to make crackling and whooshing noises when I used the phone from now on so people didn't get the wrong idea about how tough we were doing this thing.

We were 150 km past the Pole and progressing well, until Peter woke and inexplicably proceeded to be sick just outside the front door of the tent. This really concerned me as I knew that there were no bacteria up here and we were both eating the same thing. Anything that happened to him affected me and vice versa and we had become very protective of one another. To his credit and testament to his mental resilience, after a terrible night he emerged from the tent with frozen vomit still attached to his beard and we managed a solid day with me leading.

It just served to demonstrate how hard we were pushing ourselves. The sleds seemed to be feeling heavier rather than lighter with our consumption 1.5 kg per day of food and fuel. Our gruelling regime of no rest days, cold temperatures and large workloads was leaving us in constant energy deficit, despite consuming our 7000 calories each day. As every scrap of fat had long since been shed from our bodies it was muscle – and, as a consequence, strength – that we were losing.

The altitude left us short of breath when working hard and the hacking coughs we'd developed from sucking in deep lungfuls of cold, dry air wouldn't abate, making sleep fitful. Importantly, though, we still felt positive about things – if we could just get over the top of the Titan Dome it was literally all downhill to the top of the Shackleton 200 kilometres further on and then down to the thicker air of the Ross Ice Shelf. I didn't want to think about the massive final push of 800 kilometres across the Ross Ice Shelf to McMurdo Base. It was a hell of a journey in its own right. We both knew too that it was the freezing temperatures and terrible blizzards of the Ross that had claimed the lives of Scott and his men all those years ago and we had no illusions about what it would be like.

An added concern was that we had organised to hitch a ride home on a Quark Expeditions ice-breaker that would be at McMurdo in January and we had to be there in time to meet it, or think of another option. I was already dreaming of sleeping in a cabin on board the ship, waking only for meals and a few drinks in the bar in the evening.

The next day was one of the worst of my life. We were ascending towards Titan Dome and the second change of underpants beckoned, so we must have been on the ice almost two months. That evening it was Peter's turn to get food from his sled and some more fuel from his bulk containers to decant into the stove. 'Oh, Christ!' I heard him swear in disbelief as he threw an empty bulk fuel container on the ground in disgust. 'What's going on?' I asked, frustrated that it was taking so long to unpack the stuff from the base of his sled.

'Look at this,' said Peter, showing me an empty canister with a 5-cm gash along its base.

It should have been full with 5 litres of white spirit – enough to sustain us for fifteen days or so of use. Worse still, its contents had leaked into the twenty or so food bags in the bottom of Peter's sled. Given that most of our food bags had torn and the food within them had been pulverised after 500 km of being thrown around in the sastrugi, the fuel was through everything.

Hastily we put up the tent and assessed the damage, going through Peter's sled until my hands were too numb to continue rummaging. It was a terrible situation, but one that was beyond debate. Best case was that we'd lost at least two weeks' worth of fuel, and much of the food in Peter's sled had been contaminated. You didn't want to be consuming powdered milk, muesli and rice laced with white spirit, that's for sure. Things were borderline enough on the health side, without poisoning our-selves to boot. I still had 21 days' food in my sled, but we still had over 1100 km to go. We might have been able to salvage a couple of days' worth of Peter's, but at the risk of poisoning ourselves.

If we were lucky, had no rest days, no bad weather days, no injuries, no technical problems and continued the merciless 30 km a day we had been managing up till now, we might get to McMurdo in 37 days. At best, though, we had fuel for only 20 and food for perhaps a couple more.

The atmosphere was dark. We were always hungry now and had been for weeks, despite consuming all of our daily rations. We were getting very gaunt and our strength was deteriorating with each day. Even the pleasure I'd derived from munching through my extra allocation of chocolate in front of Peter each night had long gone. (I carried more due to my size.) I had consumed it without fail by late morning.

There were a number of choices. We could call for an air drop of food and fuel or we could go on. We called ANI to discuss the logistics of an air drop, knowing that it would have ruined the unsupported nature of the trip and correspondingly destroyed our focus. What kept me going most days was the knowledge that we were doing this without any support. I didn't want to do this trip like so many others who get sup-ported then claim to have done it on their own. It would just tarnish our world record to the Pole and that was very impor-tant to preserve. ANI told us that an air drop would cost at least $200 000 Australian. It just wasn't an option.

Going on inevitably would have meant a hazardous and costly air rescue on the far side of the continent at the very least. It would have allowed us to post a distance record of sorts, but then again according to Neil we had already achieved that by taking our first steps past the Pole. Either way, that wasn't important to me.

At worst, we would have travelled as far as our depleted food and fuel allowed us before trying to arrange for a rescue, perhaps dying alone and starving as Scott and his men had. Ironically, we would have run out of food or strength or both somewhere in the middle of the Ross Ice Shelf, just as they had. The difference was that Scott and his two remaining men had died heroically, unable to summon the energy to lift themselves to reach their final food depot, 'One Ton Depot', just 17 km away. We would have had 400 km to go. Although the mind may have the will, however you look at it, as soon as food runs out and your body fails you, Antarctica will dispatch you with ease. It can go on forever; you can't.

It occurred to me how incongruous it was that Scott was known as 'Scott of the Antarctic', as if he had some particular affinity with the place or some canny ability to eke out an existence from it. The harsh reality was that neither he nor anyone else could really be 'of' this place. Antarctica is somewhere where people come to find out something about themselves by pitting their mind and body against it – but it remains impervious. Even as the bodies of Scott and his men remain entombed in the ice of the Ross Shelf, the final word will be with Antarctica. Their bodies will one day be cast into the Ross Sea, calved off in a berg as the ice of the shelf moves north at the rate of about a kilometre each year.

Polar expeditions are all about managing risk but, had we continued, our running out of food and fuel was a foregone conclusion. It was a cruel blow after all the hardships we'd suffered and obstacles we'd overcome: massive loss of body weight, frostbite, Peter's fall in the mountains, a number of scares with crevasses, problems with our GPS unit, the need for serious repairs to most of our electronic equipment due to the extreme cold, and damage caused to our harnesses and skis in the sastrugi.

This was one problem we just couldn't solve. In the spirit of the unsupported way the expedition had been mounted, however, we felt we should be responsible for our own 'rescue' back to a safe pick-up point. A week later we arrived back at the South Pole, except this time from the opposite direction and under very different circumstances.

There's no doubt I was disappointed, but on the journey back I dreamt of the recognition we would get for having achieved the record fastest unsupported time to the Pole and the record unsupported distance for an Antarctic journey. It would change life forever, surely. Not only that but we'd reached the Pole in record time with the weight of food and fuel for twice that distance. Not a bad effort and more than I ever dreamt would be possible. I knew how desperately hard I'd worked and was confident no-one would manage it faster for a long time to come. I didn't want anything to detract from that. Now that the pressure was off, the magnitude of what we'd achieved began to really sink in.

Once again the buildings of the Amundsen-Scott South Pole base loomed into view. The governments of various nations had all staked their claims to bits of Antarctica years before, the triangular pieces of the pie radiating out from the Pole. The US missed out, so constructed their Amundsen-Scott base right in the middle at the South Pole itself in 1957, based on the fact that it was something of a neutral spot. It was a somewhat dubious claim but I didn't care – it was great to get back to it. As I approached I found myself alternating between thinking about meeting friends and family again, how our success would be received and bracing myself for the invasion of our private world by other people after months alone on the ice.

We crossed over some vehicle tracks, which we had also noticed when leaving the Pole, and I wondered what they were for. A scientist later told me that they were the tracks made by a vehicle that periodically goes out to take background readings of atmospheric air quality, the South Pole being one of a few locations worldwide where these baseline measurements are taken. They were the only signs of humanity I ever saw in Antarctica apart from the Amundsen-Scott base and the small collection of tents at Patriot.

We could almost feel people watching us as we approached the base for the second time. Even under such disappointing circumstances, I had to laugh at what they might be saying to one another as they observed our steady progress towards them. 'Christ it's those goddamn Australians again, they must have forgotten something. Now what do they want?' We were again met by a welcoming committee, although with all of their cold weather clothing on I couldn't recognise any faces.

'We didn't think we'd see you again!' said a familiar voice. It was the scientist with my camera films.

'I just came back for the camera film – couldn't trust you to send it!'

He burst out laughing. 'You are a pair of mad bastards.' I guess we were.

I dragged my sled up to the mirror-ball that officially marks the South Pole itself and undid my harness for the last time, dropped it on the ground and stood waiting for reality to catch up with me. People were now crowding around us and asking questions, and despite the fact they are not meant to offer help to private expeditions it wasn't long before they invited us inside.

The central part of the base is housed under a geodesic metal dome that, although not warmed, protects the buildings beneath it from the worst of the weather. The dome is gradually sinking into the ice and so these days is half-buried. To get into the base we therefore had to descend into it via a tunnel, emerging into a James Bond set of heated shipping container-style buildings under the dome. We were invited in for breakfast (by our watches it was the middle of the night but I was prepared to compromise). I sat down between a coffee-making machine and a Christmas tree emblazoned with lights and it was all too much to take in. After almost 70 days in the tent in bitterly cold temperatures I could now sit still and absorb the heat without having to move to generate it for myself. I can't honestly remember what I did during that hour, but can remember answering lots of questions and drinking coffee. I was brought to my senses by a wet sensation on my legs. I looked down and realised I was sitting in a large pool of something. For a moment I thought the worst. Then I realised that all of the accumulated ice from 70 days of sweat and condensation in my clothing had melted. My clothes assumed a fabric quality that I had not felt for months. I was content.

'Do you want any food?' someone shouted over. 'Couldn't possibly,' I replied with sarcasm lost on our new hosts. What followed was a spectacular display of eating that even the base personnel, renowned for their large appetites, probably found revolting. We were watched like animals at the zoo as we consumed plate after plate of scrambled eggs, waffles, toast and sausages. Someone claimed that Peter had eaten 21 sausages and probably had photographic evidence. Afterwards I felt quite sick and ironically had to go outside for some fresh air. Now at the safety of the base, the polar plateau looked benign and I struggled hard to remember what all the fuss had been about. I knew the memories would come back to me, but now it was too soon.

Probably as a means of stopping us from eating any more we were offered a shower, which was absolute bliss. In the medical quarters they also had a full-length mirror and for the first time I saw my scrawny, dishevelled, smelly body with skin hanging off me and grime ground into every pore. The scales confirmed I had lost almost 20 kilos despite our 7000-calorie-a-day diet, confirming my fears. It made me hungry and I went back for more.

Over the next few days we were given a tour of the base and met some great people there. The base is home to a series of X Files-style projects, including the AMANDA project that has sensors buried deep in the ice for measuring subatomic particles with no mass (called muons and neutrinos) from deep space. I assumed that they measured these particles from the Southern Hemisphere but was told that to the contrary, they were using the Earth as a filter to shield the sensors from noise that other particles generate and in fact were measuring their muons and neutrinos from the Northern Hemisphere. Of course they were. How silly of me.

The National Science Foundation (NSF), which runs the base, is not meant to offer any assistance whatsoever to private expeditions but unofficially we were well looked after. However, the line was drawn at actually staying in the base and we were quartered in a little hut some distance from it, in probably the most spectacular location for a storeroom you could want and infinitely better than the tent. Soon we got into an interesting routine at the base, meeting with people at meal times. We were some eighteen hours apart in terms of our body clocks and watches, but united under a common time zone by the convergence of the lines of longitude at the Pole and an overwhelming desire to eat.

Christmas and the new millennium were now fast approaching, however, and we needed to get ourselves away from the base. Using our satellite phone we called up ANI in Punta and got through to Kevin and Dave. They were ready to come when we wanted but ANI first needed to be sure that they would get paid before they would let them come to get us. We were now stuck at the South Pole and conscious of not overstaying our welcome but didn't begrudge Kevin and Dave, as they were just obeying orders.

Finally a deal was struck and Kevin and Dave flew down to the Pole and we were reunited after almost 80 days, after having spent a great Christmas down with the NSF people.

I lay dozing in the early hours of Christmas Eve our time (sometime in the afternoon on Christmas Day for our American hosts) when I heard the door to the hut open, an object get placed inside and the door quietly close. I got up and opened the package. It was a six-pack of beer! 'Peter, beers!' He was half-asleep. 'No bears at the South Pole, mate,' Peter murmured, turned over and kept sleeping. There was a note from Father Christmas, too, wishing us a Merry Christmas. It occurred to me that he had come a bloody long way to deliver these as we were literally as far away from the North Pole as you could get.

The next day we were about to say goodbye to our NSF friends and thank them for their hospitality, when a plane landed. On board were some BBC journalists who had planned to take some footage at the Pole for the new millennium. They were excited when they heard we were still there and before I knew it I was in front of the cameras as a joint UK passport-holder, speaking to the folks back in the UK. An old friend of mine, Sara, said she was at a party in Belfast and the TV was on in the background. She almost fell off her chair when she saw my frostbitten, bearded mug appear on the screen broadcasting from the Pole, wishing everyone a happy new millennium and talking about the records we'd achieved.

Minutes later we taxied down the runway and were airborne and on our way back to Patriot Hills in the Otter, saying little as we contemplated the magnitude of what we had just achieved.

The irony of the situation was not lost on us. We had sought to undertake the journey that Ernest Shackleton had dreamt of so many years before, and had been forced to make a decision to turn back, much as he had done on his unsuccessful attempt to reach the South Pole in 1910. 'I'd rather be a live donkey than a dead lion,' he'd said of his decision to turn around only 100 miles from the Pole at the time. In our case, however, we were ecstatic with our achievements, not least of all the world records for unsupported Antarctic manhauling (1600 km), and the fastest time for an unsupported journey to the South Pole of 47 days (completed with the extra weight of food and fuel for a journey of twice that length). We were not only proud of what we had achieved but felt that our difficult decision to stop – in our case based purely on a mechanical problem – somehow brought us closer to knowing him.

Four hours later the mountains of Patriot Hills loomed into view, and a few minutes later we bounced along the runway and came to a halt. We erected the tent and considered our next move. It was 31 December 1999. Financial and logistical problems now existed with our pull-out via the Hercules back to Punta. There was talk of us having to wait for over a week so that our journey could be combined with a flight to pick up some climbers attempting to climb Antarctica's highest peak, Mount Vinson, some 200 kilometres away. We weren't happy and it looked like we were going to be stuck here for some time. Kevin and Dave flew off to Mount Vinson to wait for the climbers and we resigned ourselves to our fate, put up the tent, climbed into the sleeping bags once again and tried to keep warm.

A few hours later I heard the sound of an engine over the sound of the wind. It must be the Hercules! I hurriedly put on my clothes and boots, clambered out of the tent and looked skyward. In the distance I saw an aircraft approaching, and then to my surprise saw someone jump out. Christ, that'd be right, there must be something wrong with the Herc and now the bloody pilots are bailing out! Then I saw another jumper, and then another, and another, until I counted over twenty people in all. The sky was full of parachutists. Perhaps someone had put on a display for the new millennium for us – nice, but honestly, not necessary.

In fact I wasn't too far off the mark. The plane was not the Herc but an Ilyushin Russian transport jet and the parachutists were Russians jumping out over Antarctica to celebrate the new millennium. Pretty soon they had all landed and began setting up a large communal tent to spend the night in. The Ilyushin landed on the ice runway and taxied over towards us. It was an immense aircraft – far bigger than the Herc and was designed as a parachute transport plane, carrying up to 150 parachutists at a time.

Only one of the Russians, 'Sergei', spoke English, claiming to have been a KGB agent in a former life. The rest of the guys were ex-military and had decided to participate partly for fun, but partly to practise the logistics of organising something like this. Why not? No more insane than our reasons, I thought to myself.

Immediately after the tent was up and the aircraft tied down with guy ropes, the Russians began digging two parallel trenches in the ice about a metre apart. The trenches were to be foot wells, with the raised area left in between forming an ice table to hold a meal of raw meat, bread and bottles of vodka. We were invited to join in and began toasting one another with things getting messy pretty quickly, despite my prepping my liver with six bottles of Christmas beer a few days before. Within an hour we were all best of friends, and had been made honorary citizens of the city of Kiev, although I still couldn't understand a word of what anyone was saying with the exception of Sergei.

Sergei told me that their trip was being supported by an arm of the Russian government called the 'Ministry of Extreme Situations'. I was tempted to say that ours was being supported by the 'Ministry of Silly Walks', which not only sounded relevant, but also marginally less daft than their name. I held back. Sergei said that the pilot of the plane was a hero of the former Soviet Union and had flown with Yuri Gagarin (the first man in space) at flight school and had asked if we wanted a lift anywhere.

We hastily agreed, not really caring where we went as long as it wasn't here and spent a restless night waiting for morning so we could be on our way. About 5 am (on my watch) I heard the jet engines roar into life and I sat bolt upright. They were leaving without us! We threw on our clothes, shoved the tent untidily into one of the sleds and hurried over to the plane to find Sergei. He laughed as we hurried over. The engines needed to be warmed up for half an hour before take-off so we could relax – oh, and by the way, we were going to make a stop in Punta Arenas if that was all right with us! What a present it was – the first day of the new millennium and we were going exactly where we wanted in South America. We lugged the sleds on the plane for the final time, jumped aboard, roared down the runway and were airborne.

The Ilyushin was a massive plane, dwarfing its load of 25 or so passengers. It had 150 seats in two parallel rows of 75 each on either side of the fuselage for parachutists, with a ramp that opened at the rear of the plane for them to jump out in rapid succession. Activity on board made for interesting viewing and we sat there watching everyone as they went about their business. Quite honestly we had little else to do as we had no reading material and had eaten almost all of our food apart from some of our biscuits. Everyone was smoking pungent cheroot-style cigarettes and no-one wore seatbelts. A 2-tonne generator unit rolled about lazily in the back, apparently not tied down to anything. It wasn't a regular flight, but then nor were any of the others we'd taken recently.

One guy in austere military fatigues was sitting in the rear section of the plane near us. I assumed he must be the navigator as he sat in a swivel chair at a large map table, wore headphones and appeared to be in conversation with someone, presumably the pilots, via the microphone on his headset. He was concentrating hard as he fastidiously twiddled the dials on the console next to him, no doubt fine-tuning some aspect of the running of the aircraft. After half an hour of adjustments he got up, put on some insulated gloves and walked over to another console. We watched, fascinated. He pressed a button and a metal tray like a filing cabinet shelf slid out. He leant over and lifted something out and put it on the table. I couldn't believe my eyes. There before us was a big, succulent mother of a roast chicken! We'd been watching his antics for about half an hour and had no idea. I laughed hard, then could have cried when they ate it all in front of us, not even giving us a sideways glance. We were just glorified hitchhikers, after all. The aroma of roast chicken filled the plane and I felt like a dog hanging around at a barbeque, looking for scraps.

As we left Antarctica behind, all of the mental and physical hardships of the trip seemed to fall away. The frostbite would recover in time, the body would mend, the mental toil was fast being forgotten, and the elation of the achievements was beginning to sink in. We touched down in Punta and the door opened. Five minutes later we were standing next to our sleds on the airport apron. We said our goodbyes and offered to pay for our lift. Sergei would accept nothing, we all shook hands and he disappeared. It was like the final scene from *Casablanca*. Very poignant as he turned and walked off without so much as a backward glance, leaving us on the apron sweating in our polar gear.

It wasn't long before a couple of soldiers saw us skulking around on the apron, looking distinctly suspicious in our cold weather gear standing by our brightly coloured sleds. They swaggered over in the normal display of South American officialdom to ask us a few questions and on hearing our unbelievable tale 'invited' us to visit passport control. We walked over to the office and began the lengthy task of trying to explain where we had been for the last three months, having literally dropped out of the system whilst down south. It took a while. I was thin, I'm sure my clothes stank, the Customs guys were unhelpful, but it was only 15 degrees outside and it felt bloody fantastic. There was something else strange going on too – it was getting dark. After almost three months in the 24-hour light of the Antarctic, the sun was finally setting on us, bringing to a close a day that at times had seemed to last an eternity but that had really been an unbelievable journey.

After battling through Customs, we took a minibus into town and back to the Condor, where our friend the hotel manager received us with open arms. Even wearing our rancid expedition clothing – a sign of real friendship. Quite honestly, I don't think he expected to ever see us again. He asked lots of questions that I did my best to answer in Spanish and then, realising we were tired, showed us to our room. We dumped the sleds in the corridor outside, thanked him for his help and shut the door. We were back where it had all begun three months before. I fell onto the bed and all was still and quiet in the room. So much had happened it was still too much to contemplate.

After a few minutes the silence began to get to me. I wanted to find out what had been happening in the world and talk to people. We wandered up the hill, meeting strange looks as we went and trying not to overheat in our gear. We knocked on the door of the ANI HQ and were received like old friends. There on the wall was a large map of Antarctica complete with coloured pins indicating our progress across its vastness. The pins were pretty close together, serving to show just how slow our movement was across somewhere the size of Antarctica, but it was heart-warming to see they had been following us so closely.

That night we feasted on steak and chips and a few drinks back at our favourite café in Punta. Our flight to Buenos Aires and then on to Sydney was the next day, and ever since our return to the Pole when we'd phoned through our situation, we'd known a big press conference was planned for our return.

Flying back into Sydney late in the morning I wondered what lay in store. I'd been given express instructions not to shave off my beard before the round of media was out the way, even though I was desperate to do so. I've never liked beards but it would look good for the *Today* show and the news programs, so

I could put up with the itching in the heat of the Australian summer for another couple of days.

As we came through the green channel into the airport we were greeted by cameras and film crews. It was surreal. I wondered who they'd come to see, until I realised it was us. Within ten minutes we'd warmed to the role of celebrities and were led away to a room at the airport where the official press conference was to take place. Microphones were set up on the table at which we sat with John Leece, and questions came thick and fast from the 40 or so assembled journos. How was it? How cold was it? Would you do it again? Why did you do it? Did you argue? Are you still friends?

We battled on manfully shaking hands and answering questions, being whisked off by camera crews to get footage and recordings for various TV and radio stations. It was exciting and tiring, but finally, three hours later, we were away.

All I wanted to do was eat some junk food, swim in Peter's pool and not have to answer any more questions for a while. My next brush with the media would be later that night when I watched my own face on the six o'clock news. Tomorrow, it would all begin again.

That night at 6 o'clock we turned on the TV and with a bit of channel-surfing managed to catch ourselves on three or four news slots. 'Two men have returned from Antarctica, breaking two world records . . .' It was a hoot. 'Christ, you look like Jesus,' said Peter, unaware of his pun, as my bearded face appeared on the Channel 9 news. I thought I looked more like something out of *Life of Brian* but maybe I did look the part. And then I realised I was being my own worst critic, knocking what I'd done despite the magnitude of it all. It had been a great achievement, no two ways about it, but the realisation of what we'd accomplished would take a while to really sink in.

11

North Pole

We were approaching the end of our journey as we trudged through the glare and shimmering heat haze rising from the ochre sand of the Great Victoria Desert. I squinted into the distance, trying to pick out the Yamarna fence line, which was our goal. Yamarna had been the easternmost limit of pastoral activity back in its heyday. It was shut now but its boundary still officially marked the end of the desert we'd been trekking across for almost a month.

It was bloody hot. My face was crusted with salt from the sweat that had dried on it and it struck me as strange that this whole trip had been conceived as training for an attempt on the North Pole. It had proved to be a tough test, made more so by the fact that I'd seriously underestimated the food requirement and was constantly hungry for the whole of the trip. Once again I felt the familiar loss of strength and weight that signifies the end of a tough journey. (On weighing myself at a nickel mine in Laverton the next day I discovered I'd lost 11 kg!) To be honest, I didn't have the burning desire to attempt this journey as much as I had with other journeys, but had harnessed my naturally competitive nature and over the weeks had warmed to the task.

Strangely, our final day felt peaceful – almost fun, probably because for the first time we knew that our momentum would now carry us over the line. It only became apparent on that last day just what a strain we had been under. Each morning we would wake in the frigid darkness of the desert night, hoping that an ache or pain from the previous day hadn't developed into something capable of stopping us achieving our goal, or that our mental resolve had evaporated as we slept.

We awoke at a leisurely 5 am, a full hour after our normal 4 am, and packed up the remainder of our now meagre possessions. We'd abandoned our carts two days before, marking their position on our GPS, and had decided to make a 100-km dash for the end of the desert with what we could carry on our backs. After half an hour or so we felt the intense cold of the predawn as the sun on the distant horizon pushed down the cold layers of night air upon us, before we felt the warmth from its first rays. I was in one of those frames of mind where I felt I could tackle anything, so when Peter's question broke the silence I was more than happy to talk about it.

'What about trying for the record for the North Pole then?' he asked. We chatted logistics. The trip is shorter than the distance to the South Pole, but it's pretty fickle. For a start, the ice needs to be thick enough to walk on and that changes dramatically from season to season. It also means that you need to be up there when it's colder, when the ocean is frozen. Then, the fact that the ice can end up drifting south at a faster rate than you trek north can make the journey impossible. And last but not least, there are loads of polar bears.

'But it's possible?' asked Peter.

'Getting to the Pole is possible,' I replied. 'I'm not so sure about the record. I think that would be down to luck.'

What a strange conversation it was, walking through the spinifex and scrub of Australia's largest desert – and I loved it. Now that the strain of this journey was almost over, it was great fun to have a no-obligations chat about a trip to the North Pole.

In fact Peter's idea of trekking across the Great Victoria Desert had been touted to the media as being a training exercise for attempting to reach the North Pole. This may sound silly. Taken at face value one is hot, sandy and dry and the other is a frozen ocean where the temperature seldom rises above zero. But the two are actually not as different as you might think. Both are vast, unforgiving places where survival involves pulling a heavy load of food, equipment and provisions.

Peter was a man on a mission to cross all of Australia's deserts unsupported and to my knowledge he is still trying to complete the set. His dream to do all of them meant he needed company to help him get across this one. It was, after all, the biggest desert at twice the distance of the Simpson and his biggest non-polar challenge to date. He needed someone with a good knowledge of navigation and an aptitude for pulling a heavy load of supplies. More than that, he needed someone he could trust. In the winter of 2001 these qualities were in short supply.

Now the solitude of the desert was somewhere to escape to. It may have been uncompromising, but at least it was an honest adversary, unlike the insipid, jealousy-inspired stuff that he'd been on the receiving end of in recent months. Now more than ever he was enjoying the desert, in particular for the solitude and anonymity it afforded.

We rounded a group of dunes much like many others that had blocked our way and there ahead of us spotted the glint of light on the bumper of our rendevous four-wheel drive driven by Neil Cocks and his wife Helen. We had made it – 1100 km in 29 days. A tape had been tied between two trees and we broke through it together as if crossing the finishing line in a race. I propped my rucksack up against a gnarled fencepost and collapsed onto the ground under the shade of a gum to be plied with bread, coffee and campfire pancakes.

∧ ∧ ∧

The idea of the North Pole trip had reared its head in January 2000 on our return from our successful record-breaking journey to the South Pole. At our press conference at Sydney airport someone had asked the obvious question. 'What about the north?' I looked up over the sea of faces and cameras, trying to address my question to the voice that had uttered it, leaning towards the microphone and giving a measured response. 'We were just considering it,' I replied dramatically. It had the desired effect and a murmur went round the 50 or so people gathered. A kind of 'you mad bastard' incredulity that we could be considering another foray into such a life-threatening and unpleasant environment so soon after finishing the last one.

I hadn't been considering it at all. In fact to that point it had never even entered my mind but it had seemed so easy to say yes at the time, and made a great one-liner. I guess returning to adulation and media attention helped. That and the fact that 72 hours before we'd been in −25°C. Now it was a balmy Sydney day of 35 degrees and soon we would be yesterday's news. We rode the media wave for a week or so, relaxed and enjoyed our incredible journey, complete with achievements beyond my wildest dreams, culminating in my reading out a letter of congratulation from Tony Blair to assembled dignitaries in Adelaide at the opening of the permanent exhibit to Sir Douglas Mawson. Again I was asked what next, and again found myself uttering the words 'North Pole'. I was beginning to feel committed to it.

A journey to the North Pole means trekking over 900 kilometres of frozen ocean. The ice may be 4 metres thick at the Pole itself but it's not like that all the way. In fact, far from it.

Down 'south' where we were to start our journey on the north coast of Arctic Siberia, the ice can be as thin as only a few centimetres thick or even worse – open ocean. When embarking on a journey like this you get yourself to the northernmost point of the land by whatever means you can, and then it's a leap of faith when taking your first tentative step onto the ice of the frozen ocean itself. Probably about as near as you're going to get here on earth to the feeling Neil Armstrong got when first stepping down onto the alien world of the surface of the moon. It was a big commitment to make.

∧ ∧ ∧

Sure enough, after articles and appearances on TV and radio the media frenzy stopped dead and we were old news. But the idea of trying for the North Pole remained, surreptitiously slipped into conversation by Peter each time we spoke.

What I didn't realise is that it had genuinely been in his mind ever since the South Pole. He saw it as his swan song before hanging up his boots permanently, a fitting way to bring to a close a fantastic career in the outdoors. He'd been subject to some pretty adverse publicity, claiming that some of his solo achievements back in the 1980s had been exaggerated. Most things are water off a duck's back to Peter, with the exception of comments about his family or his expedition achievements. Of the former, luckily there were none. Of the latter there were many. Perhaps he saw the North Pole as his way of finally vindicating himself.

When embarking on any serious trip you need to have a really firm goal or reason in your mind for doing it. This is so that when things become really tough, you can draw upon it to get yourself through. It may be one reason, or it may be a combination of reasons, but to my mind, regardless of whether it's ego, public recognition, or to make money out of it, your ultimate reasons must be your own personal ones. Of course it's difficult to separate one from the other, as the ego boost you get from public recognition can seem very much like doing it for your own personal reasons. Although they can be similar, there's a subtle difference.

The media and ambiguous descriptions by people of their polar trips would have you believe that many have trekked unsupported to the South or North Pole. In fact this couldn't be further from the truth. Only a very small number of groups have trekked to the Poles unsupported, carrying all their provisions, and receiving no assistance in the form of air drops, or dogs or kites to pull them along. In fact the total number of groups who have trekked to a Pole unsupported is less than the number of people who summit Mount Everest on a busy day.

This is because one of the most difficult things about polar travel, mentally and physically, is the effect that the workload of pulling a heavy sled has on your body weight, strength and your ability to keep warm. Undertaking a supported trip means that these encumbrances are greatly reduced and safety, morale, and physical preservation are vastly improved. And yet there are still many who claim to have made it without any assistance.

And so there are people who have reached the Poles with weekly resupplies of food, pulling a sled of only 40 kg instead of 160 kg. There are those who have used kites to get there, allowing them to travel 150 km a day expending only 2000 calories instead of 7000 dragging a sled 25 km. If they want to claim these journeys as unsupported, that's up to them. It's just that our version is fundamentally different, that's all. The point is, if you do these trips for your own reasons then it doesn't matter what others do.

In the case of Antarctica, I embarked on that journey not because I had a fascination with the South Pole, but because I wanted to see myself there. I wanted to get there under my own steam and that meant no help of any kind. That's what kept me going. Not the fleeting recognition from people who didn't know me and who would undoubtedly forget my name shortly after hearing it.

The North Pole was the logical next step for someone who has been to the South and I guess it was in my mind to attempt it at some stage, but not as soon after the South as Peter was suggesting. Nevertheless, I was soon convinced that the North was there for the taking. I was sure that I would rise to this challenge just like the others. It was going to be incredibly hard, though – of that I had no illusions.

In order to get media interest and corporate funding for expeditions you need to have a hook that will interest them. The trip needs to be the biggest, furthest, fastest. To be the first Australians to get there was one thing, but Peter had it in his mind that we should go for the record fastest time to the Pole. It didn't take much effort to sow the seeds of this idea in the minds of the media and sponsors. In fact, as we had the record down south, it seemed logical that we should go for it. I wasn't as confident.

It goes without saying that the prospect of a trip across such a treacherous landscape didn't thrill my partner, Caroline. She and I met while training at a gym just before the Great Victoria Desert trip and although I'd talked her through things, she was concerned it was the last she'd see of me if I headed north across the sea ice. I promised her I would only be making one attempt and that research and careful planning would mean it was a safe trip. That wasn't the truth.

∧ ∧ ∧

I'd researched where to embark on a journey to the North Pole and come up with two options: Canada or Russia. This is because the North Pole is situated slap bang in the middle of the 15 million square kilometres of the Arctic Ocean. Getting to the Pole meant trekking straight across the frozen surface of the ocean.

I decided the best place to start from would be Russia, for a whole series of reasons. Firstly, the pressure ridges tend to be smaller and the terrain a bit less obstructive to pull a sled through because the predominant drift of ice tends to be from east to west, meaning that it accumulates on the Canadian side. This accumulation causes it to contort and buckle up under the pressure and form bigger pressure ridges. Secondly, I really like the Russians. When the chips are down, they're the kind of characters who come looking for you when everyone else packs up and waits for a break in the weather. Last but not least, it was much cheaper to mount a trip from there.

Having said all that, there are of course lots of good reasons to go from Canada and not Russia. The northernmost tip of Ward Hunt Island in the Canadian Arctic is almost 100 km closer to the Pole, and this thicker ice means there's also less chance of falling through. Falling through the ice was our biggest fear. A fall into the icy water of the Arctic Ocean will kill you in no time if you can't get out, as your limbs refuse to do what your brain commands after only a couple of minutes. Rumour had it that the thickness of the ice also meant that there were fewer bears on the Canadian side as they tend to loiter where the ice is thinner – it being where seals, their principal food source, can find breathing holes.

I'd never been to Russia before and was intrigued to see what the place was really like. I flew into Moscow in the middle of the afternoon and emerged from the controlled environment of a BA jet into the crowded airport and the back of a large queue.

The terminal was nicotine-stained and dirty and had that distinctly utilitarian feel. Both it and the queue felt reminiscent of 1980s newsreel footage of communist Europe I'd seen – people standing in line simply because one was there and the fact that there might be something worth having at the head of it all. Being of British origin means I'm genetically predisposed to orderly queuing. After half an hour it didn't feel like it as prickles of sweat began to form on my back.

A solid slap on the back gave me the fright of my life. I looked at the face. It was Serov. 'Tim – welcome to Russia!' We embraced. It was great to see him. I knew two Victors – Victor Serov and Victor Boyarsky. Victor Serov was trained as a physicist, but like everyone in Russia had a second job as an expedition guide that earnt him the real money. A stocky guy in his mid-forties with blond hair, blue eyes, a keen sense of humour and an incredible tolerance of the cold, he was bloody good at it, having taken a group of people to the South Pole a few years prior with the experienced British guide Geoff Somers. They had gone from Patriot Hills and been heavily supported by aircraft resupplies but Victor and Geoff had done a fantastic job getting everyone through the journey.

The temperature outside the airport was bitter, causing my breath to condense in a cloud of steam in front of my face every time I opened my mouth. Luckily we were ushered into a warm van and quickly made our way into town. I was starving and the prospect of the overnight train to St Petersburg to meet with Boyarsky meant we needed to eat our fill now. After a couple of beers and some beef stroganoff at a café in Red Square with the imposing walls of the Kremlin framed through the window, I felt much better.

'So what's your plan, Tim?' asked Victor. I explained we wanted to attempt the North Pole the following year and were open to suggestion re start dates and where to set off from. We'd also want some time at the start of the journey to acclimatise and test equipment.

Serov didn't see this as a problem. He explained we would go from Moscow on a commercial flight up to a place called Khatanga in northern Siberia. From there we could go via either a plane or helicopter to fly up to Sredniy Island in Severnaya Zemlya. I knew of the Severnaya Zemlya islands off the north coast of Siberia – enigmatic and isolated from the rest of Russia, let alone the rest of the world. It was exciting to think we would go there. The Arctic Ocean surrounds them on all sides, with the sparsely populated forests and tundra of Siberia the closest coastline to them in the south.

'There we have some friends who live in a radio station on the island,' Victor continued. 'We can stay with them, and then fly up to the northernmost point of the islands where you set off from.'

It sounded easy. I asked if we could spend time at Sredniy Island testing equipment and getting used to travel on the ice. 'No problem. Sredniy is a very narrow island and the radio station is at the end of it, so the ocean surrounds the hut on three sides. You will have plenty of opportunity there and we can also test out the gun and emergency flares.'

We talked for several hours until it was time to head to the train station for the overnight to St Petersburg and the meeting with Boyarsky. Serov was an expert in sea-ice travel and filled my head with all sorts of information about the strength of the sea ice and how we would be able to judge whether or not it could hold our weight by looking at its colour and texture. He had never been to the North Pole but understood what it would take to make it.

We arrived in St Petersburg after a poor night's sleep in a shared cabin with two strangers and made our way to Serov's apartment. Serov and his wife lived in a small apartment in a five-storey block in the leafy suburbs. After breakfast and a shower we headed to pick up his car, arriving twenty minutes later at a ramshackle collection of wooden garages. A gruff-looking guy doffed his hat when he saw it was Serov and slunk back in to his sentry box. We opened the door of an old garage and I expected to see a Lada parked inside. Instead there was a shiny new VW Golf. Victor smiled knowingly. The guiding business was obviously more lucrative than I thought.

We drove to the Russian Museum of the Arctic and Antarctic, of which Boyarsky was director, and on the way I got a feel for the incredible beauty of St Petersburg. Relatively young at 300 years old and founded by Peter the Great, St Petersburg sits astride the Neva River. The buildings are exquisite and most of them are of similar age and architecture, making them even more striking with their classic columns, and pastel colours of green, yellow and pink. The whole city is given a wonderful proportion and feeling of space by the width of the river, over 800 m wide as it passes through the city.

The museum was a wonderful old building fronted by large neoclassical columns. Inside all was musty and dark, with a scale model of Antarctica, items of scientific equipment and machinery and stuffed animals including an imposing polar bear guarding a corner of the museum. We went upstairs to a scene of a dozen or so people drinking vodka around a table. We shook hands and were invited to join the group. It was someone's birthday and not normal to be putting vodka away at 10.30 am; a bit early even by Russian standards.

Boyarsky was someone I'd always wanted to meet – a true polar legend who in 1990 as part of an international team had undertaken the longest ever journey in Antarctica. The six-man team had traversed the full length of Antarctica by dog sled, getting fresh teams flown in every month or so. It had been a four-month, 4000-km journey for which Boyarsky should have been made a hero of the Soviet Union. In any case, he was a living legend to all who knew him.

We went into his office to talk. He was 6 feet tall, but exuded the presence of someone much bigger, like a bear, with a thick orange beard, permanent smile and – like Serov – a wicked sense of humour. We discussed everything. Best start dates, our route, how best to negotiate our way through the ice, bears, equipment needs and a wishlist of questions I had compiled over six months of planning.

Boyarsky, like Serov, filled my head with facts about ice colour and texture and how through reading it you could tell whether or not it would hold the weight of sled and man passing over it. 'You will meet many leads,' [open sections of ocean] said Boyarsky. 'Best when you do to check your thermometer. If it is below −25°C then the ocean will freeze solid enough – about 10 cm – to walk upon in three or four hours.

My hands went clammy at the prospect. 'How wide are the leads?' I asked.

'Depends. They can be 1 metre or they can be 500 metres.'

I imagined the prospect of the two of us getting halfway across a recently frozen lead, hundreds of metres from solid ice only to have the ice break, plunging us in. It would mean certain death.

'How big will the pressure ridges be?' I asked. The two Victors conferred. Finally Serov replied that some years it is small, only a metre or two. Other years it is very large – 5 or 6 metres. It depends on the drift of ice, how cold the winter has been and a whole series of things. He could have put a positive spin on it, but that's just not the Russian way. They tell it to you straight and then you know exactly what to expect. No point going up there with a false impression of what it would be like. One or two metres would be bad enough. I remembered back to the seventeen days spent toiling desperately in the sastrugi up on the polar plateau in Antarctica and felt that had prepared me for anything the Arctic had to offer.

The best time of year to start the journey was apparently in March, when the Northern Hemisphere winter is coming to an end and the 'warmer' weather of spring is coming on. The extremely low temperatures at the end of winter provide the greatest chance of the ice being thick and strong enough to support your weight. This means the temperature for the first few weeks of the journey can hover down around –40 degrees or lower, a full 10 degrees colder than Antarctica was for much of the time. Start any earlier in the year and it is simply too cold to endure; any later, and you face the grim prospect of plunging through thin ice into the sea.

With this in mind Boyarsky suggested taking extra fuel. 'If one of you does fall in and you can get them out quickly enough, you can use the extra fuel to dry their clothes. It means carrying extra weight but it is the only way.' He added, with a smile, 'The only problem of starting the journey at this time is that it is when the polar bears come out of hibernation and are at their most hungry. At this time they will eat more or less anything and they are not afraid of humans, so you must be vigilant.'

The start point, too, needed careful consideration. The predominant drift of the ice is east to west, but this can change dramatically to southerly or even the opposite direction on a whim. Any journey to the Pole would need to consider the general drift once on the ice. On a good year you might just crab-walk a bit. On a bad year you might find yourself on a conveyor belt of ice going the wrong way. A British team who had attempted the Pole a few years earlier gave up after two months, having covered less than half the distance of 900 km due to backwards drift. An ocean of 2000 metres deep with a couple of metres' thickness of ice on its surface equates to something like a leaf on the surface of a deep pond in a stiff breeze. Under the force of wind and ocean currents the ice can move huge distances, normally towards the open ocean of the Northern Atlantic where it finally breaks up. Occasionally large bergs from the ice caps of places like Greenland reach the Atlantic where they can cause hazards to ships, the most famous victim, of course, being the *Titanic*.

It was a relief that after four hours of discussion Boyarsky suggested we adjourn to his summer house or 'dacha'. A timber mansion set amongst a winter treescape on the outskirts of St Petersburg, it was a kind of *Dr Zhivago* version of Russia. After a wonderful reindeer stew and a few icy cold whiskies (in my honour rather than vodka) things looked more rosy. The North Pole was another challenge and that was what I was after, although trying for a world record did seem silly given the number of things that could conspire against you. Luck would probably play as big a part as anything else in getting there quickly.

I now had no illusions about the difficulty of the journey. The Arctic would be demanding right from the outset. The ice is thinnest when you start your journey, when you're least used to the conditions and before you can get a feel for the strength of the ice. The Inuit apparently have 100 words for snow and ice and I was beginning to see why. We would have to learn ice conditions via trial and error, through assessing its colour and texture and hope for the best.

The trip would also see us pitted against my old adversaries from Spitsbergen. Polar bears are beautiful but fearsome creatures with good camouflage and an acute sense of smell. They are the largest bear in the world, completely carnivorous, aggressive and unafraid of humans. Two slow-moving obvious targets like us would fit the bill nicely as an hors d'oeuvre before maybe a seal or two.

Dinner over, Boyarsky and I drove down to St Petersburg's grand central train station for the overnight journey back to Moscow. Again we shared a cabin with two strangers, to whom Boyarsky managed to humorously translate my questions about thin ice and polar bears, causing great mirth. By lights out we'd had a couple of customary vodkas and were all old friends. It felt exotic as I was gently rocked to sleep by the train rolling through the Russian night, bound for Moscow.

The following morning I'd cogitated on what Victor had told me the night before, and I had a question about the helicopters that would take us in to the start of our journey and out at the end. These weren't just any old helicopters, they would be large military-issue Sikorskys; the kind the Russians used to good effect as helicopter gunships in the fight against the Mujaheddin in Afghanistan. They would be used to drop us onto the ice quite simply because the terrain was far too rough and unsafe to even attempt to land a plane. But what payload would we have?

'I would say you will have at least 2000 kg,' Victor said. I knew that Peter and I would use around 500 kg give or take, and asked about the rest. 'You have paid for the hire of the helicopter, so you can use it for what you want,' replied Victor.

Suddenly it became clear to me. We could offer our potential sponsors a trip to the North Pole.

∧ ∧ ∧

Back in the UK and visiting my parents in their house in Cheltenham, in England's Cotswolds, I frantically rattled off a long email to Peter outlining my thinking re the helicopters. Within an hour he had emailed back, ecstatic about the prospect. We had been talking seriously with a few sponsors who probably needed only a little nudge to get them on board, and this was it. They would not only sponsor our trip to the Pole but they would get their own trip into the bargain.

My visit to Cheltenham this time was not only to see my parents. The small market town of Malmesbury, only 30 miles from Cheltenham, has a strange claim to fame. It is the improbable home of none other than 'Snowsled' – a company run, managed and owned by Roger Daynes, an eccentric salt-of-the-earth Englishman who is CEO, shopfloor worker, chief accountant and bottle-washer of the UK's biggest sled manufacturer. I had approached Roger to help me find a second-hand sled for the Spitsbergen trip years before and now I was looking to use one of his sleds to undertake one of the toughest polar journeys imaginable.

Opposite an old church and graveyard down a narrow alleyway, I finally found the Snowsled 'factory' – a small, artisan's lockup tucked away in rural obscurity. Safe to assume he doesn't rely on passing trade, I thought to myself as I drove up. Roger knew his stuff, though, and had supplied sleds for all sorts of journeys, including for Ranulph Fiennes, whom he counts amongst his friends. He knew what would be required for a North Pole attempt.

'It'll need to float, obviously, and to be stable enough to ensure there's no chance of your falling in. Trouble is, in order for it to be stable enough, it really needs to be about a metre wide, but that will mean it is absolutely impossible to get through the terrain.' What Roger designed was a pole for attaching the sleds together side by side to provide sideways stability. The intention was then to use either a ski or snow-shovel to paddle across any leads we might encounter, a treacherous but necessary process to keep us moving north.

∧ ∧ ∧

I returned to Australia after a tiring but fruitful trip. The next time I would see Roger and the two Victors would be when I came through en route to the journey to the Pole.

Back in Adelaide I called Peter and he updated me on progress. One of the main potential sponsors we'd been talking to was Sanity Music. Sanity is owned by a guy called Brett Blundy. A self-made multi-millionaire, risk-taker, and owner of the famous Sydney Harbour Bridge Climb, he was attracted by the madness of an attempt to walk to the North Pole on foot and unsupported. The fact that he would get the opportunity to come and meet us at the Pole swung it. He was in, and the Sanity logo of an inverted capital 'I' declaring our insanity appeared on our jackets supplied by our South Pole equipment partners Helly Hansen.

We continued with the now familiar routine of training and acquiring the food and equipment needed for the journey, with both Arnott's and Westons Biscuits coming to our aid. Now the biscuit diet would be a mixture of Tim Tam chocolates and Westons shortbread made with extra sugar and butter.

Training consisted of sessions conducted on rowing ergo-meters supplied by Concept 2 in Geelong, enabling Peter and me to train independently but update each other on our training regimes and compare notes. We both imposed goals upon our-selves, requiring improvements to be made by certain milestone dates in preparation for the trip.

Christmas 2001 was now fast approaching but Peter was not

progressing as well as expected. This was a problem. We knew the terrain of the Arctic Ocean would be at least as bad if not worse than the sastrugi we had experienced down south, and would require a certain amount of brute strength as well as Peter's unquestionable endurance and mental toughness to get through.

Achieving the Pole at all was going to require a broken routine of periods of gut-wrenching effort to pull the sled over the obstructive pressure ridges we would encounter, followed by the already gruelling routine of pulling the sled across the 'flat' sections. One only had to look at the images of Peary, purportedly the first man to reach the North Pole using dog sleds, to understand the nature of the terrain. I had seen images of him and his dog teams strung out up the steep face of a 20-metre pressure ridge of uneven blocks of ice, some the size of cars, struggling to get any purchase to propel their heavy load forward. I knew that we might face the same.

Instead of a long-distance effort, where at least you could get into a rhythm, our journey would consist of a succession of short lung-busting hauls to cover the ground. This style of travel had manifested itself in amongst the regular steep-sided, sandy dunes of the Great Victoria, some of which involved climbs lasting hundreds of metres while pulling a cart that weighed over 200 kg. The more I researched, the more I suspected that kind of effort level and style of travel were close to what we'd need in the pressure ridges of the Arctic and it concerned me.

Despite all this I trained as usual, interspersed with acquiring information about typical ice movement, and researching equipment options. I changed my training to more interval-based short, sharp bursts and with each gruelling session felt my strength improve. We maintained our conviction that this would be a great achievement and, the media having picked it up, that it would be a world-record-breaking attempt. I had doubts about the achievement of a record, but was determined that I would achieve the Pole.

In keeping with the charitable nature of the trips, I was approached with the idea of getting involved with the Smith Family. The Smith Family is a private charitable institution that provides not only assistance to poor families but also has a program that provides funding and educational support to kids from underprivileged backgrounds to ensure they receive help in getting a normal education. I liked its philosophy of trying to give yourself the chance to achieve, and saw parallels with what we were doing. We were putting ourselves in the position where we had the opportunity to learn a lot about our potential and so were kids via the Learning for Life program. It gave them a chance. It was up to them to take that chance and make something of it, as it was with us.

A contact of mine in Adelaide, John Hart, ran a promotions company called Supporterzone and came up with a brilliant fundraising idea for the Smith Family. Corporate and private sponsors could donate money to the Smith Family and get their signature or corporate ID placed on a flag to be planted at the North Pole by us. It was a fantastic idea, reliant, of course, on our getting there, but the Smith Family loved it and soon their PR machine was at work spreading the word.

We convened a press conference at the Smith Family's HQ in Sydney. Peter, myself and Brett Blundy our major sponsor were there, all kitted out in our matching Helly Hansen cold weather jackets, each with our name embroidered on it. We were a team. Without Brett's support we wouldn't have been going anywhere. The next time we'd see him after the press conference would be at the top of the world as he flew in to the Pole to pick us up.

12

The land of the gulag

Peter and I arrived back in the UK and managed to check in the boxes of equipment and food into left luggage at Heathrow. Peter had arranged to stay at a friend's place in London and I travelled out to the west country to stay with my folks for a few days R and R and to pick up the sleds from Roger at Snowsled.

It was relaxing being in Cheltenham away from the cut and thrust, other than the niggling concerns I had about the media's spin on why we were attempting the journey and Peter's mindset for doing it. The media were now confidently touting the story that we were going for a second world record to be the fastest to both Poles. We would do our best to get through as quickly as possible, but I knew that it would be down to providence as to whether we made it, let alone in record time.

I arrived at Snowsled and Roger talked me through the sled design over a mug of tea. They were huge 2-metre-long high-sided boats – and needed to be, so that we could retreat to them in the event of the ice opening up beneath us. I had read a story of an explorer who had two smaller sleds, left one behind to ferry the other over some thin ice and returned to find the first one had sunk. He narrowly escaped death.

After six days of home-cooked excess and deliberate weight gain, Dad, the two boats and I made a conspicuous and probably highly illegal journey to London in Mum's hatchback. It was comical. The sleds took up the whole car and stuck out about a metre at the back. Needless to say we caused great interest and backward glances from passing motorists as we trundled along in the slow lane, sitting one behind the other like bobsledders, the sleds completely obscuring visibility out of the rear view mirror. It was one of the multitude of unusual journeys I was to make in the context of the trip. Dad dropped me off and wished me a safe journey, and I watched him drive away, hoping it wouldn't be the last time I saw him.

I had arranged a meeting with Alexandra Shackleton (or 'Zaz', as she's known to friends), granddaughter of Sir Ernest Shackleton – the most famous and well-respected polar explorer of them all – to thank her for accepting the role of international patron for the trip, John Howard having again agreed to be patron. We'd met at an exhibition titled 'South' at the Greenwich Maritime Museum. The exhibition was a celebration of the incredible achievements of her grandfather, and Scott and Amundsen in the Antarctic, and I'd been invited by the Royal Geographical Society after the successful South Pole journey. We were introduced by a close friend of hers, Geraldine, whom I met admiring one of the exhibits and got talking to, and the three of us are now firm friends.

I arrived at Zaz's house and the three of us sat down to dinner. We shared a couple of bottles of red and chatted and Zaz asked me how I was feeling about the trip. I explained my concerns honestly to her, but said that I felt confident of our ability and that we'd done our research well. It was amazing having Zaz agree to lend her support and her name certainly opened all sorts of doors. A fun personality lying just below a demure exterior, she was great company – honest, frank and warm.

'I have something to show you,' she mentioned after dinner,

carefully placing Sir Ernest Shackleton's polar medal on the table. He had been awarded it in recognition of his incredible feats of exploration and human endeavour. It was certainly an inspiration and it added to my resolve to make the trip a success. Zaz and Geraldine wished me luck and I promised to call them from the Pole on the satellite phone when we arrived.

∧ ∧ ∧

Two days later and Peter and I arrived at Heathrow airport's Terminal 4 laden with polar equipment, and even at the busiest airport in the world created a stir. I could see the look on the airline rep's face as we approached the check-in counter with our ten boxes of equipment and sleds. A kind of 'as long as you don't intend to check all that lot in' look. I explained we had been given permission to travel with everything and she quite naturally asked to see some kind of proof. I couldn't oblige, because of course there was none. All I really had was the evidence of having travelled from Sydney to Singapore without being charged excess baggage, implying that some kind of agreement was in place. I suspect that had been to do with the fact that the check-in person had been swayed by our media coverage on the Australian TV before we left. Now in the UK we were, relatively speaking, unknown and it was up to us to bluff our way through. 'The total weight is 305 kg, at $40 per kg.' Our allowance was 25 kg each. Twenty minutes later after making a nuisance of ourselves to a series of airline staff we conceded to pay $1000 – a fraction of what was owed. The process was becoming stressful, especially as I'd had to do the same in Singapore where I'd broken the journey on the way over.

Now it was Peter and I standing side by side sweating at the back of a huge queue in the Sheremetyevo terminal. This time it wasn't just the warmth. Our sweating had something to do with the fact that each of us had US$20 000 hidden in our clothes. You need to declare more than $1000 but that would cause hassle for Boyarsky's company VICAAR (Victory in Arctic and Antarctic Research) from the authorities and so the need for our subterfuge. Plus Boyarsky didn't trust banks. I felt like a drug smuggler and remembered what happened to the guy in the book *Midnight Express* when incarcerated. The Russians took this kind of thing extremely seriously and if we were caught we might just see one of the famous Siberian gulags closer up than I'd intended.

'Anything to declare? Goods, currency?'

'No nothing,' I replied, smiling nervously, a $3000 roll of 50-dollar notes bulging conspicuously in my pocket. Even a basic search would have found most of the money on me, the remainder being in my wash bag and unimaginatively stuffed inside a couple of socks.

Unsmiling, the official gestured me through, and I was out. The two Victors strode over and gave me a manly hug and I introduced Peter. We chatted nervously, having reached another milestone on our journey, and waited for our baggage to arrive. One by one our hard-won boxes appeared on the carousel, creating great interest and murmurings in the crowded baggage hall.

Soon we had a battered and bruised full complement, followed shortly by the sleds that appeared via a side entrance due to their size. They were indeed massive – much bigger than our South Pole sleds. They needed to be able to float with 150 kg of food and fuel in them and with us sitting on top, for paddling across open water.

A group of Victor's henchmen appeared, burly and no-nonsense, and soon had all ten boxes and our sleds in the back of a truck and we were again on our way, leaving questioning looks from many back in the terminal. The ground was covered in snow and the temperature well below zero as is customary for Moscow in February.

We arrived at Moscow's domestic airport after one and a half hours of driving. I chuckled to myself, imagining a tourist trying to walk it with a luggage trolley from the international terminal, thinking it was just round the corner and getting lost in the snow. You didn't need to go to Siberia or the North Pole to die in the cold of Russia, that was for sure.

I knew we were bound for a frontier when all the people boarding our flight had the rugged look of hunters and fishermen. Ahead in the queue, the metal detector light went on. After a cursory search a large bowie knife was produced by the equally large guy who had set off the detector. He looked incredulously at the authorities. 'What this?' he seemed to say, unsure what all the fuss was about, reluctantly handing it over. That was Russia: massive overreaction about a camera and complete understanding over a guy trying to take a knife with an 8-inch blade onto a crowded passenger plane.

It was 5 hours before I felt the plane begin to descend. Ten minutes later we dropped out of the clouds, affording a first look at the land. It was the twilight of late afternoon, the sun sitting low and orange in the sky. All round the Arctic tundra stretched into the distance. This was Siberia, synonymous with hardship, and vast untamed wilderness.

We bumped down onto the runway at Khatanga at the mouth of the mighty Khatanga River. The only thing north of here was the Taymyr Peninsula, still home to huge herds of reindeer and elk that migrate across it each year, and to local tribal peoples who live a pretty much unchanged nomadic hunter–gatherer existence. North beyond Taymyr was our stopping place – the islands of the Severnaya Zemlya group. Locked in the ice of the Arctic Ocean, they were an enigmatic destination with names like October Revolution Island and Bolshevik Island serving to remind you that this part of Russia would have been absolutely unreachable back in the communist days. Locked behind the Iron Curtain and under Arctic ice in equal amounts – a perfect place to send political dissidents, many of whom served out their lives in abject misery and perished in the terrible Siberian 'gulags' (prisons) during the communist years.

Khatanga was a collection of stark low-rise flats interspersed with modest housing. Temperatures here in winter frequently hovered below −30°C for months on end, and yet when summer comes, the place becomes a breeding ground for mosquitoes. We emerged from the plane into −35 degrees of cold. Severnaya Zemlya was still 600 km to the north and the Pole an elusive 900 km beyond that.

A truck pulled up and took us and our sleds to the 'Hotel'. The only one in town, it resembled a prison block – dark, grey, and bleak, with windows shut permanently by multiple layers of paint. Our room was utilitarian, and an eerie twilight filtered in through the iced-up window. It would be our home for the next few days.

Our plan was to rest up and test equipment in Khatanga and then fly up to the radio hut on Sredniy (middle) Island in Severnaya Zemlya for final equipment checks and testing and a couple more days' rest and overeating. From there we would fly via helicopter to the northernmost tip of the northernmost island in the group, a place called Cape Articeskiy. There was nothing beyond Articeskiy except the vagaries and dangers of a swirling mass of thin sea ice that forms the surface of the ocean we would walk on for the next 50 days.

The hotel didn't serve food, so an hour later we joined the two Victors and the team and headed out on foot to a local eatery, giving us the chance to look around. It didn't take long. Other than the wonderful wooden church complete with an exotic-looking Eastern Orthodox dome overlooking the frozen harbour, the town consisted of about a kilometre square grid of drab buildings, the biggest of which was our hotel at six or so storeys high. The awnings over the windows of houses had a pretty collection of ice crystals hanging from them caused by the moist air from inside freezing as it came into contact with the bitter temperature outside. A stack stood in the middle of town churning out acrid black smoke from its coal-fired burner and people hurried about snow-covered streets, rugged up in multiple layers, heads hung low for protection from the frigid wind, faces hidden behind goggles and masks.

Dogs of every description hung around everywhere, rifling through refuse tips and rubbish bins, eking out a sad existence. There were some really scrawny creatures but there were some beautiful huskies too. They were the kind of creatures that Peary had used to get to the Pole – strong but gentle – good foils for the fiercely driven egos of the men who went with them.

Over the next few days we unpacked our boxes and went through the equipment, getting the two Victors' advice. On my first trip to Russia, Boyarsky had given me a list of items he felt I would need to make it through and I'd tried to address each of his points. One of these had been a pick to chop through the icy rubble that would block our path each day. With saving weight in mind, I had been given a super lightweight titanium ice-axe by Grivel, the leading ice-axe manufacturer, thinking this would be perfect for the job. Boyarsky laughed out loud, his whole body shaking with mirth at the sight of the axe. He left the room and returned a few minutes later. It was like the scene from the movie *Crocodile Dundee* where Dundee confronts the mugger threatening him with a flick-knife. 'That's not a knife. *That's* a knife.' he says as he pulls a huge knife from its sheath, scaring the mugger off. In like fashion, Boyarsky handed me a huge pickaxe. It must have weighed 4 or 5 kg and was totally at odds with our weight-saving philosophy. 'This you need,' said Boyarsky. 'The blocks of ice will be big – the size of a bed, and a metre thick, but a few solid blows with this in the middle and they will break in two. Better than climbing over them with the sled.'

So it was with the gun, too. I had in mind a Magnum pistol or a lightweight hunting rifle. Instead, we were given a bloody great big pump-action 303, delivered to our room dramatically in a rough-weave sack under cover of darkness from an anonymous source. Its chamber took six bullets and Serov was confident of its bear-stopping ability, although again I didn't like the weight implication. Why didn't we just take a bazooka and make really sure?

Everything for the North Pole seemed to be bigger and clumsier than it had needed to be for the South Pole. Reinforced jerrycans to handle the impacts of the sled being dropped off great pressure ridges many metres high, complete with extra fuel for drying ourselves off if one of us should fall through the ice and make it out alive. A heavier and stronger sled, a huge rifle, the construction worker's pickaxe and a flare gun. I wasn't sure whether equipment for the North Pole needed to be so heavy duty, or whether it was just that everything in Russia seemed to be made from heavy steel rather than more modern alloys.

The bottom line was that our sled weights increased each day as we substituted and modified bits of equipment. Day four in Khatanga and Boyarsky was not happy with our ski bindings and I had to confess that I too had my concerns. Our Berwin bindings were made from plastic and looked childlike in amongst all our other heavily reinforced equipment. Victor suggested replacing them with a metal binding that he had devised. Adversity is the mother of invention – a concept that can be applied to Russia in large doses, even more so to Boyarsky, and for polar travel it is an absolute prerequisite. By the following day he and Peter had improvised a metal binding that would fit Peter's boot which then left me with my Berwins plus Peter's pair and four spare pairs. That surely should be enough, even with breakages.

It was with relief that we finally went through the last of our equipment and the Victors seemed satisfied. The strange thing about polar travel is that because so few people have been to the Poles unsupported there is only a very small number of people who can comment or offer advice about the range of things you are likely to experience. Neither Victor had made the journey from land to the North Pole, although both had many kilometres of polar travel under their belts and I trusted their judgment implicitly. Our making it would be testament to that judgment as much as to our mental resolve and physical ability.

We got the word that we would be leaving the following day and were asked if we would visit the kids at the local school to talk to them. We sat in front of 50 or so kids of all ages and via translation by the two Victors gave a little presentation and then answered their questions. The kids were fascinated. A mixed group of blue-eyed blond-haired Russians and indigenous kids all living together harmoniously, according to Serov. It was nice to see. We were received like returning heroes even though as yet we'd done nothing. We asked the kids about what to do if we met a polar bear and they suggested running would be a good idea. They asked us about Australian animals and Peter's kangaroo impression had everyone captivated, me included. After an hour and a half we retreated to the staff room for tea, cake and of course vodka with the teachers and were presented with some souvenirs of Khatanga, which was celebrating its 375th anniversary. I could only imagine what the place would have been like back in 1626.

That night we got ready to head down to the restaurant for the final time, sleds packed and ready to go. The temperature outside was –47 degrees – the coldest I had ever experienced and a light breeze would be in our faces if the plume from the power station was anything to go by. People often ask if it is easy to tell the difference between –20° and –40° and it is, although explaining the difference isn't easy. I stepped out into the breeze and it was bitter cold that made your lungs ache when you took a deep breath, and started to constrict blood supply to the extremities almost immediately. It was with relief that we reached the restaurant for a hearty meal of potato soup and reindeer stew washed down with large amounts of ice-cold vodka.

We finished our meal with another of Boyarsky's many exuberant toasts. 'Timushko, we toast to the success of your terrible deal!' and we all knocked back our vodkas. It was the Russian way of saying 'break a leg' – tempting bad luck and hopefully meaning a great deal would be struck; in our case, that the trip would be a success.

We left the restaurant warmed with the food and vodka. Some low cloud had appeared above us, obstructing my view of the stars. I looked up at it and to my surprise the cloud began to swirl around strangely. As I watched, it changed in colour from grey to emerald green and then to blue and back to green again. It was the northern lights – the aurora borealis – a spectacular display of charged particles from the sun that are attracted towards the Earth's magnetic poles, releasing energy in the form of auroras as they strike atoms and molecules in the atmosphere. It was magnificent: better than any fireworks display ever could be, moving as if it were alive. Both my previous polar trips had been in the summer when 24-hour light prevented aurora being visible but now our arrival at the end of winter had allowed us to see it. It felt like a good omen.

That night in bed my mood changed. I lay there awake thinking about things and I have to confess there were some doubts creeping in. Other than the seriousness of the journey we were attempting and the bears we might meet, the sea ice was of concern. Ever since I'd pored over the satellite images of the Arctic Ocean provided by Radarsat two weeks before, I'd been uneasy. The key for the images clearly indicated that the ice for the first 300 km of the journey had large sections of only 20 cm thick, and some much thinner. I hoped that had improved.

There were a lot of unanswered questions to think about. Boyarsky had been a bit uncertain about the age of the fuel in the drums in his lockup and I'd noticed a bit of residue in it when we'd decanted it into our jerrycans. The MSR stoves we were again using were fantastically efficient but tended to be a bit sensitive to blockages if dirty fuel was used and that could be serious. There was no other fuel around, though, so we had no choice.

Walking around in Khatanga I was reminded of what the South Pole trip had taken out of me. Even in the five-minute walk down to the restaurant each night my right thumb had gone a bit numb and ached. It had never been the same since I had brought it back from its blackened point of no return in Antarctica and I worried how it would handle the intense cold we were about to subject ourselves to on the ice. The irony is that although your mental tolerance for polar travel improves with successive journeys, your physical ability deteriorates, such that I think someone only has two or three really serious polar journeys in them.

We seemed to be experiencing problems, too, with the system we'd set up for Boyarsky to be notified of our position on the ice. The French Argos Beacon was a sealed waterproof box that we would switch on to provide our position and status. It relied on a relay of a message back from the French government SPOT satellite via the Argos HQ in Toulouse to VICAAR back in St Petersburg and then a phone call from them to his Iridium satellite phone at a predetermined time for updates on our progress. Being a sealed unit the beacon would provide nothing back to us, just an invisible message to Victor. We set it off with an all-clear message each day in Khatanga to test it out, but only on the day before we left did Boyarsky finally receive a call from St Petersburg telling him that Argos had been in touch – four days after we transmitted our first message.

I knew the problem lay at our end and not with the beacon, but it didn't instil confidence. Despite the serious ramifications, listening to Boyarsky calling from Siberia trying to explain in heavily accented English to a French person at Argos HQ in Toulouse that he was a representative of an Australian team trying to go to the North Pole had me in stitches. 'I am Boyarsky. I am callink from Russia. We are usink a beacon in Siberia for the Australian North Pole team. It is not workink. Can you please check this?'

I was also worried about Peter. He had not been his normal focused self. He'd had a lot on his mind apart from the trip, and he seemed concerned too by the Victors' account of how obstructive the pressure ridges would be and was worried about the quality of his training for the trip.

Tired after considering all the known facts for a couple of hours I finally fell asleep, waking in the morning ready to get on with things. After breakfast we packed up the sleds for the final time and it took four men to lug them clumsily down the stairs and, with one mighty effort, lift them up onto a flat-bed truck parked outside.

Khatanga's small military airport strangely had a Customs point. That meant there was the requirement for the normal subterfuge when dealing with the Russian authorities. In our case it meant no mention of guns, flare guns, fuel, large sums of US currency or video and still cameras within our sleds. We were happy to oblige, the language barrier ensuring we didn't say anything that the Victors didn't want us to.

The cargo plane we loaded the sleds onto was taking up supplies for a small base of troops that were still stationed on Sredniy – a hangover from the Cold War days when they had manned a missile early-warning listening station. According to some, they had missiles of their own stationed up there. One thing's for sure, had there been any exchange of missiles between North America and the Soviet Union quite a few would have followed the route we were going to take over the Pole as the most direct line between the two continents.

Loading complete, the ramp closed and we blasted down the icy runway bound for Sredniy, all on board (with the exception of Peter and me and the Victors) standing around casually smoking as we took off. An hour and a half later we touched down on Sredniy's snow runway to be greeted by a friendly-looking guy in a truck. His name was Igor and he and his wife and young son together with another couple had manned the weather station on Sredniy for years.

Sredniy is a long, thin island about 15 km by 1 km, so nowhere is far from the sea. You wouldn't have known it, as all was frozen and covered in snow as far as the eye could see – the sea being distinguishable from the land only by the former's tumultuous surface of pressure ridges and strange formations. After 45 minutes or so of ploughing through deep snow in the truck we pulled up at Igor's hut, which sat at the very end of the island, the frozen ocean surrounding it on three sides.

It was a truly spectacular location. The heavy weather-beaten wooden hut had originally been designed to provide meteorological information to the early-warning base that had been here. Now the base was largely gone, having been dismantled at the end of the Cold War when missile attack was no longer a serious threat. Bits of abandoned machinery still poked through the deep blanket of snow. Igor and his crew, too, had sadly been largely abandoned, their salaries unpaid for years according to Boyarsky. Still they steadfastly continued to go about their jobs, recording weather data and manning the radio, sharing night duty on a rotating shift so that the radio was manned 24 hours a day, 365 days a year. To whom they provided this information I had no idea, and I had images of the information being recorded conscientiously for no purpose, being sent through to an abandoned military command centre somewhere in Moscow. But they had nowhere else to go, and had become accustomed to the solitude and harsh beauty of the place, so they remained.

Their income was supplemented by people the Victors brought through, several having attempted the Pole before us from here, bringing with them valuable US currency. The families were also masters at eking out an existence by salvaging things they needed from the old base. Their radio was housed in a separate hut and this was full of spares from trucks, old radios, bits of switchboards, and reels of copper wire.

A third hut housed the diesel generators that provided power and warmth, the fuel having also been acquired from the old base. They had been using this old diesel for years and reckoned they had a stockpile of several years' worth to go. When they ran out they'd find some other way of making ends meet.

A wire about 10 metres off the ground ran between the huts and I assumed it had something to do with power supply until a large black husky bounded round the corner, almost bowling me over. His lead was attached to a chain that ran up to the wire. He was perimeter protection against bears and would raise the alarm if one approached, having a reinforced kennel to retreat into if a bear actually tried to attack him.

We settled into life at the hut with ease. It was wonderfully warm inside, as were our hosts, who cooked hearty meals of stew and soup for us throughout our stay, one of the cargo plane's reindeer carcasses ending up in the pot. The hut was basic but cosy, with the exception of the cold room. Rather than being refrigerated, it was simply kept unheated, easily keeping everything frozen as the outside temperature hovered around −30°C much of the time.

We went about our business of checking our equipment for the final time and went out onto the sea ice to test the gun and fire a few flares. The gun had a recoil like a kick from a horse but it instilled confidence and that was the important thing. Our shooting range was a spectacular frozen section of ocean a few hundred metres from the hut with views back to it and the early-warning base that was built into the low hill of the island. All around was frozen ocean contorted into strange shapes and the sun sat low in the sky, giving off weak rays.

Even taking a leisurely trip out in the cold made you extremely hungry and I relished each meal, building up the reserves that I would need for the journey. No-one other than the Victors spoke any English, so all communication was done with the aid of Boyarsky or Serov translating or with sign language honed over the course of nights of vodka consumption. I would go to sleep at night looking out of the window at the raw beauty of the Arctic. In a few days we would be somewhere 100 km or so north of here in a tent on the ocean. In Spitsbergen I had taken paper maps. In Antarctica I'd taken maps of the key bits of the journey. Here there were no maps, just a vast ever-changing ocean of ephemeral sea ice. It was an exciting prospect.

Day five came and we sat in the warmth of the hut, nerves jangling, waiting for the sound of the truck that would take us to the helicopter and to the beginning of our journey. We felt ready, having tested most things – with the exception of finding thin ice to get used to. Around Sredniy it was solid. That in itself didn't represent a problem. If it was like this here it might be like this further north where we were going and, strangely, I felt pretty relaxed about it.

The wind was strong that morning and visibility was reduced to only a few hundred metres. The truck appeared out of nowhere, taking me by surprise. With hugs all round, we said goodbye to the two families who had kindly shared their lives with us over the past four days and were on our way. As we left, the mind again played tricks. This little radio hut had seemed like the end of the world when we first arrived. Now it seemed like civilisation and it was hard to leave behind.

An hour's journey through drifted snow and we arrived at the airstrip and loaded the sleds onto the helicopter. I marvelled at the way these guys could drive a 25-year-old conventional two-wheel-drive truck through metre drift snow without getting bogged.

The helicopter was an old military-issue Sikorsky, with a crew of four rugged-looking characters. They stood around laughing and joking, cigarettes in mouth to a man, occasionally stamping the ground trying to keep circulation going in the bitter cold as we waited for the helicopter to be refuelled.

Soon the wind became too much for all of us and we sought shelter in the helicopter. None of the guys spoke any English but were keen to talk. Boyarsky translated and we answered questions about Australia and what it was like. I'd never been in a helicopter before and this was going to be an incredible first journey. Minutes before embarking on my first flight I thought a good question for them was whether they had ever had any serious problems. Boyarsky translated their response. 'No, they have had no problems,' he replied. As Boyarsky spoke, the navigator, a small indigenous Russian from Khatanga, appeared to remember something worthy of recounting and started speaking. Everyone listened. Judging from everyone's reactions he had an amusing style of telling a yarn, and I watched people's faces, trying to anticipate what was going on.

The story went on and as it did, the whole crew, Boyarsky included, began to roll with belly laughs, until they were all crying. Finally after about five minutes Boyarsky had composed himself enough to tell me the gist of the story. Apparently the guy had been navigator with another crew flying over Siberia one summer. Siberia can be as hot in the summer as it is cold in the winter and the temperature in the helicopter was sweltering on this particular day. To cool down, one of the crew suggested they stop and go for a swim in the lake they were flying over. The problem was that all the ground around the lake was marshy and unsuitable to put down on, so a bright spark on board suggested they put the helicopter on autopilot and hover low over the lake as they all went in for a dip.

All was well and they had a great swim and cooled down. Now it came time to get back in. Unfortunately, after ten minutes of hovering, the helicopter had burnt off quite a bit of fuel and this, combined with the fact that the crew were paddling around in the water below, meant it was now quite a bit lighter and the ladder was now a few centimetres higher. Where they were swimming was too deep to stand, and try as they might they couldn't reach the ladder to climb in. After a period of fruitless endeavour, they decided that they had better try to find a boat to paddle over to the helicopter so they could stand in it and reach the ladder. They returned an hour and a half later, rowing like crazy in their underpants in a rowing boat they'd borrowed off a local fisherman, only to witness the helicopter run out of juice and crash spectacularly into the lake.

I probably would've laughed more than they did, if it weren't for the fact I was about to get into just such a helicopter and fly over the frigid water of the Arctic Ocean. A figure appeared at the helicopter's door. Refuelling was complete. We were off.

13

Into the labyrinth

We approached the northernmost point of Russia, and as if to herald our arrival in its domain, a polar bear appeared below us on a large piece of pack-ice, standing defiant on its hind legs as we thundered past. Only ten minutes later the chopping rotor blades slowed and we dropped down gently onto the snow. This was Cape Articeskiy, the end of land, marked by a solitary fuel tank in the icy wilderness. The remoteness was spectacular, with snow and ice as far as the eye could see lit by the sun's amber rays as it sat large and bright on the horizon. Our next stop would be the frozen ice of the ocean.

Ten minutes and we were airborne again. I hoped the ice would be more substantial than the fragmented patchwork quilt of brash ice we'd flown over to get here. It was nothing like the stuff around Sredniy. Perhaps it was all a bad joke. The crew looked relaxed. For them it was just another flight. For us it was a bit more than that.

As we flew along the coast looking for a suitable place to put down, I got the essentials to hand. Surely we weren't going to be cast adrift in this broken jigsaw of pack-ice. Sure enough, though, we were descending. Boyarsky turned to me and shouted over the sound of the engine, 'Are you ready?' I nodded confidently, amazed we could put down here, and wondering what lay ahead.

We hovered at 30 metres or so, the blades blasting the ice below, and then gently touched down to test the strength of the floe. It creaked under the weight of the helicopter, so the pilot gunned the engine to give us some lift. The wheels now just touched its surface.

'Okay, go,' shouted Boyarsky. We piled out of the chopper onto the ice and many hands lugged the sleds forwards to the hatch and shoved them down to us. Boyarsky and Serov jumped down onto the ice and we embraced as the blades of the chopper whipped round dangerously just above our heads. 'Go well!' shouted Serov, raising a clenched fist, and with that he and Boyarsky were back into the chopper and the hatch shut. The pilot gave me the thumbs up and gunned the engine, sending the massive machine skyward and blowing the sleds away from us with the force as we shielded our eyes.

After the noise and pandemonium of our exit from the chopper all was suddenly silent. Within the space of a minute the helicopter had become just a dull buzz like an insect in the distance. Here we were on an ice floe in the Arctic Ocean, complete with contorted ice formations and the bitter cold – an alien yet strangely familiar world. I put the compass round my neck, kicked on my skis, loaded a bullet in the breech of the gun, and strapped it to the top of my sled. Peter was waiting for me by the time I had done everything. 'Ready?'

'Ready.' We headed where the compass pointed – north.

Our plan was to head slightly north-east so as to counter the likely predominant drift of the ice, which was from east to west. If we headed straight for the Pole we stood a good chance of being pushed away to the west of it and then having to turn to head into the teeth of ice moving directly against us on our final run into the Pole. That was a long way off. Now the key was to get moving, keep warm and get used to travelling in this strangest of places.

The temperature had already started to eat into us and manual dexterity began to ebb away. It was one of the worst things about polar trips. The time you need manual dexterity most is when you are packing and unpacking equipment at the beginning and end of the day, and this coincides with the time when you have the least. When you commence the day you have to force your body to work by getting moving and gen-erating heat. This gets blood coursing around your body until you stop and, via an inbuilt system of self-preservation, your body constricts your blood vessels to conserve heat in its core. The blood is the fuel to make your hands work. As soon as this is cut off, your hands begin to perform with a mind of their own.

The sled weighed a tonne, bringing back memories I had not felt since the South Pole and the trek in the desert and I took a deep breath and prepared myself for the next 50 days of super-human effort and mental resolve that I knew would be needed to make this journey a success. I leaned into the harness and the sled shuddered forward in fits and starts.

More or less in line with our north/north-east bearing was a massive iceberg that had been frozen into the sea ice, towering above it like a white table-top mountain. I remembered my naivety at the beginning of the South Pole journey where I had allowed myself initially to think of the total task in hand and became demoralised. Now my goal was no more ambitious than to go and have a look at the iceberg.

To the uninitiated, scale was impossible to gauge, but at a guess I would have put the berg at least 10 km away from us. The terrain between us and it was, however, desperately obstructive and difficult. A landscape of strangely shaped ice blocks stretched to the horizon, like a city reduced to rubble by heavy bombing. It was as obstructive as the sastrugi but more angular and this was to do with the way that it had been formed. The sastrugi down south were formed by the wind that ravages Antarctica. Here up north, the ocean ice was a thin layer, a metre thick in places and perhaps 3 or 4 metres at most but at the Pole itself the remainder was wafer-thin by comparison, perhaps 20 to 30 centimetres thick.

The Arctic Ocean sits almost land-locked at the top of the world, hemmed in by the long coastlines of Alaska, Canada, Greenland and Russia, with only a few gaps allowing water to circulate in and out of it, the biggest being the opening into the Northern Atlantic between Greenland, Iceland and Norway. It is extremely deep at over 2000 metres in many parts and yet the icy crust on top of it is so thin that the Russians have even taken a nuclear-powered ice-breaker right through the North Pole in recent years.

The consequence of the depth of the ocean and the thinness of the ice on its surface is that ocean currents and wind move vast sheets of this ice around on the surface of the ocean with ease. As they move they regularly shunt into one another, causing buckling and warping due to the enormous pressure involved, reducing the surface to piles of icy rubble. New ice then forms as the ocean opens up into a lane of water, or 'lead', as named by whalers who first experienced them. The lead then freezes over, forming a conspicuous momentary area of flat in amongst the tumult, before it too is broken and contorted by the force of another plate of ice ramming into it.

Pulling the sled through this landscape was incredibly hard. It would snag behind even the smallest obstruction, its snub-nosed shape getting caught disappointingly easily. I pulled for an hour, stopping on a wall of icy rubble some 2 metres high, the sled perched crazily atop it while I surveyed the misery of the terrain that lay ahead. It was more of the same as far as I could see, but I convinced myself that we hadn't come far and it could all change tomorrow.

Peter appeared behind me and put my thoughts into words. 'Worse than sastrugi,' he gasped.

'Yeah,' I replied, 'definitely worse.'

'Still, could improve tomorrow, eh?' I managed.

'Yeah, hope so,' replied Peter. With that I moved off, having picked what I thought was a decent route through the rubble, not a straight line, but manageable with the weight of the sled in tow.

By the end of the day we were still short of the berg, but it did look spectacular and couldn't be far off now. It was truly amazing to behold and must have been calved off an ice sheet from one of the big Arctic caps – perhaps Spitsbergen or Franz Josef Land, or even Greenland, where the world's thickest ice can be found at over 4 kilometres thick.

Bergs are dangerous, not only because of their ship-sinking potential but also because they have a tendency to topple over without warning. For this reason it is safest to go nowhere near them, just in case they decide to roll over onto you. When they can be as big as a city you can see it's a good idea to give them a really wide berth.

Our berg was still a fair way away. A bigger concern for us was the thickness of the ice we made camp on. We pushed the aluminium stakes into the snow that had drifted on top of the ice and clambered inside. We were back in the same type of Bibler single-skin Gore-Tex tent as we'd used down south. As we lay there it was an eerie sensation to think that less than 30 cm below us was cold dark ocean, perhaps a kilometre deep at this point. One of our biggest concerns when pitching the tent was not only where to pitch it in amongst the tumultuous surface of ice, but where there was the smallest chance of the ice opening up beneath us and dropping us into the ocean during the night. We had decided we would pitch the tent immediately next to an old pressure ridge, where the ice was piled up high from two plates having collided. We guessed that the ice would be thickest and strongest here and least likely to break apart again, like a weld joint being stronger than the surrounding metal it has bonded together.

I was tired and fell asleep easily – strange, given the number of things we had to be concerned about, including bears, the ice cracking beneath us and the throbbing sensation emanating from my old frostbite injury to my right thumb.

The next day we woke at 5 am and I remembered just how miserable life in a tent in the polar regions can be. I was warm in my bag, but the temperature in the tent was not – according to the thermometer –25 degrees. Breakfast was not the average meal that suburban families enjoy waking up to either. Snow needed to be heated on the stove to rehydrate our powdered milk, a frozen block of olive oil stood next to the stove sweating as it gradually thawed to be added to our muesli, and the piss bottle sat on the lid of the pot, its frozen contents gradually melting so we could pour them away before setting off.

Two hours later we had finally finished melting the snow required for our drinking water for the day and I added more clean snow to the dirty residue in the bottom of the pot to make a hot chocolate before setting off. Whilst this was going on we progressively dressed, our legs still inside our bags to retain as much warmth as possible until the very last when we would pull on our boots, pack our bags away and be on our way.

There was one additional task up north. That was to check the GPS again in the morning to see whether we'd drifted as we slept, as this would have implications for the bearing we were to follow. Sure enough, the unit revealed we had drifted 1 km backwards and about 500 metres to the west, making us even more determined to keep to our north/north-easterly bearing. It seemed amazing that we were on top of such a thin layer of ice; for all intents and purposes it looked like solid land. It was a depressing thought that we'd effortlessly drifted backwards through a kilometre of hard-won ground.

The berg was waiting for us when we emerged from the tent. It had obviously moved in the same direction as us during the night, as a north/north-easterly bearing still took us straight past it. I agreed I would lead again today and made the pickaxe secure and accessible on the top of my sled alongside the gun and spare rope. Unlike down south we used rope for our traces from our harness to the sled, to make it easier to get back to the sled quickly. This was so that I could get to the pickaxe more easily to chop away blocks of ice that blocked our path, and to give us easier access to the gun or rope in an emergency such as a bear attack or one of us falling through the ice. We couldn't afford in either case to waste any time buggering around with mitts and unclipping harnesses.

The rubble seemed worse today than it had been yesterday, or maybe it was the fact that we were to spend seven hours toiling in it today, unlike the five of yesterday. It wasn't 100 metres before my bearing took us to a 3-metre-high wall of rubble around which there was no obvious route. I was annoyed as we had not yet had the chance to warm up and our hands were numb from the cold. I decided to give Boyarsky's pickaxe a burl to warm up and to vent some of my frustration, flicking off my outer mitts so they hung round my neck on their lanyards. Gripping the wooden haft of the pickaxe in my gloved hands, I took a huge swing at the nearest block that stood in my way. The blow cleaved the massive block into two metre-long pieces, which I broke up into smaller bits to stand on and take my next swing, doing this repeatedly until I stood atop the wall of rubble, having heaved the sled up behind me hand over hand.

I looked round to see Peter behind me shaking his hands hard in an effort to keep the circulation going in them. It was the problem with leading and following. The leader gets tired as he does most of the work, but the seconder has to wait, unable to do much, and so gets cold with inactivity as a result. The view from the top of the wall was of a chaotic surface of blocks of ice with awkward gaps in between, designed to snap ankles and twist knees if your leg should plunge into them. There was no choice but to remove my skis to climb down, involving an awkward balancing act while I strapped the skis atop my sled. Further blows with the pickaxe and I had made a passable ramp down off the wall, filling the gaps with rubble from blocks obliterated by my efforts. The sled, however, was now firmly stuck behind the lip that marked the crest of the wall. Any attempt to move back towards it let off the tension on the rope, causing it to slide back down the other side. Yet try as I might, I couldn't get the thing up and over the crest of the wall from where I was. 'Come on, you bastard!' I screamed, but it wouldn't move.

Peter had realised my position and suddenly the weight lifted and the sled moved. He had taken off his skis and ascended his side of the wall and was now pushing. As the sled got to the top of the wall it suddenly tipped over the edge and slid down onto my side, picking up speed quickly and almost knocking me off my feet. I looked at my watch. We had been going for just over half an hour and had covered about 100 metres. This was going to be hell.

In between the pressure ridges were flatter sections which had escaped being buckled up into barriers of broken ice, probably because they were more recently formed. Their time would come. These sections allowed us to get into a kind of a rhythm before the next inevitable pressure ridge blocked our path – anything from a metre to 5 metres in height, they came with depressing regularity.

The travel in amongst the pressure of the Arctic Ocean allowed for no free thinking time like Antarctica had. In some respects this was good, as down south the problem had often been trying to keep the mind occupied. Here it was the opposite; constant requirement to keep an eye on the compass bearing and concentration to find the best way through the labyrinth of pressure ridges, and constant vigilance for thin ice and bears. It was exhausting.

We both struggled with the weights of the sleds, but Peter found it especially difficult being of slighter build than me and 20 kg lighter. We sat and talked over a cup of hot soup and some energy biscuits at one of our breaks on the afternoon of day 2. 'How're you feeling?' I asked. 'Good enough to do a lead?'

'Don't think so. Not just yet. If it's okay with you, I'll follow and if you struggle to get over a ridge of pressure I can help push your sled over. I think we'll make best progress like that.'

I agreed. It wasn't an ideal situation, but it would work until we'd used up a few days' worth of food and fuel, reducing the sled weights, and we'd got more used to the workload. Plus the pressure could abate a bit and we might find ourselves in more open sections.

That night we checked the GPS, having covered 14 kilometres in seven hours. Not too bad, considering. Now we were at the mercy of the elements again and waited to see how far we'd drifted during the night and in which direction. A light wind had been in our faces for much of the day, so I psychologically prepared myself for the fact that it would be backwards – it was just a case of by how much.

We woke in the icy cavern as usual, the sound of Peter's sleeping bag unzipping returning me from my dreams of other places. My nose was freezing cold too, it being the only thing that protruded from my cocoon. I rolled over onto something large and lumpy – the GPS unit, which now permanently lived in my sleeping bag to save time warming it up for use in the morning. I started getting dressed before I checked the unit, just to get some momentum going in case the news was bad. My Hellytech jacket used as a pillow during the night had already assumed the qualities of a suit of armour and I beat it to break the ice that encrusted it. I pulled it on and shuddered, feeling the sensation of ice on the neck and arms from the sweat that had frozen into it from the previous day's effort.

On checking the GPS it was a pleasant surprise to discover we'd actually gone forward about 500 metres along with a sideways move of about 2 km to the west. At least it was progress of a sort and something we could build on psychologically. I set off and decided to try to start using the same mind games I'd used down south to good effect. I wouldn't think about the big task but just about reaching the next piece of pressure, and see if I could improve my 'technique' for getting through the ridges with each successive one I encountered. In this way I turned each wall I met into a kind of learning opportunity – something to test myself.

It seemed to work today, buoyed with the good news of some forward progress during the night and unless it was my imagination the pressure also seemed to have got slightly smaller and was spaced further apart. It reminded me a bit of the dry stone walls and hedgerows you'd get around fields in England's Lake District, and by the middle of the day we'd crossed at least twenty fields and walls and had made a good distance. The more open terrain also allowed us to get into a rhythm and keep warmer, which suited Peter's style of travel far better. All was well.

The conditions also showed no sign of changing and if it was going to be like this all the way, we'd be okay. At one point I actually found I was talking to myself, 'This is nowhere near as bad as people led me to believe, I can do this.' Staring at the distant horizon I convinced myself that the early pressure ridges we'd experienced were just caused by the ice meeting the north coast of Siberia. Now that we were 50 km or so off the coast, we were free of the worst of it. The theory held no water of course, and I knew it, but it served its purpose today – I was in a good mood and nothing was going to stop me.

The next day we woke and the temperature was inexplicably warm by the standards we'd come to expect of the Arctic at this time of year, the thermometer showing only –12°. Pulling the

sled was still hard work, but the warmer weather made the interface between the runners and the snow melt more easily and
allowed them to run a bit rather than drag as was the norm. We
had only set ourselves a target of 20 km a day and we'd managed
it yesterday with eight hours of hard pulling. All we had to do –
and I say 'all' advisedly – was sit on this distance and hope the
ice didn't drift us too far backwards.

Still, there were the occasional massive outcrops of pressure-
fractured ice. I stopped on the shoulder of one and to my
surprise noticed a huge piece of driftwood protruding. It
reminded me that despite the fact that we battled to get through
this terrain, it was nothing more than a thin layer of ice on the
surface of a deep ocean.

From the mound I surveyed what lay ahead. A few hundred
metres ahead I spotted something – a ribbon of black in amongst
the white of the ice. It was a lead. We arrived near it and I unclipped myself from the sled to take a closer look. Despite what
we knew to be true, three days of travel across this landscape with
no sign of water and it still took some convincing that you were
on the surface of an ocean. I approached the edge cautiously. It
was about a metre across and the water looked inky black against
the white of the snow and ice. I knew it was clear and that it was
only the lack of light that gave the impression of darkness as
I could clearly see in profile in the water the thickness of the
ice on which I stood. Turquoise and white, it was no more than
30 centimetres thick, which for some reason came as a shock to
me even though I'd been walking on it for over three days.

Boyarsky reckoned 10 centimetres was just about safe to walk
on with a heavy sled as long as you didn't hang around too long.
Still, I didn't want to try jumping the lead just in case the edges
were brittle. Eventually cold got the better of me. Even –12°
was cold enough not to be standing around inactive and
I decided to lay the sled across the gap like a ladder and climb
across it. It worked and Peter followed suit. Negotiating the lead

gave us confidence and we felt positive. Then we reached the next one a few hundred metres later. This one wasn't quite as easy to cross, being 4 metres or so across.

We went our separate ways to the left and right and luckily a few minutes later I heard a shout from Peter that he had found a point narrow enough to step over. We repeated the process a few more times that day, each lead causing us to stop and consider our options. Luckily in each case we found a narrow enough point so that we didn't have to attach the sleds together and try paddling across. I couldn't believe that the two sleds attached together, with over 300 kg of food and equipment in them and with me on top, would float.

That night we'd again covered 20 km but it had been a real effort. Smaller pressure reminded me of how difficult the sled was to pull in 'normal' conditions without leads or big ridges. Peter was feeling philosophical in the tent that night and decided he'd have a go at leading the next day, the smaller pressure being a bit less to cope with, and with 5 or 6 kg less weight in his sled.

I went through the routine of getting the evening meal ready as quickly as I could. The warmth of the stove and the infusion of a steaming broth of rice and noodles saturated with olive oil was always a greatly anticipated event. It was the one time you had the chance to talk and download the multitude of thoughts you'd had during the day as you plodded along in isolation. Try as I might, though, the stove would not light. The spare was in the sled and I was in my bag trying to get warm. My hands were too cold and too numb to try to fix anything and certainly too cold to try to tie bootlaces and go back outside to search for the spare stove in the sled. I lay there trying to warm my hands between my thighs. Fifteen minutes later, having taken the stove apart, I wiped the last of the telltale residue of dirty fuel onto the stove bag. The stove reassuringly burst into life and we ate hungrily.

The next day the Arctic ruined our plans for Peter to lead. Almost immediately after setting off, we encountered bigger pressure. Progress was painfully slow. After an hour and about a kilometre, we agreed it was faster if I went first, with Peter following up to help me get my sled over the ridges we encountered. Once a bit more weight came out of his sled he'd be leading half the time like he had down south. I knew Peter. He is a phenomenally determined, driven individual who wouldn't shirk his responsibility in any way. It was just better all round for the success of the expedition if I led and he seconded for now. It would change later.

The next couple of days I led as the expedition began to gain momentum and we crossed the 800 km to go mark, meaning that we were now 135 km off the north coast of Siberia. It was good to cross that milestone as mentally we'd tended to think of the journey as being 1000 km and so looking at it in those terms, we were almost 20 per cent in. That was a big chunk, but it had been hard-won.

Day 8 was again not that cold at −15° and we woke to a terrifying scene. A massive expanse of ocean had opened up just ahead of us. We had made camp the night before in amongst big pressure ridges but the snowy landscape that had lain ahead of us was now just a distant land on a far shore about 400 metres away. Worryingly, our tent was not 3 metres from the edge of the huge lead. Had it opened up another 3 metres to the south we would have been gone. We decided to move. If we couldn't find a way round it, we'd at least get further from its edge.

We decided to head east, as north-east was the general direction we were trying to head in, against the predominant drift of ice trying to take us towards the open Atlantic to the west. An hour or so later and we had managed a couple of kilometres east across incredibly obstructive terrain. It was demoralising working so hard just to head sideways, but we had no choice. Paddling across leads on the sleds relied on their being no more than 30 metres wide. That allowed us to tie the middle of our 60-m rope to the sleds so that the man following could pull the leader back if he got into trouble and the man in front could pull the follower to the other side once across, saving the need for both to paddle. After two hours we decided further searching was pointless. This open section could go on for miles.

Reluctantly we camped 10 metres or so from the edge of the lead. We'd have to revert to plan B, which involved waiting to see if the lead either closed up or froze over. The consensus was that at −25 degrees open ocean freezes over sufficiently to walk on in three or four hours. The temperature, however, was only −16° and this lead wasn't a lead as much as it was open ocean. The only choice was to sit it out for the night and reassess the situation in the morning. The worst part of any expedition is sitting out bad weather. It is demoralising, forcing a period of inactivity where you know that not only are you making no progress towards your goal, but that you are probably reducing your chances of making it as you consume valuable food and fuel.

By morning the lead and the temperature had plunged back to a more seasonable −30°. This made us feel safer about the strength of any ice we were about to cross, although it made dragging the sled more difficult as the snow we pulled it over would not melt at the interface with the runners. Such is the Arctic. The lead had narrowed but was still 100 metres or so of open water where we were. As I stared at the inky water, wondering whether it was likely to freeze over in a hurry, a head appeared in the middle of it, making me double-take. It was a seal, the first living thing I'd seen in the polar regions since the birds of the Spitsbergen trip years before. It lifted my spirits immeasurably – making the place feel less harsh and giving me hope that I could look forward to seeing some occasional wildlife in amongst the interminable white of the ice. After a minute or two of watching us, it disappeared and we headed off.

We again headed east, encouraged by the fact that the lead had at least reduced in size and that during the night we'd actually drifted 2 km north. After twenty minutes of searching we found a point where the lead had constricted to about 20 metres wide and decided the time had come to try paddling.

We moved as quickly as we could to keep warm, conscious of the fact we needed to do it properly as setting up the sleds to cross the sea – even a bit only 20 metres across – was potentially very dangerous. If one of us had fallen in it would have meant making camp, getting the stove going and trying to thaw our our only clothes. Clothes that even when dry and functioning normally only just made the bitter cold tolerable and life sustainable in this harshest of places.

It was time-consuming work attaching the sleds together, even though the mechanism for doing it was straightforward enough. First we had to find the two poles that threaded through the fibreglass housing in each sled and then wearing thick gloves attach the butterfly clips that held the poles secure. It was a fiddly job at room temperature but at −30°, cold hands began to numb after contact with the metal, even through several glove layers. The sleds made a pretty stable platform but it still seemed incredible to think that they would float with the massive weights still in them. We both held onto the rope as we gently inched them towards the jagged black edge of the lead and lowered them in.

Sure enough they floated, although there was only 10 cm or so of freeboard above the water level and I was still unsure of how they'd go with my 105 kg on top. I gingerly lowered myself on, spreading my weight between each pontoon as best as I could. The sleds lowered noticeably so that the freeboard was even less than before but I was still dry and afloat; that was the important thing. Peter handed me the aluminium snow-shovel and I began paddling, warily at first, but a bit more aggressively once confident of the stability of the sleds. Initially I made good progress across the open water, until I got halfway across where I encountered a lot of loose brash – lumps of ice about the size of basketballs or slightly bigger – just beneath the surface of the water. It was like trying to paddle through wet cement. After five minutes I had managed about a metre. I decided to try using a ski as a punt, pushing off against big pieces to try to propel myself forward. It was demoralising, exhausting work, and only slightly better than trying to paddle with the snow-shovel, especially given that the sleds presented a metre-wide bow to try to force through the ice-clogged water.

In desperation I tried using the ski to prod away as much of the ice as I could, but it was difficult to get leverage gripping the ski high up, balanced on the sleds, and the ice was extremely difficult to move. It was difficult, too, to put too much force into it as the ski would slip off the slippery surface of the ice and throw you dangerously off balance. Twice I almost fell in. I resorted to punting and paddling carefully.

Depressingly, by the time I had cleared a channel and turned to paddle with the shovel, much of the ice had closed back in again, blocking my path. It was ball-breaking and thoroughly depressing and the fact that it stood out as such in a place where ball-breaking is pretty much par for the course says something about how bad it was. After half an hour I still had 3 metres to go to reach the other side. Prod with the ski paddle, prod, paddle, prod, paddle . . . Finally, after a difficult manoeuvre to bring the sleds parallel to the far side to be able to climb out, I flopped onto the ice, exhausted.

My feet were completely numb from the inactivity of sitting on my haunches paddling for 45 minutes and my gloves were wet despite my being careful to try to avoid splashing. I stomped up and down to get some circulation back. Even when working hard, if the exercise is specific to certain muscles, others end up being deprived of blood flow and become numb. I had experienced it with my hands when climbing through the Dufek

Mountains in Antarctica, when my legs required all the oxygenated blood that my body had to give. Now it was the other way round.

I looked across the miserably small body of water I had just negotiated to see Peter swinging his arms, trying to maintain circulation in his hands before climbing onto the sleds for the crossing. All was well and he seemed to have got across okay, but when pulling the sleds out, his left foot slipped and plunged into the icy water up to his thigh.

At least we were both across. I worked hard to keep my focus, convincing myself that the past nine days had not been as incredibly slow as they felt, but that they and the painful crossing of our first wide lead were just the way things were in the Arctic. With the sastrugi down south, as the conditions became worse we compensated by lifting our game and, amazingly, covered some of our biggest distances in amongst the thin air and big sastrugi of the polar plateau. So it would have to be here. I put any thought of the 'fastest time to the Pole' attempt out of my mind. This trip was going to be about managing one problem at a time and taking each day as it came.

We sat on the sleds, ate some chocolate and stared around at the place. Large pressure ridges and chaotic blocks of contorted ice surrounded us. At least it sheltered us from the wind that had picked up. The wind was now at our backs and that could only be good. It may have taken us 45 minutes to negotiate a 20-metre lead but in that time we, and the whole landscape through which we travelled, may have moved ten times that distance north. I really hoped so.

14

On thin ice

Peter's foot was now becoming extremely cold from its dousing and it was time to move. I put on my skis again and stood up to move off, checking the compass for our bearing. It pointed to an area of pressure and I psyched myself up for the effort and got moving. We battled through the pressure for two or three hundred metres until, to our intense disappointment, we saw another sliver of black a few hundred metres away on a more open section of ice. It was another lead – this time about 15 metres across. The pressure all around us was enough of a deterrent to want to go in search of a better place to cross and without speaking we kicked off our skis and made ready the sleds for another crossing. It was a repeat performance of the last one, although my technique had improved slightly so that we were over in about 20 minutes of swearing and hard upper body workout.

We fell into the tent that night utterly spent after the mental and physical challenges that the day had thrown at us. I had to confess my head had begun to hang on spotting our fifth lead in near white-out conditions only half an hour before the end of the day. We decided to spend a bit of extra time getting across it just in case it opened up during the night and presented us with an ocean to cross in the morning, and once a safe distance the far side of it called it a day. It had been one of the toughest days of my life: ten hours of constant slog and focus to get through what the Arctic put in our way. We had climbed over constant pressure ridges that seemed like mountains to our tired bodies, and then just as we became warm from our exertions found ourselves again faced with dark, jagged leads.

In my sleeping bag with a warm cup of tea in my hand the world seemed less malevolent, although the stove had again blocked requiring a hand-numbing session of cleaning. In three months down south the stove didn't block once. Here on day 10 it had already blocked four times. My suspicions about the fuel were right – it was dirty for sure, but seemed to be manageable as long as we kept cleaning the stove every few days.

The stove was unbelievably important, providing precious temporary warmth before the heat escaped through the thin tent fabric out into the frigid Arctic night. Without fire you can't melt water to drink or to add to your dehydrated food and that would spell disaster.

I looked forward to the tent each night and to reading my diary, but never more so than that night. My partner Caroline had spent ages preparing a diary entry for me for the trip. Jokes, poems, brain teasers, little-known facts, photographs of stuff we'd done and places we'd been – it was great. I loved her very much and knew she'd been concerned about the trip since it had reared its head. She'd been concerned about the Great Victoria Desert crossing too but that was a cakewalk compared to this. I read my nightly brain teaser and after a few scribbled thoughts shut my diary, the cold being too much to write any more.

The following day the pressure was a bit easier and we crossed a huge expanse of open flat ice with not a ripple on it. It was reminiscent of South Australia's vast salt lakes – flat and white with a thin crust on the surface. Initially we approached it with a bit of trepidation, thinking it might be quite thin, but Peter stepped out onto it and decided it was solid enough. Not 50 metres in, he stopped suddenly and started backtracking, difficult with the sled on ropes. 'Get back!' he shouted, only narrowly avoiding falling in as a section fell away under his weight.

It must have been a huge area of ocean that had only recently frozen, and we gave the area of thin ice a wide berth and continued on. Still, we took the smooth surface of the ice gratefully, as it trended in the direction we wanted to head. Soon we were striding out across it and again I found myself thinking confidently about making the Pole in good time. If only I could hold on to that thought.

Three-quarters of the way across, my right binding crapped itself completely. Obviously it had fatigued over the last ten days and now my taking big strides across open ice was too much for it. I fossicked around in the sled for the leatherman and a spare binding. It would be cold enough on the hands doing a simple replacement, let alone trying to do a clever repair using bits of wire or rope. I decided I'd have a look at the broken one in the tent tonight to see if a repair was possible.

In the tent that night I looked at the binding and realised it was beyond repair. It was what I had feared when I'd first set eyes on Berwin bindings – just not strong enough for the task. They had been designed for cross-country skiing and a big mukluk-style boot. In their defence, the weather here was extremely cold, which tends to affect plastic badly, and the terrain and loads we were pulling meant we were putting a lot more force on them than they were probably designed for.

I had five spare bindings, so tried not to worry about it. If each lasted ten days then I should be okay. I'd just have to try to be careful. In any case I was in good spirits as our GPS showed we'd travelled 24 km – our best day yet. I went about cooking the evening meal while Peter changed into his spare thermal leggings and socks to warm up his left foot which was still numb. For some reason he'd been plagued by foot problems since the beginning of the trip, suffering badly with the cold and prolonged numbness long after he was in the relative warmth of the sleeping bag. Taking off his inner sock for the first time since the trip began he was concerned by what he saw. His right foot was white but functioning okay. His left foot wasn't so good, with several of the toes turning distinctly dark grey – frostbite. It was ironic – despite the extreme cold of the Arctic, our feet were better insulated than they had been down south.

We were both extremely concerned. The expedition had just begun to gain real momentum, especially with our having achieved our best distance to date, but his foot didn't look good. We both wore exactly the same equipment, so whatever was causing his foot problem was down to his ability to keep warm. The obvious answer was that it was because he was following rather than leading. Leading was desperately hard work but it at least served the purpose of keeping me warm. In fact most days I had to be careful not to overheat and sweat. I would often look round after chopping through a pressure ridge to see Peter throwing his arms downwards to try to get blood to his hands and stamping up and down to try to keep his feet warm. We obviously needed to do something or his frostbite would worsen and he'd be in strife.

We resolved that Peter would lead for a couple of hours the next day and I'd do the rest. The next day I finished my first session and Peter took the compass and set off on his lead. Fortunately it coincided with a section of slightly smaller pressure and the two of us started moving well.

Following is so much easier than leading. It was bliss to follow for a while, not having to be responsible for making the pace, navigating, chopping through the pressure ridges, or watching out for thin ice and bears. I was happy. The two of us were functioning like we had down south. Like a unit capable of achieving a record fastest time, sharing the leading and moving at a good speed.

At the next break, I asked Peter how his feet were and whether moving along at a steadier pace with him leading was keeping him warmer. He replied sullenly that it didn't seem to be making a difference and that he'd had no sensation in his left foot since breaking camp. We moved off, with me again leading, the weight of responsibility now firmly back on my shoulders. I did my couple of hours in amongst a labyrinth of interminable pressure, only getting a view of more than 5 metres ahead of me when I ascended a ridge before being plunged back down into the tumult at ground level. That session felt very lonely as I stared at my next obstacle wondering whether Peter would mentally and physically bounce back from the period of despondency he'd been in. He was normally unflappable and it worried me.

We sat on the sleds for our break and talked briefly about our predicament. We were both doing it tough. Peter was understandably preoccupied by his left foot, which had now been numb for a good six hours and he knew it was getting worse. My concern related to his ability to get through this, combined with my own level of resolve and physical tiredness. My frostbite injury had for some reason not troubled me as much as I'd thought it would – probably as I was doing a lot of chopping work with my arms and hands and that was keeping it warmer. It was the sheer unpleasantness of the place and the difficulty of the terrain that got to me.

That night we talked more. We'd done a good 20 km and that was all we needed as an average to make the Pole in around 46 or 47 days. Peter went about tending to his left foot, and to the two toes that were fast becoming black. I recalled my feelings only ten days from the South Pole, when I'd wondered whether I'd end up losing part of my right thumb. I knew how concerning it was, not only because of the loss of digits. The

bigger issue was the gangrene that can set in and cause septicemia or blood-poisoning, and that can be fatal.

We spent a cold night in −30 degrees and our sleeping bags
no longer seemed to be insulating us as well as they had been.
I put it down to the fact that they were progressively becoming
affected by moisture from our bodies that was freezing into the
lining of the bags and reducing their insulation capacity. Each
night when we made camp, with cold hands we would have to
literally fight to unroll the sleeping bags, which had frozen into
a tight ball with moisture from our bodies from the previous
night's sleep. Now part of my evening routine became breaking
up the ice that seemed to coalesce into large golf ball sized
lumps in the liner of the bag before I climbed into it. By
morning these would have again turned into an evenly distributed layer of moisture in our bags by our body heat during the
night and the process would repeat itself.

This increasing moisture didn't bode well for Peter's
recovery. If you're not keeping warm when you work and you're
not warm when you sleep, it doesn't leave many options for the
body to recover its strength or repair itself.

I made a final check to see that the gun was sitting in its cover
in the annex of the tent, within arm's reach. If I heard something I would need to react quickly and I half-unzipped its cover
for ease of access, just in case. It would have been nice to have
the gun closer but to have it in the tent with us would have
meant it stood a good chance of becoming clogged with ice
from moisture in our breath condensing and freezing inside the
barrel, and this would be enough to render it useless.

Despite a cold, unpleasant night, our routine gave our lives
structure and helped us keep mind and body together and our
sanity throughout our ordeal. We'd called friends and family
the night before to boost our spirits. These calls were always a
bit stilted, partly due to the strangeness of the circumstances,
the requirement for economy due to the limited batteries we

had and the fact that it was difficult to get intimate with loved ones when you sat about 60 cm away from someone who listened to everything you said.

I told Caroline that progress was good, and that spirits were good, really wanting to tell her that the environment was in fact extremely harsh and that I was concerned about Peter. She told me all was okay back home, and asked if we'd had any problems or seen any bears. I assured her we hadn't, not wanting to tell her that we'd already walked across several very thin sections of sea ice that had bowed under our weight and had quite a few things happen to us already, but thankfully no bears, although I'd love to see one under normal circumstances. Peter spoke to his wife Beth and mentioned his frostbite and his concerns about it. I have to confess I listened to his words to see if I could pick any underlying reasons for his frame of mind. But I couldn't pick up anything beyond the fact that he mentioned to Beth how cold he found it and how the terrain prevented him getting into any kind of rhythm.

Our brief calls always left us dissatisfied but we only had enough batteries for about 4 hours' worth of calls for the whole 50 days if we were lucky. Our decision to forgo the solar panel we'd had down south was based on there not being enough northern sunlight, but looking back I'm sure it would have worked fine, especially as solar panels don't need much direct sunlight to work, and they actually work much better in the cold than in the heat.

Inside five minutes we had made our calls and there was complete silence in the tent with just the sound of the wind gently flapping the fabric. We lay back in our bags analysing every word of our respective conversations. I had told Caroline how sensitive you become to bad news when on the ice, and so she never gave me any. It only served to have me try to read into her choice of words to judge if all was really okay.

The following day the pressure was bigger again, so big that even after almost two weeks of well-honed pathfinding technique I couldn't find a decent way to head directly north, being forced instead to head east and then west round huge walls of icy rubble 7 or 8 metres high. It was soul-destroying but we were slowly edging north and significantly the drift of the ice had been kind to us, only having sent us backwards for three of our thirteen days. Amazingly, we were still on track.

In the morning, the whole place was a mixture of pressure and open channels of water. After two hours we were only 600 metres or so from where we'd made camp. Ground was hard to win as we went round and round, doubling back on ourselves and taking chances in desperation to get through – jumping leads, and hurling the sled off the top of pressure ridges and climbing down after it. My skis regularly snagged, causing me to stumble. In frustration I took them off, making travel over the pressure ridges far easier, until my foot plunged through the ice into water. On one occasion it sank in up to my thigh when in a trough between two piles of icy rubble. Quickly I threw my weight forward, grabbing a big block of ice, only narrowly managing to pull myself up before I plunged through alto-gether. It was desperate.

A pattern developed in response to the terrain we found our-selves in. I would put my skis back on until the frustration of stumbling over blocks of ice got the better of me again and I'd throw caution to the wind and remove them. The terrain now consisted of huge pressure ridges interspersed with short sections of ocean clogged with tightly packed blocks of brash ice. The need to get through things made you experiment with techniques and I found that if the water was filled with enough large chunks of ice it would support your body weight as long as you had your skis on and moved quickly. Too slowly and you'd begin to sink.

The pressure ridges, too, could be negotiated by getting your body weight on the far side of the ridge and using your body as a counter-balance to pull the sled up the ramp created with the pickaxe. By the end of the day, ten hours of travel saw us cover 17 kilometres, but the price was utter mental and physical exhaustion and another Berwin binding giving up the ghost. To add insult to injury, I had to carry it, my environmental morals not allowing me to jettison it in the pristine Arctic wilderness.

Somehow each day we'd lift ourselves to the task again and again, putting up with the cold of the tent and dampness and increasing discomfort of our sleeping bags to spend the whole day battling in amongst the pressure. I would hold on to any positive thought I possibly could, and a significant one was the fact that although we were drifting it was mainly west/north-west and not south as we'd feared may be the case. While we slept on our fourteenth night we drifted an utterly amazing 18.5 kilo-metres – just over 13 km west and about 5 km north – a fantastic result and incredible to contemplate. After five days of slightly northerly drift, though, it began to become something I'd rely on to supplement our daily distances and I had a stern word with myself for lowering my guard. I knew if I came to expect a gain I was setting myself up for a fall as soon as the ice started moving us backwards, as I was sure it would at some stage.

Peter's frostbite, meanwhile, was getting worse. Two of his toes were black as coal and he was getting increasingly worried about what to do with them. I'd read up a lot about frostbite since the South Pole trip in anticipation of having to manage my old thumb injury throughout the trip. Unbelievably it had been okay. I had blackened fingertips on my right hand as usual, as being right-handed I tended to expose that hand more, but no deep tissue frostbite as far as I could tell, although I seldom checked my feet. Peter had been immersing his left foot in warm water each night to try to thaw his frozen flesh and stimulate some circulation, sitting up and putting his rancid foot into his food bowl, it being the only container he had. He'd then clean out the bowl with a bit of snow and use it for breakfast the following day. Hygiene standards were not high.

Even in amongst the misery we had to laugh at the comical nature of what we were putting ourselves through. Peter bent at a funny angle to immerse his foot in his food bowl, dislodging ice and rime from the roof of the tent down onto both of us as he manoeuvred. We both laughed long and hard. The cold was desperate but it produced some funny moments. I couldn't help but laugh at the icicles that had accumulated on Peter's balaclava. He looked at me and laughed even louder. 'Talk about the pot calling the kettle black.' I apparently had a silly icy protuberance emanating from my nose. A frozen lance of snot, to be precise. 'You don't need the bloody gun, Tim, you could kill a bear with that,' Peter joked.

Cooking each night, too, would create steam in the tent worse than any white-out conditions that we might meet out on the ice, such that we'd have to wait a few minutes before it cleared enough to see what we were doing. Sitting in a white-out in the tent was one of the more ridiculous scenarios that faced us each day.

We lived in a world full of a myriad of 'learning experiences' as I jokingly referred to the day-to-day problems we'd face – broken bindings, gruelling workload, dirty fuel, thin ice and huge pressure ridges, but there was one really serious problem – Peter's condition. Other than a few fleeting glimpses of the fantastic teamwork that had led us to the world record in Antarctica, our relationship was being put under increasing strain by the circumstances.

I'd led every day of the trip bar a couple of hours and it was beginning to get me down. The pressure of having to make the pace and do all the stuff that leading requires, without the confidence of knowing whether Peter was ever going to improve enough to make it either mentally or physically, was utterly demoralising. I went from feeling philosophical about it to feeling very bitter. The topic of my leading and his seconding never came up unless I brought it up and it was starting to get to me.

I didn't blame him for his frostbite, of course, nor would I wish that on anyone. What did annoy me, however, was that he tended to retreat into his shell and say nothing about our current situation, which obviously wasn't going to be tenable forever. I felt I was busting my balls to get us through the trip: navigating, trail-breaking and, to my mind, keeping the mental focus for both of us to give the expedition its momentum.

There was a tremendous weight of expectation on us too – from the kids at the Smith Family we were trying to help, to our friends and relatives, our main sponsor Brett Blundy from Sanity Music, and the PM and Zaz Shackleton. It was a hell of a position to be in.

You get to know one another's mind very well on these kinds of journeys as the extreme nature of what you're doing lays bare all societal pretensions and strips life back to basics. Food, warmth, survival and a determination to reach a goal are what it's all about. In fact you often know how the other will react to a situation better than they themselves know. The good thing about this is that you can draw energy from the other and help them out when they're down. The flip side is that you know pretty much how much mental and physical resolve they've got left in the tank when things are bad and this has the opposite effect. If something's wrong with them, then basically something's wrong with you too, as their problems and doubts prey on your mind.

Peter functions brilliantly physically and mentally if he's moving forward, even if he's slowly chipping away at the task in hand. He is very goal-driven and relishes forward momentum both to keep him warm and to keep his mind from dwelling on the pain and suffering. The North Pole doesn't allow you this. It toys with you. Just as you get some momentum going, the fickle ocean currents can drift you backwards all of the distance you have made that day. Climbing onto your sled to paddle across open ocean involves taking off your skis, attaching the sleds together for stability, getting the rope out and taking off your outer gloves to enable you to paddle. You cross a section, spend ten minutes readjusting everything to get moving again to warm up, and 20 metres later behind a wall of ice there is another lead lurking that forces you to repeat the demoralising and dangerous procedure. All the while your heat reserves are being sapped by the cold and the clock ticks on.

∧ ∧ ∧

The next day my mood swung again. We found ourselves on a recently frozen section of ocean, as it turned out about 10 km in extent, judging from how long we spent on it. I marvelled at the scenery through which we travelled and found it hard to remember the circumstances that had led me to be here. I felt strangely out of body, like it wasn't really me walking out across this vast wilderness. It felt exciting to be heading off towards an uncertain destiny, and it was great to get the heart pumping and actually make progress again. I lengthened my stride as a wave of euphoria came over me – things were okay again.

All good things must, of course, come to an end and by early afternoon the open flat sea ice had become a mixed landscape of runways of good ice, criss-crossed by canals of open water, requiring paddling or bridging with the sled to get across. As we moved so too did the whole landscape, the ice slabs growling and creaking as they shunted up against one another. As I looked to the horizon there was no stable point of reference to judge which bits were moving and which bits remained still as we rushed from one unstable piece of ice to the next as if the bit we were headed for represented something better than what we'd just left.

Several times we discovered to our dismay that the bit we rushed onto was a tiny slab of ice with leads opening on all sides of it, no bigger than your caricatured tropical island complete with its single palm. And so we leapt across channels that grew before our eyes on to the next piece of ice, occasionally breaking away the thin edges of slabs and immersing a booted foot in icy water. Adrenaline flushed through the system. It was one of the most dangerous environments I have ever been in. A fall through the ice or into a lead would mean serious hypothermia at best, and at worst death, given our limited ability to attempt a rescue and the impossibility of setting up the tent to get warm on this fractious thin layer of swirling ice that stretched for kilometres in all directions.

After over three hours we were finally able to stop, reaching the relative safety of a 5-metre-high ridge of old pressure, breathing deeply from the exertion and pumping adrenaline, legs burning with the lactic acid. I never thought I'd be pleased to reach a high wall of pressure, but its thicker ice was reassuring after the thin veneer of moving ice we'd just come from.

I looked down at my feet and realised that in all the hurrying my right binding had again broken and was hanging on only by a thin shard of plastic. 'For fuck's sake,' I muttered to myself. Peter had the leatherman in his pocket and offered to change the binding over for a spare to save my exposing my right hand. I gratefully accepted. As we concentrated on the repair I suddenly became aware that something was moving behind him. I stood transfixed as a vast slab of ice appeared out of the sea, creaking and squealing as if alive, being pushed up at an angle of 45 degrees by some combination of immense forces. Here the ice was thicker, perhaps 50 centimetres, with colour gradations from translucent white, to turquoise and blue hues. I watched, awe-inspired, for about 30 seconds before I realised it was coming our way and we needed to move.

Peter hurriedly finished the repair and we moved out of its path and watched as it lifted further and further up, until it had gone from horizontal to a height of 3 or 4 metres, at which point a slab about 3 metres long broke off under its own weight. The slab fell onto the ice, punching a hole through and exposing the dark ocean. It was an amazing sight to behold. For all of its danger and hardship, this was a truly surreal and spectacular environment through which to travel.

∧ ∧ ∧

Day 15 came and we had covered 300 km at an average of about 20 km a day. I regarded it as a real landmark. Now we were getting stuck into the guts of the journey and with every step we took further north we not only increased our chances of making it to the Pole, but decreased the chances of meeting bears, which tended as a rule to stay south of the 84-degree line, according to Boyarsky.

Despite the first few days of relative warmth, the weather was becoming progressively colder. I awoke at 5.30 am on day 16 and the transformation of the tent into an icy cave was complete. Long icicles of frost hung from the roof in a layer several centimetres thick. The temperature was bitter, and I lay there summoning up my strength to get moving. I unzipped my bag and sat up, my body heat escaping into the tent almost immediately, warming the frost layer on the roof and causing it to drip onto us. I pulled on my jacket, hitting the side of the tent with my arm and dislodging great clumps of frost that cascaded down on Peter. 'Piss off,' he muttered at the conditions rather than at me. We pulled on our clothes, soft the day before and as usual now stiff with frozen sweat.

Peter's foot was worse again. He had barely been able to get any sensation in the toes of his left foot during the night, which was very unusual as normally after a hot meal you would experience at least a brief spell of overheating in your bag before cooling down. I would rely on this flush of heat to force warmth into any extremities that might need it. I'd been lucky. The only extremities I'd ever had problems with had been the fingers on the right hand and in particular the serious deep tissue frostbite to my right thumb.

I emerged from the tent and the temperature was off the

thermometer, meaning it was somewhere below −30°. Beyond that I wasn't interested. We got moving and I again got ready to lead. I walked round to the back of the tent to pull out the tent stakes and there in front of me were some huge bear prints, not 3 metres away. Not only were the pads of the pawprint clear but so too were the claws. They must be fresh. The question was, had they appeared during the night? It didn't bear thinking about. Our tracks were clearly visible away to the side of the bear's but I don't think I could have missed them when we made camp in the clear mid-afternoon light. I got the gun and followed the tracks 20 metres or so before they disappeared into some pressure. I was sure I hadn't seen them the night before when we made camp. It was time to move.

We packed the sleds, keeping an eye out as we went. Peter put the flare pistol around his waist just in case. A flare fired at a bear's feet will scare him away, probably for good, but if not it at least gives time to get the gun ready in the event of an attack. I spent much of that morning wondering why the bear had left us alone. Perhaps it had already eaten. Perhaps the tent and sleds were of no interest. Maybe the prints had been there already, but I'm sure they hadn't. It was exciting to think he was out there somewhere nearby as we moved along. Ironic, too, that he had appeared just after we'd crossed Boyarsky's 84° north.

The pressure again was mountainous as we moved onwards and I took out the pickaxe and swung it angrily at the ice in front of me, cleaving a huge block in two with one massive blow. It felt like a victory and I again broke the halves into fragments that I could build into a ramp for climbing up and through the gap I'd made in the wall. Peter was 20 metres back and becoming noticeably slower with his injury, but stoically battling on, saying little but no doubt with plenty on his mind as he fought his own private battle.

The pressure was so large and continuous that despite negotiating our way round big walls of ice wherever possible, every

20 minutes or so we had to smash our way up and over one and pull the protesting sled with us all the way. To save time I decided to keep the pickaxe to hand by strapping it on top of my sled. The leads were still present but thankfully small enough that we hadn't had to paddle for the last couple of days. I didn't miss it.

I arrived at the face of a wall, unable to find a roundabout route to avoid it. I decided I was going to have to build a ramp and then punch a hole in the top and pull the sled through hand over hand. At the base of the wall I planted my ski stocks and shuffled back to the sled to grab the pickaxe. It wasn't there. I had repeated the exercise of chopping through pressure at least a hundred times and was sure I'd strapped it securely on to the top of the sled. But it was missing. Peter was a hundred metres or so away and I shouted for him to look out for it as he approached, just in case it had fallen off in the last few minutes. I thought back to when I'd last used it. It was at least 20 minutes, maybe as much as half an hour before. I was distraught. The pickaxe was the most important item of equipment for getting through the pressure. Without it we were alone and at the mercy of the pressure that could pretty much determine which way we went. Either that or we would have a much, much harder time climbing up and over it. It was already plenty tough enough.

Peter hadn't seen it in the last hundred metres. The only option was to go back and look for it. Now the choices were whether we both went and whether we took the sleds. We decided to take the gun and a bit of food and leave the sleds positioned atop a high piece of pressure, their position marked with the GPS. I delved into my sled and got the GPS out, marking the sleds using its 'man overboard' emergency function, a legacy of its originally having been developed for sailing.

We searched for over fifteen minutes but could see nothing. It was all we needed. Peter was already suffering badly. Now I'd lost the pickaxe and we'd left the sleds behind to go looking for it. Searching for the pickaxe told me a couple of things pretty quickly. First, it showed me how relatively easy it was to cover ground without having the 135 kg sled in tow. Second, it made me realise how completely reliant we were on the sleds for our survival and made us feel extremely exposed.

We stepped over a few leads, bridging the gaps more easily on our skis. Now we were a good kilometre and a half from the sleds – more than we would have covered in twenty minutes of manhauling. Any one of the leads we stepped over could have opened wider in the interim, preventing our getting back to the sleds. It was a very dangerous thing to do, but it saved us valuable time and energy and, quite honestly, I couldn't face back-tracking with the sleds. It was bad enough going forward. Unless we spotted the pickaxe on the way back to the sleds, though, it was gone.

We didn't. It was an absolute disaster and I was furious with myself. Grim prospect though it was, I could see myself leading for much of the remainder of the trip, but without the pickaxe it would now be even harder.

That night in the tent the mood was at an all-time low. Peter was despondent and so was I. These trips rely on physical and mental teamwork to boost one another's inevitable bad moods and bouts of depression. Now neither of us had anything much to give.

Peter broke the stalemate. 'Look, the pickaxe is one thing, my frostbite is quite another. I've had no sensation in the toes of my left foot for the best part of a week and I know my moving slowly has got to the point where it's becoming unworkable. I've got two black toes that I doubt will recover and I'm worried about gangrene and septicemia.' I agreed, intent on listening to what else was going to be said. 'I'd understand if you didn't want to continue.' The words carried great weight and I couldn't believe what Peter had just said. Strangely, they didn't come as a great surprise.

My first reaction was anger. 'What do you mean, *me* not want to continue?!' I screamed. 'It's your decision, not mine. Don't think that after all the effort I've put in I'm going to be the one to call it a day. Christ, you must be fucking mad.' I calmed myself down. 'Look, I'm feeling good about things. Angry with myself about the pickaxe, sure, but otherwise okay. You're right – it's your injury that's the issue. If you want to stop it's your decision, not mine. I'm not going to take responsibility for being the one to pull the plug.'

I thought about what had been said. I think Peter was doing what he thought was the right thing. By giving me the call, he at least allowed me to say that as a team we weren't going to make it to the Pole. In a moment of frustration I'd reacted as if he was trying to get off the hook by getting me to make the decision. Either way, it was a tough call.

I was confused. I wanted to continue. Quite honestly, I'd never given any consideration to the idea of not continuing. Then again, I didn't want to continue the way we had been going, with me doing much of the work and wearing myself down with concern as to whether Peter was going to be able to continue or not. It was a grim prospect, too, thinking about the mental and physical focus I'd need to muster in order to spend the next 30 days leading through an endless maze of ice with no respite.

'Look, I think you've handled your frostbite incredibly well. But remember, I had it too down south and we managed that – and look at what we achieved.' Even as I said the words, I recalled the desperate feeling of being alone with such a serious injury in such an unremitting cold place, knowing that each day you were going to force your tired body on through the conditions that had caused your frostbite in the first place. But I continued, trying to put a positive spin on things. 'We're a team and we can get through this trip. We'll just build in warming up your foot into our routine each day, in the morning and evening with warm water from the stove.' Peter agreed to give it a go, and I respected his ability to keep pushing himself.

The terrain the next day was tumultuous. It was surreal going through the motions, unsure now as to whether we would continue or not. I would ascend to the top of a pressure ridge and all ahead was chaos. Like a city after an earthquake, except the debris was ice and the forces that had caused it were current and wind. Without the aid of the pickaxe the sled was even less manageable than before, like trying to pull a large filing cabinet full of cement bags over 5-metre-high obstructions.

We toiled for a long tough day, skirting round the pressure, without the wherewithal to punch through. Still Peter had no sensation in his foot, but it was good at least to be moving. Unlike every other day, now I dreaded reaching the tent for fear of the discussion we might have.

'If it doesn't improve tomorrow I don't think I can go on.' I'd never heard Peter utter such words – they were the words of a man who could not see a way forward. His injury was serious enough not to continue – not for fear of the toes he might lose but ultimately for the more serious issues of gangrene and possible blood-poisoning. With a month to go, his condition might become critical long before we ever reached the Pole.

Quite honestly, at that precise moment I didn't want the trip to continue either. I was feeling bloody-minded about it. If we continued on as we had been and had ultimately made it, it would have been largely based on my effort and not Peter's. He had led only once in three weeks, and even though I'd seen a glimmer of the old stubborn resilience that I had come to expect from him, he now seemed a spent force. Peter is fiercely proud, with a will of iron. This time, though, he was not himself. He didn't say it, but I don't think he would have wanted to reach the Pole under these circumstances either – taking a back seat. He'd just have to accept that on this occasion he just wasn't going to make it.

The next day we found ourselves in awful terrain and our stopping now appeared a foregone conclusion. Mountainous broken walls of ice with open sections of ocean in amongst them that we stumbled into. You couldn't move with your skis on as the ground consisted of broken uneven blocks of ice. Any decision to remove your skis left you open to the possibility of falling through the slushy thin ice in between and into the frigid water below. It was hellish and from the tops of the highest ridges of ice we could see it was unrelenting where we were headed.

As the writing had potentially been on the wall for a couple of days we'd taken the precaution of letting Victor know the state of play regarding Peter's injury. We'd also let him know that the fuel had been dirty, causing problems throughout, and asked him to bring some more with him, just in case. He had mobilised the helicopter a few days earlier, which luckily was in Sredniy anyway. They were about 400 km away and we knew that we could attract their attention with the flare gun once we could see them.

We lay in the tent, having said all there was to say and examined all the available facts to death. A final decision needed to be made and Peter needed to make it. To my mind it wasn't just a case of whether he could go on or not, it was a case of whether he could go on as a participating member of the team. It was difficult. Either way was going to be tough on both of us.

The atmosphere was tense as Peter sat up in his bag, propping himself up on his arm. 'Sorry, Tim, this is one of the hardest things I've ever had to do, but I just don't think my foot is going to recover.' I muttered a response under my breath. Quite honestly I didn't really have anything to say. I was desperately disappointed, but I knew it was coming and nodded solemnly. Peter picked up the satellite phone and dialled the numbers. Boyarsky answered, Peter gave him our GPS coordinates and agreed to phone through our position every couple of hours, given that we could drift a long way between the time of our call and when the helicopter came. Evidently Boyarsky tried to get Peter to reconsider his decision, but I heard Peter say, 'No, it's not possible' and 'We've tried that' before finishing the call. The long-range forecast was good and the helicopter could be with us within seven or eight hours.

I could have cried. It was so bloody sad to have to stop after putting in so much effort to get to where we were. We lay there, saying little. Only hours earlier I had again been on a high, convinced we were on our way to the Pole, having covered over 400 km. Now the unfamiliar sense of failure pervaded the tent. It was the opposite of everything I liked about attempting these trips, and I wanted to be away from the place as quickly as possible.

'You could always go on alone,' said Peter, breaking the silence. I could barely speak, I was so angry at the suggestion. It was all well and good saying that. We had a cash deposit sitting with Boyarsky for a pull-out and we were about to use all of it to get Peter out. My going on alone would have been an incredibly dangerous proposition. It is one thing setting out on a journey alone and making contingencies. It is quite another to decide on a change in plan halfway through perhaps the toughest journey in the world. My single sled would have been too unstable to cross leads, for a start. Had I been attempting the journey solo, I would have had floating stabilisers to make such crossings possible. My sled on its own would have been a death trap, and without help a fall into the water would have meant a quick death, as befell the Japanese explorer Hyoichi Kohno. Any solo journey really needed to employ dry-suit tech-nology at the very least to enable survival after a fall through the ice.

It was a pretty open-and-shut case based on that fact alone, but on top of that there were other things that preyed on my mind. Psychologically we had each taken responsibility for

certain aspects of the technology to do with the trip. Peter concentrated on communications and the video camera, having
developed a knack with the idiosyncrasies of the satellite phone.
I concentrated on the GPS, still camera and stoves. There was
too much information to download from him to be sure I didn't
miss anything.

Yet, over the next six or seven hours, I tortured myself about
it. I knew I could make it but thought back to what had gone
before. My mood swung between anger at Peter, anger with
myself for not considering going on and guilt at the prospect of
stopping. I had never been in that situation before. Peter had
made his decision, now I needed to make mine. I was into
testing myself, that's for sure. But going to the Arctic to push
the envelope is one thing; to die out there on your own because
you made a stupid decision was quite another. I remembered
again Shackleton's letter to his wife when he turned back just
100 miles from the South Pole. It would be madness to go on.
I knew what my decision would be.

Despite this, I was still considering my options when I heard
the distant clatter of an engine. It disappeared and then returned
again, coming and going with the wind. It was definitely the
helicopter. Suddenly I felt rushed, as if the last seven hours
hadn't been enough time to consider the only option I really
had. We put on our boots and left the tent and as the helicopter
neared, fired the flare gun. The copter landed near us, hovering
over the flattest area it could find a few hundred metres away.

We pulled the tent down, chucked the things in our sleds and
climbed aboard. Boyarsky suggested checking Peter's frostbite
to give his opinion on how bad it was. Peter declined. The
decision was made, and that was that. I have to say I would have
done the same thing myself. If the injury's bad enough in your
mind to stop, then that's all there is to it. The helicopter lifted
off and it seemed like we'd been in it just yesterday rather than
almost three weeks earlier.

As we flew off I looked out on what we would have had to face, had we continued on. It looked easy from here but I knew it was an illusion. It reminded me of the old surfboat rowing days where the surf always looked deceptively small from the comfort of the beach. When out in the boat that same surf would have transformed into growling, malevolent walls of grey water and I knew the same was the case here, but probably multiplied twenty times over.

We arrived back at Sredniy and took our first shower in almost three weeks. The sensation was familiar to me, except that last time I had experienced it was at the South Pole having broken the records for fastest time to the Pole and, covering 1600 km, the record for the longest unsupported journey. This was different. This felt bitter. I knew it would take me a long time to recover.

Beyond the Poles

So what's happened since the North Pole trip? Well, we returned to Australia and Peter's foot luckily recovered as far as I know. In the few months after we returned we kept in contact and I know he didn't lose his toes or develop gangrene. He mentioned to me, however, that he now has permanent nerve damage in his toes, which are still numb.

We've lost touch since the trip, not because of what happened up north, but mainly because the thing that brought us together in the first place was the journeys. Peter has decided to hang up his polar expedition boots and so we have less in common than we used to. We always worked well together as a team on the trips but tended to lead quite different lives when we got back home.

The legacy of what happened up north is that I feel very upbeat about things, for a few reasons. First, falling short of the North Pole has given me a sense of belief in the rhetoric I've been spouting since the South Pole trip. Stuff like striving to achieve your goals being important, regardless of the outcome, that even attempting dreams is an achievement in itself, and that not achieving your goal at least serves to demonstrate you're pushing your own envelope.

I feel positive, too, about the relationship I have continued to have with the Smith Family welfare organisation and in particular their 'Learning for Life' program, which aims to help underprivileged kids help themselves via the provision of grants for education. At time of writing I am a strategy committee member for the Smith Family in South Australia and enjoy the role.

The North Pole trip didn't end quite the way I'd hoped but at least our sponsor Brett Blundy got his trip to the Pole. He was understanding of what happened. He is a major risk-taker himself and always knew the potential for things to go awry. I had the option to fly there with him, but I only want to see the North Pole if I've got there under my own steam. Brett took the flag bearing the names of all our sponsors who supported the trip – and by association, the Smith Family – all the way to the Pole and planted it there for us. The publicity and money raised went to support the Learning for Life program. To everyone who supported us directly and via sponsorship of the journeys I am eternally grateful.

The journeys I've undertaken have taught me lots of things; about myself, about polar travel and about life. As I write now, my North Pole experience is one tinged with a sense of sadness at the outcome. The overriding feeling I have is one of optimism. If someone had said to me ten years ago that I would break the world record to the South Pole and achieve the greatest unsupported distance ever covered in Antarctica, or be trekking across Spitsbergen keeping an eye out for polar bears, I wouldn't have believed them.

I look at all the trips as having been successful. They are the most ambitious journeys I could think of and I'd rather 'fail' trying for really ambitious things than succeed with a series of easily achievable challenges.

I guess I could make the trips more manageable if I relaxed some of the ground rules, for example, have a food drop or two flown in or use a kite to pull me along, but that would change the whole nature of the thing. Attempting these journeys unsupported is for me the most important thing. Back in the heroic era in the first quarter of the twentieth century, the likes of Shackleton, Mawson, Amundsen and Scott all undertook journeys where they knew that there was little or no chance of rescue if things went wrong. We by comparison live in a world of improved communications and technology where the possibility of rescue at least exists. If explorers from the heroic era were the proverbial iron men travelling in their wooden boats, then perhaps we as modern day polar explorers are wooden men in iron boats.

However, I think the significance of twenty-first century communications and technology can be overstated. For 500 km of our journey to the South Pole, for example, the sastrugi meant that rescue for us was out of the question as no aircraft would have been able to land to help us. No helicopters operate in Antarctica due to its immense size. Rescue also relies on your being in a position to make a distress call. In many cases that just isn't possible either. I remember Kohno, the famous Japanese explorer who died trekking across the ice of the Arctic Ocean a few years ago. He had an emergency beacon but for some reason was unable to activate it – probably after a fall through the ice. Remember the story, too, of the mountain guide Rob Hall who died atop Everest whilst on the sat phone to his wife. They knew exactly where he was, they just couldn't get to him because of the altitude and the weather.

The chances of rescue then can be extremely limited, and modern journeys of exploration can still be immensely dangerous and committing. Personally, though, I feel that to compensate for the fact that the possibility of rescue at least exists and to break new ground, it is important to try to do things as independently as possible. The more challenging the journey, the greater chance you have of discovering something new about the world and your place in it and the greater the satisfaction you get if you achieve your goal. Although a direct comparison is impossible to make with the journeys of old, unsupported journeys at least serve to recreate some of the hardship and challenge the early explorers might have felt; the journeys are as unadulterated as we can make them in the 'modern era'. They are important for me because one of the most difficult things about polar travel, mentally and physically, is the effect that the workload of pulling a heavy sled has on your body weight, strength and your ability to keep warm.

Another important realisation, reinforced time and time again during my three polar journeys, is that you need to do the trips for your own reasons, and those reasons have to be the right ones. Unlike sport, there is no cheering crowd to boost your energy or morale. Polar journeys are a lonely, often solitary, unglamorous pursuit. When embarking on any serious trip you need to have real cast-iron reasons or goals in your mind for why you are there. Otherwise, when times get tough beyond what you thought possible you will forget why you are there. It is not enough to say, 'I want to reach the Pole' – that is not a reason. It is a goal, behind which lie other more personal reasons, whatever they are. I had a great childhood. I travelled widely and got the opportunity to experience many things growing up in the tropics with my parents. More than that though, childhood seemed to be full of interesting characters who took some interest in what I was up to. I look back now and can see that this came from the combination of growing up as a foreign kid in the Far East and returning to the UK each year where I was surrounded by friends and family. It all made me feel part of something much bigger. I still miss the excitement of childhood.

Back in the UK's relatively structured world at the age of eighteen, I felt like a displaced person, the Far East a mere memory. This sense of isolation has always made me feel most at home travelling, meeting new people and finding myself in new situations where there's a bit of unpredictability. In fact I've always felt most alive when doing it. I know now there's a big difference between living and really being alive, that's for sure.

So my sense of adventure may or may not have something to do with trying to 'rediscover' aspects of my childhood. Whatever the case, growing up overseas undoubtedly fuelled my inquisitive nature, my confidence, desire to see more of the world's out-of-the-way places as well as feeling comfortable with taking a few educated risks. Strangely though, my parents don't seem to give themselves any credit for nurturing this adventurous spirit. My mother always wonders where the adventurous genes come from. She's sure it isn't her, and is quick to remind me that Dad only ever went camping once and on that occasion wore his pyjamas. Personally I don't think they give themselves enough credit.

As life has gone on I've just pushed the boundaries of what I attempt further and further to find that buzz of excitement.

Perhaps there's an element of needing to be recognised – something I got from sport and living in foreign places and am now trying to recreate by doing trips. Perhaps it's basic inquisitiveness, an enjoyment of camaraderie (despite the fact that polar trips can appear very singular pursuits) and a love of excitement, and unpredictability. This applies not only to doing the trips but to planning them as well, where because of the unusual nature of what you're attempting you find yourself in some strange and exciting situations that can be journeys in their own right before the literal one has even started. It is exciting to see what providence throws your way as you start planning a big journey.

Breaking down boundaries is one of the most enjoyable aspects. I've often found myself in boardrooms surrounded by sombre-looking people in suits, asking if they'll help fund a madcap polar expedition. It's a blast; seeing that spark of recognition as they warm to my enthusiasm for the idea and identify with the idosyncratic collection of reasons for attempting it in the first place, and leave half an hour later feeling like I've just met up with old friends.

Expeditions for me are all about challenging myself and being different. I have always enjoyed expressing my individuality and inevitably a major driver behind my expeditions is ego. I don't see anything wrong with this. Some people wear the latest fashions, some pierce themselves and drive cars with big spoilers. I personally enjoy trying to do things that no-one has done – a combination of self-expression and finding out what I'm capable of. I've tried my hand at lots of sports with varying degrees of success, travelled widely, crossed deserts, lived with isolated Mayan Indian communities and cycled across Mexico. Almost without exception such experiences foster a resourceful, strong side of your personality. Challenges tend to bring this out, which I love.

I enjoy expeditions too because although they can be brutal and very complex, serious affairs, they give you the opportunity to try ideas that are childlike in their simplicity: I want to climb to the top of this, or get across to the other side of that. It's particularly satisfying when people say, 'You can't' or 'That isn't possible', which of course makes it all the more appealing.

Isn't it ironic, then, that growing up, we find out about ourselves and the world around us by trying things and learning through our experiences. Somewhere along the line, though, the responsibilities that represent adulthood seem to suppress this 'give it a go' spirit, replacing it with an increasing reliance on second-hand sources, and the opinions of others.

That spirit often lies dormant for years, until one day we wake up and look back with regret and no real answer as to why we didn't find time to try to realise at least one or two dreams. In many cases it's because we're too often told that things are not possible for us, or not as simple as they appear to be. In some cases this is true, but it's dangerous to lump everything together in the same basket. If you do you'll find yourself not trying anything new or challenging at all. After all, if the complexities of attempting to walk to the South Pole do turn out to be as great as everyone says – so what! The reward is that much greater if you make it.

The memories of my polar journeys are vivid as I write, but perhaps more than these memories, I now live with their life-changing legacy.

The Poles are utterly awesome: vast and unforgiving – but I wouldn't want them to be any other way. They are nature on a massive scale that dwarfs anything humans can muster. I take comfort from the fact that these places still exist and that we have not been able to subjugate them as we have so many other wild places on the planet. It seems ironic, though, to think that we might be able to destroy them without even setting foot there. Global warming, caused by emissions into the atmosphere thousands of kilometres away, may perhaps be their biggest enemy.

I've experienced great camaraderie with Peter and Ed on the trips. Going through the emotional highs and lows, you form a bond that you never forget – and I valued those moments even as they were happening. I've also experienced the sensation that I've heard others talk of, where in your moment of need it is as if someone is there with you – and I don't mean your travelling companions. I mean when you are in a crisis, struggling to keep going and find yourself having to dig deep, you feel as though someone is there with you. I've thought about this a lot, and I attribute it to being in the presence of that part of your own personality that under normal circumstances you are unaware of.

I've learnt that with all the extreme physical discomfort and danger of these places, survival is as much mental as it is physical. The journeys involve the slowest means of travel imaginable, across some of the vastest areas of wilderness on the planet. The juxtaposition of the two means that it is important to break down the journeys into small, manageable portions to be able to get through them. More than a fleeting contemplation of the whole task would leave you unable to muster the energy to keep going. You go to these places and you just do what you can – nothing more. Antarctica and the Arctic will both take what you have to give and then some. It is only the imposition of your own routine upon the vastness of these places that allows you to keep body and soul together.

This mentality I have brought back with me to 'everyday life', whatever that is. I use it to break down large tasks into manageable ones, complete with their own discrete milestones and achievements. People who meet me for the first time these days tend to think I am very driven and task-based, always aiming for some milestone or another. If anything, my fear now is that I run my life like an expedition, whether it be the planning or execution of the trip. I only hope I haven't forgotten how to relax. Perhaps I'll go for a few beers after this.

Spending time living in these places also makes you appreciate what you have when you deprive yourself of the creature comforts and security that we surround ourselves with in our modern world. I once read a book by the Dalai Lama in which his interviewer asked why there needs to be bad in the world. Surely some omnipotent God would eradicate the concept of bad altogether? His response was that bad exists so that we appreciate the good. I think we can all identify with that, although perhaps not when the bad has just befallen us. The Poles are harsh but at least honest, and they really help you appreciate 'normal' life.

It is also challenging to be in a place where you are entirely responsible for your own actions. Sometimes those decisions can make the difference between life and death, or at the very least serious injury. In our increasingly litigious world we could do with more shouldering of responsibility.

The Poles, too, taught me a new approach to looking at problems and I've also found myself applying this to everyday life. I think it was the Dalai Lama again who said there are two kinds of problems. There are those you can overcome, and so you needn't worry about them. Then there are those you can't overcome, in which case there's no point worrying about them. I laughed when I read that but in fact it suits polar travel down to a tee. Every day we systematically overcame problems – problems with the sat phone, the solar panel, our skis, our bindings, the harnesses, the stoves, and our sleeping bags. Not to mention fillings dropping out, frostbite to fingers, toes and noses, muscle wastage, eye damage, sensory deprivation and bouts of extreme depression.

I'm no Buddhist initiate, so I had my own take on the philosophy. I looked at problems as learning experiences. I tried to look at the inevitable equipment failures and breakages as opportunities to be resourceful and learn new skills. I tried to look at my overcoming injuries and accidents as in some way making me a better person for the experience. And so when the weather was bad, instead of thinking that someone up there hated me and was making it bloody difficult for me, I told myself that I was pleased that the conditions were tough, the way they were for Scott, Mawson and Shackleton. I managed to persuade myself I would have felt in some way cheated if I'd had blue skies, unseasonably warm temperatures and no wind the whole way down south and a conveyor belt of northerly drifting ice on the Arctic Ocean.

With that in mind, I learnt also that the idea of getting a world record to somewhere like the North Pole is a flawed concept. I guess I always knew it was before I went but when the media picked it up and ran with it I found myself going along with it. The reality is in a place like the north you are lucky to make it to the Pole, let alone do it in a world record time. Whoever makes it there fastest will likely be the one who experiences the most favourable northerly drift of the ice.

My achievement of the South Pole in record time forced me to face some interesting personal issues. We all have them. Like many people, one of my pet issues is that I tend to be my own worst critic. As Groucho Marx so eloquently put it, 'I don't care to belong to a club that accepts people like me as members.' The ergo title changed that predisposition to a certain extent and encouraged me to try other things. The South Pole blew it right out of the water, forcing me to give myself a bit of a break. I still have the fire in my belly to try more, but it's a far more positive energy than it was. A kind of contentment at what I have achieved, rather than trying to prove myself. Something that for me was brought about by having reached the South Pole and knowledge that it is within my means to achieve the North.

Now I tend to see life as a series of opportunities. Contrary to conventional wisdom, I don't feel like taking my foot off the accelerator, instead I want to push it down a bit harder and see what happens. For me this will mean more trips and more challenges, and not all of them will involve polar expeditions. I set out to see what it's all about and what's possible. I was unsatisfied that the life I was leading was it. Everyone has dreams and it's great to see whether one or two of them are possible. With each achievement you get greater confidence to try to achieve something else and so it becomes addictive as you discover more and more about your capabilities. It helps redefine who you are.

The polar trips have also given me the opportunity to stand up in front of groups of people and, in the course of telling an adventure yarn, put across positive messages about all these sorts of things, from the environment to setting personal goals and getting the most out of life. That, too, has been a good opportunity to push myself. Speaking in front of a group of 1500 people can be as frightening as any given day at the Poles!

I hope that by the time you read this I will be about to

attempt to retrace the famous journey of Sir Douglas Mawson down in Antarctica, although I hope to not suffer the same fate as either of his two colleagues, Ninnis and Mertz, who tragically died on that trip.

After that, who knows? Just as Peary failed to reach the North Pole on many occasions before he was ultimately successful in 1909, I too know what I would do differently next time. And yes, there will be a next time. Don't get me wrong – I have a positive take on the North Pole trip, but still feel that there's unfinished business up there.

However I look at it, I want life to be interesting, and that motivates me to get off my backside and attempt these journeys, regardless of the obstacles. The more I've tried, the more I've felt like doing. If you're successful in something it gives you the confidence to try the next thing and you find all sorts of weird and wonderful ideas appearing on your radar. Perhaps scientist Marie Curie said it best: 'Life is an adventure or it is nothing at all.'

Acknowledgements

There are many people I would like to thank for the part they have played in this story so far and in helping make both the expeditions and this book a reality. There are too many to mention, but most of them know who they are. In particular I'd like to thank the following:

My parents for their love and support and for instilling in me a spirit of adventure that they never seem to give themselves credit for. Alexandra Shackleton, the Right Honourable Tony Blair, Prime Minister of Great Britain, and the Honourable John Howard, Prime Minister of Australia, for having the confidence to provide their patronage for the trips and all of the kudos and support that brings. John Leece whose role in both the North Pole and South Pole trips cannot be understated – without his moral, financial and logistical help the trips simply wouldn't have happened. Andrew 'Ed' Edwards and Peter Treseder for being such accomplished companions, able to put up with the unrelenting conditions – sharing a tent with me and the extreme cold and danger in roughly equal amounts.

Our principal sponsors of the South Pole expedition, Arnotts Biscuits and Lachlan Murdoch and News Ltd, and major sponsors, Virtual Communities, Youth Hostel Association, Marsh Swiss Re, Helly Hansen and Australian Geographic; and Sanity Music and Helly Hansen as major sponsors of the North

Pole expedition. Scouts Australia for their help with the North Pole expedition, and to all those who contributed money to the Smith Family (our nominated charity) as well as a warm thanks to Kathy Gale and all at the Smith family who worked so hard to make it all come together. Particular thanks must also go to Brett Blundy owner of Sanity Music for being game enough to fly to the North Pole in our helicopter to plant our flag there on behalf of all those who contributed money to the Smith Family.

To a succession of employers who have turned a blind eye to my planning these trips while holding down a 9 to 5 job, and in particular Jim Mantle at PPK, John Fargher, Merv Jones and Dave Williamson at URS, and Charlotte Divall who kindly helped me with the graphics and wording of countless sponsorship proposals.

Of friends, supporters and advisers there have been many, but particular thanks also to Anj Vaughan, Dave Cowell, Alison Glazebrook, Roger Daynes, Dr Taher Omari, Sally and Colin Luke, Borge Ousland, Bruce James-Martin, Bruce Macky, Beth Treseder, Lucy Kerr-Lewis, Dr Chris Forbes-Ewan, Martin Betts, Neil Treseder, Mike Stroud, Kurt Lance, Sjur Mordre, Craig Cobbin, Guan Oon, Geraldine Martick, Nigel Venning, Peter and Mike McDowell, Jay Timmerman, and the staff of NSF at the Amundsen-Scott South Pole station.

To Jane Southward and Heather Curdie at Random House for having faith in both me and my story and putting up with my bad handwriting. Victor Boyarsky and Victor Serov and all the team at VICAAR in Russia for never letting Russian bureaucracy get in the way of making a great trip happen.

Last, but not least, I would like to thank my partner Caroline who has given me love and support throughout both the trips and the writing of this book. She has given both the confidence to keep going and a healthy dose of dressing down to keep my ego in check. To her I am extremely thankful.

References

Bstan-'dzin-rgya-mtsho, Dalai Lama XIV, *The Art of Happiness*: a handbook for living, Riverhead Books, New York, 1998

Fiennes, Ranulph, Sir, *Living Dangerously*, Atheneum, New York, 1988

Fiennes, Ranulph, Sir, *Mind Over Matter*: the epic crossing of the Antarctic continent, Delacorte Press, New York, 1993

Fiennes, Ranulph, Sir, 'Ranulph Fiennes: You ask the questions' in *Independent News*, UK, 16 October 2003

Goulet, Chris M, 'Magnetic Declination: frequently asked questions', Alberta, Canada, Version 4.4, October 2001, http://www.geocities.com/magnetic_declination/

Krakauer, Jon, *Into Thin Air*: a personal account of the Mount Everest disaster, Villard, New York, 1997

Mawson, Douglas, Sir, *The Home of the Blizzard*: a true story of Antarctic survival, St. Martin's Griffin, New York, 2000

Shackleton, Ernest Henry, Sir, *South*: a memoir of the Endurance voyage, Carroll & Graf, New York, 1998

Sponsors

South Pole

Principal Sponsors
Arnotts Biscuits

Major Sponsors
News Ltd
Marsh Swiss Re
Virtual Communities
Helly Hansen
Australian Geographic
Youth Hostel Association

Sponsors
Concept 2 Rowing
Mountain Equipment
Phoenix/Clayton Graham
Leki
PPK Environment and
   Infrastructure
Merit Apparel
Alfa Boots
Rottefella Bindings
Asnes Skis
Grant Minervini
Quark Expeditions
Silva
Oakley
Borough Mazars
Eveready
Continental
Arrowpac
Panasonic

North Pole

Principal Sponsors
Sanity Music Ltd

Major Sponsors
Helly Hansen

Sponsors
Dick Smith
URS Australia
George Weston Foods
The Hayson Group
The Smith Family
Mountain Equipment
Leki
RadarSat
Arnotts Limited
Grant Minervini
Silva
Foodex
Borough Mazars
Sanitarium
Oakley
Kingtread Pty Ltd
M & C Saachi
Continental
Arrowpac
News Limited
Horizons Golf Resort
Telstat
Stratos
Panasonic